CW00585152

Controversial Issues in
the Curriculum

Controversial Issues in the Curriculum

Edited by J J Wellington

Basil Blackwell

© Basil Blackwell Ltd
First published 1986

Published by Basil Blackwell Limited
108 Cowley Road
Oxford OX4 3JF
England

All rights reserved. No part of this publication may be reproduced, stored in a
retrieval system or transmitted in any form or by any means, electronic,
mechanical, photocopying, recording or otherwise, without the prior permission
of Basil Blackwell Limited.

British Library Cataloguing in Publication Data

Controversial issues in the curriculum.
1. Social Policy—Study and teaching
I. Wellington, J.J.
300   HN29

ISBN 0–631–15127–3

Typeset in 10 on 12 pt Sabon by Oxford Publishing Services, Oxford
Printed in Great Britain

Contents

Notes on contributors 175

Index 177

Introduction

The title of this book is intentionally ambiguous. It might lead the reader to expect a collection of articles solely on handling controversial issues in the school curriculum and the classroom. Many of the chapters *do* discuss ways of approaching controversial issues in the classroom, and some of the contributions on specific issues go on to consider particular teaching strategies and teaching resources in a selection of controversial areas. But the book has an additional theme. Part of its aim is to consider controversy surrounding the curriculum itself. What is the status of certain new subject areas, such as Peace and Conflict Studies? Should unemployment be dealt with, either implicitly or explicitly, in the school curriculum? If so, how? Indeed, should controversial issues of any kind be included in the school curriculum? Such key problems will be introduced later in this chapter, and will be discussed by different contributors in different ways throughout the book. These questions form the unifying threads in this collection of papers on controversial issues in the curriculum.

As result of the intentional ambiguity in the title, and the consequent wide variety of the contributions, it is hoped that the book will appeal to a diverse range of readers. First, the book should prove useful to teachers who deal with controversial issues of any kind in their own curriculum. To this end, a number of chapters have been written on specific issues which are, and have been, tackled by teachers from a spread of subject backgrounds. The book is intended to provoke discussion and provide classroom ideas, as well as offering guidelines to resources for such practitioners.

Indeed, the book itself should prove a useful resource for students of education, whether on undergraduate, postgraduate or in-service courses, who wish to examine the role of controversial issues in the curriculum. Finally, for those who wish to make an extensive study of controversy in the curriculum, the articles are intended to provide original contributions in themselves, as well as guidelines to the relevant literature.

Three of the important themes running through the book are introduced briefly below. They are the problems of *definition*, of *justification*, and of *approach*.

Definition

The first key problem in discussing controversial issues in the curriculum is that of deciding what is to count as a 'controversial issue'. This may appear to be an academic question, but in my view it is fundamental to curriculum practice. At a time when people of varying political persuasions and from various quarters (including parents and pupils themselves) are demanding that controversial issues should be excluded from curricula, the problem of justifying their *inclusion* is a very real one. The problem of justification rests on the prior problem of definition.

Thus the problem of deciding what constitutes a controversial issue is in itself controversial. For example, the decision to treat the nuclear issue as controversial and even to label it as an 'issue' at all may be seen (in some circles) as politically biased and problematic. Discussion of the meaning of 'controversial' is therefore a matter of some importance, and not simply a philosophical exercise.

Several important views have been expressed in writing. I shall briefly summarise three of them, with a view to arriving at a workable definition of a controversial issue.

The Humanities Curriculum Project (HCP) is well known for its efforts in introducing controversial issues in the school curriculum. A recent publication of HCP provides a useful starting point:

> The crucial problem in handling human issues is that they are controversial. By a controversial issue we mean one that divides students, parents and teachers because it involves an element of value judgement which prevents the issue being settled by evidence and experiment.[1]

In other words a controversial issue cannot be settled by an appeal to facts, empirical evidence or experiment alone. It will involve matters of value as well as matters of fact. This definition is questioned by Dearden in a rigorous and carefully argued paper.[2] He claims that many purely factual matters are controversial and therefore that controversy need not involve value judgements. Two examples are controversies in science, eg whether light is particle or wave-like in nature, and controversies in mathematics, eg over the largest prime number. Dearden's point must be granted as a 'philosophical truth', but surely any controversial issue worthy of inclusion in the whole school curriculum must involve values and value judgements?

A final useful point is made by Gardner.[3] He argues that for an issue to be counted as controversial it must be felt to be important. I can perhaps illustrate this point with an analogy from the world of football. A decision which gives a throw-in to the wrong side may arouse feeling but will hardly be described in the papers next day as controversial. However, a decision to allow a disputed goal or to award a crucial penalty in the last minute of time will generate 'heat'. It is this factor which Gardner feels to be essential to a controversial issue. As he puts it:

'It was controversial but no-one thought it to be of any importance' is a contradiction.

In my view, the criteria discussed above provide a working definition of a controversial issue, ie a controversial issue must:

• involve value judgements, so that the issue cannot be settled by facts, evidence or experiment alone;

• be considered to be important by an appreciable number of people.

Such a definition obviously rules out certain controversial issues, eg scientific and mathematical controversies, by the first criterion. It also rules out disputes or controversies which are simply a matter of taste. The definition can therefore be used in deciding what counts as 'a controversial issue worthy of inclusion in the school curriculum'. The problem of defining a controversial issue is explored fully by a number of other contributors to this book.

The next question to turn to is the justification of why controversial issues should be included in the curriculum at all.

Justification

Perhaps the onus of justification should fall on those who wish to *exclude* controversial issues from the curriculum. In other words, they should argue the case for excluding the controversial issues of medicine, science, religion, and society from the education provided in the school curriculum. In practice, however, the case for the *exclusion* of contentions or controversial matters is rarely, if ever, rationally argued. It is simply asserted that they should not be included, thereby leaving the onus of justification on those who would wish to include them.

Perhaps the best justification for including controversial issues is offered by Stenhouse. He argues that any 'education' ignoring them would be seriously inadequate and hardly worthy of the name. Issues should be tackled which are matters of 'widespread and enduring significance'. Using this criterion, the topics chosen for enquiry in HCP were: war and society; education; the family; relations between the sexes; poverty; people and work; living in cities; law and order. I would also have added: the provision and distribution of energy for the world's people, and the appropriate use of new technologies (information technology and biotechnology) in mankind's future. These are surely matters of 'widespread and enduring significance' for the next century.

Dearden[5] also argues, from a subject-centred approach, that a discipline in the curriculum is misrepresented if no mention is made of its controversial elements. Such a narrow treatment is likely to omit the 'historical context' and give students a totally false impression of the subject. In my view, science teachers are especially guilty of misrepresentation of science, often presenting it as unproblematic, value free and non-controversial.

Both the above justifications are *content-based*. In other words, the inclusion of controversial issues is justified in terms of the content of the material which is presented to students. An equally convincing justification can be based on the *skills and processes* which students can learn by examining controversies, ie a process-based justification.[6] Students can learn to weigh up evidence, to search for information, to detect bias, to question the validity of sources and to present their own considered viewpoint. The skills of communication, listening, working collaboratively and cooperating in group sessions can all be enhanced. Clearly the development of these skills will depend on the approach or pedagogy of the teacher.

Teaching approach or pedagogy

Three of the crucial notions often employed in discussing the 'correct approach' to controversial issues are the ideas of objectivity, balance and neutrality. All three are linked to the role of the teacher as 'an authority' in the classroom as discussed by R S Peters.[7] The key question in discussing the handling of controversial issues is this: to what extent should teachers act as an authority in the classroom? This question is especially difficult for teachers who are handling matters of *value* as well as matters of *fact*.

A teacher may well be able to adopt the role of a factual authority – for example, in settling a dispute over the facts involved in a controversial issue. Thus, in discussing nuclear energy, a science teacher could usefully correct the mistaken belief that a nuclear reactor could (in the event of an accident) explode like an atomic bomb. But should he or she act as 'an authority' in settling matters of value? Clearly, a teacher who did so would not be acting objectively, neutrally, or in a balanced way. Should teachers therefore confine themselves solely to matters of *fact* (as science teachers were advised to do by Sir Keith Joseph[8]) and avoid, or stop short of, questions of value? This exhortation rests on the belief that there is a clear distinction between facts and values, a distinction which more than one contributor to this book has questioned.

I would suggest, in this brief discussion, that the criterion of objectivity is extremely difficult to apply in handling controversial issues which involve facts, values, value-laden facts, and values dependent upon people's perceptions of the facts. What could possibly constitute an *objective* viewpoint in such cases? How could a teacher apply a criterion of objectivity in handling a discussion of complex controversial issues, except perhaps by acting as an objective authority in advising on the occasional clear-cut matters of fact?

The two other notions often discussed are the procedural principles of neutrality, and of balance. Both rather different notions are considered fully by a number of contributors to this collection.

I sincerely hope that this book will be of value to students, teachers, lecturers, advisers and indeed any reader with an interest in controversial issues and controversy within the curriculum.

J J Wellington
Sheffield 1986

Notes and References

1 This definition occurs in *The Humanities Curriculum Project: an Introduction* J Rudduck (Schools Council Publications, 1983) p 11. A similar definition can be found in *The Humanities Curriculum Project: an Introduction* L Stenhouse (Heinemann, 1970).
2 'Controversial issues and the curriculum' R F Dearden, in *Journal of Curriculum Studies* 1981, Vol 13, No. 1, pp 37–44.
3 'Another look at controversial issues and the curriculum' P Gardner, in *Journal of Curriculum Studies* 1983, Vol 16, No 4, pp 179–85.
4 *The Humanities Curriculum Project: an Introduction* L Stenhouse (Heinemann, 1970).
5 Dearden, *op cit.*
6 This distinction is developed in *Teaching Controversial Issues* R Stradling, M Noctor and B Bains (Arnold, 1984).
7 A discussion of Peters' views on authority is given in *Ethics and Education* (Unwin, 1966).
8 Sir Keith Joseph's spoken views were reported by *The Times Educational Supplement* 18 March 1983, p 1.

Chapter 1

A strategy for handling controversial issues in the secondary school

Jean Rudduck

The school does not give people their political ideals or religious faith but the means to discover both for themselves. Above all it gives them scepticism so that they leave with the ability to doubt rather than the inclination to believe.[1]

Would that it were so! The critical thinking that fosters scepticism and independence of mind is too much absent from the curriculum of the comprehensive school. The man who made the statement quoted above was head of an independent school, and one recalls Stenhouse's challenge: 'Is the entry into critical thinking to be the privilege of an educated oligarchy? Is it being stifled in the state system?'[2]

I start with the ideas of 'critical thinking' and 'independence of mind' because these are the capacities which, I think, the active exploration of controversial issues in schools can help to develop. They are also, at least in embryonic form, a precondition for handling such issues. Pupils should be helped to approach controversy not with the expectation that authority figures can resolve issues for them but with a recognition of their right to arrive at their own judgement.

The problem is that teachers and pupils often conspire in perpetuating a false security that manifests itself in a reliance on right answers and on a view of the expert as one who knows, rather than as one who uses knowledge to refocus doubt. Teachers, prompted by a kindly concern for the young people they teach, often over-simplify the complexities of living and learning; they seek to protect their pupils from uncertainty by holding out intellectual safety nets. Consequently it is not easy for pupils to escape from what Giroux calls 'the tyranny of imposed meaning'.[3] We must first strip away the layers of unexamined reality that hide behind 'the facts' and help pupils and teachers sever their dependence on the chimera of intellectual certainty. Many teachers in their period of professional training have not acquired the intellectual tools they need in order to view knowledge as problematic. Many pupils find it hard to conceive of questioning adults after years of regarding knowledge as something that lies between the covers of an official textbook or exists in the teacher's mind.

In short, the classroom has *not* generally been an arena for the exercise of critical thinking. Even academic sixth-form work, which is often regarded as an appropriate context for the development of intellectual independence, is seriously constrained by the protocols of the examination system. A recent study sponsored by the British Library shows this quite clearly. An A-level teacher interviewed in the study explains how difficult it is to challenge the assumptions that sixth-form students bring to their work:

I feel that our pupils expect that tradition of being spoon-fed. We will give them notes. We will give them essay plans. We will tell them exactly which pages to read. And they don't seem to have the initiative themselves . . . They complain if they are told to go and find out about something. They expect to be told where and how. It's very difficult to abandon that system when you know it works and pupils will get through their A-levels. And *they* know that that's the system that got the last lot through their A-levels, so they are very loath to lose that system.[4]

Another A-level teacher interviewed in the study highlights the tension between examination success and the development of intellectual independence:

I think the problem is you have to balance whether you want results and feed the information or whether you want them to develop their own ideas, through which they tend to fail the exam.[4]

Interviews with sixth-form students showed the extent of the anxiety that students experience when confronting diverse views and interpretations that are not mediated through and evaluated by their teacher. These three A-level students find it difficult to deal with the claims to truth made by different experts in books and articles and confessed in interview to being bewildered about how to proceed:

I mean, there is two people there who supposedly have been paid an awful lot of money for writing books on it and they have two entirely different opinions. I mean, what am I supposed to think?

You get one book and you find one thing and then you open another and find somebody else arguing a completely different thing and of course you have got to put that in your essay. It is a bit of a fiddly subject.

Every now and again you get two ideas and each of them have points backing them up and then it starts getting difficult. I usually try to actually make a choice out of the two because I end up getting in a muddle if I try and work from sort of two positions.[4]

Were they supposed to summarise the different positions or use them to formulate a personal view? These were the dilemmas. Controversiality was new, and it was difficult to handle. Entwistle[5] (summarising Perry[6]) discusses the difficulty students face in moving from 'dualistic reasoning' where they believe that there is always a right and wrong answer to any question, to 'contextual relativistic reasoning' in which the partial validity of contrasting interpretations of reality is accepted. The evidence gathered through interview in the study of academic sixth-form learning supports Perry's observations.

The comments quoted above were made by sixth-form students grappling on their own with controversy and finding that their experiences of teaching and learning so far have not equipped them to respond adequately. But a strategy was developed in the late sixties and early seventies (I was a member of the development team[7]) for helping young people handle controversial issues in a group situation. The strategy was not designed for the minority who pursue academic sixth-form work but for 14- to 16-year-old pupils in the last years of compulsory schooling. We felt it important that pupils should have some experience that would prevent them from moving from intellectual dependence on the authority of the teacher to intellectual dependence on other authority figures in their working or social lives. We wanted young people to recognise their right to think for themselves. Our evaluator saw clearly how difficult the task was likely to be: by the time they are 14, pupils have developed 'a trained incapacity' for thinking independently: they have been successfully socialised into a tradition of teacher dominance and custodial attitudes. The difficult step, initially, is persuading children that alternatives are possible within the school system as they know it.

The starting point for our work was this question: faced with the task of handling controversial issues in the classroom, what strategy can the teacher adopt which is socially and educationally justifiable, given the pluralist community in which teachers work and whose future citizens schools have a responsibility to educate? The aim of the work was to help young people 'develop an understanding of social situations and human acts and of the controversial value issues which they raise'. An issue was defined as controversial if people were divided about it and if it involved an element of value judgement which prevented the issue being settled by evidence and/or experiment alone.

Our approach had five premises:

1 that controversial issues should be handled in the classroom with adolescents;

2 that teachers should not use their authority as a platform for promoting their own views;

3 that the mode of inquiry in controversial areas should have discussion rather than instruction as its core;

4 that the discussion should protect divergence of view among participants and not force a consensus (unless of course group action necessitated a common perspective and plan);

5 that the teacher as chairperson of the discussion should have responsibility for ensuring proper exploration of the issue, using evidence as appropriate, and for quality of understanding.[8]

The distinctive features of the approach were *discussion* as the medium of group inquiry; the availability of *evidence* to feed the inquiry; and the role of the teacher as *neutral chairperson* in discussion.

Discussion is, logically, an appropriate strategy for exploring controversial issues in that it supports the interplay of various perspectives on a closely focused issue or task and permits individual members of the group to arrive at their own understanding in the light of evidence that has been critically examined. *Evidence* is crucial. Without it young people have only their own, often limited, perspectives to draw on. Evidence helps them to see how other people from different backgrounds and in different situations experience events and talk or write about them. The availability of appropriate evidence gives depth and breadth to an inquiry. It guards against the mere 'pooling of ignorance' – which may occur in discussions of social issues which have no formalised way of helping pupils consider and take into account views and experiences of other people in society.

In the project, core collections of 'evidence' – views and experiences of people in different historical and social settings, presented through words and images – were built up round a number of topics. The materials (transcripts of interviews, passages from books and newspapers, reproductions of pictures, photographs, poems, statistical data, etc.) are 'evidence' in the sense that artefacts are regarded as evidence in archaeology: they help archaeologists to explore particular questions that they are curious about. In our discussions, the evidence was available to help the members of the working group explore and deepen their understanding of the issues that, as a group, they were concerned to explore. The topics around which balanced collections of evidence were gathered were all judged to be capable of raising fundamental issues which young people should be helped to think about in a reflective and serious fashion before they leave school. The topics included the family; relations between the sexes; people and work; law and order; race relations; wealth and poverty.

Neutral chairing was also fundamental to the approach. Our assumption was that schools would not want to assert an institutional position on controversial issues in the face of the diversity of views held by teachers. We also assumed that teachers would be cautious about exposing their own views unless they could be sure that their authority as teachers would not lead pupils automatically to accept their view as the right one. To adopt the view of a respected other is a beguiling temptation, but to do so without critical scrutiny of the foundation of that view, and of its strengths compared with other views, denies pupils the experience of thinking things out for themselves and achieving some depth of personal understanding. This is what primacy of conscience is about.

Neutrality is not as awesome for pupils as some teachers suspected. A teacher acting as a neutral chairperson is, as pupils see it, 'just not taking sides in *our* discussion'; he or she is acting more as a referee – a role that pupils can comprehend and respect. The chairperson is there to ensure quality and fairness in discussion. Given the complexity of the task of learning through discussion, sensitivity and careful chairing is a way of demonstrating to pupils the teacher's respect for the seriousness of the task that they are engaged in. For teachers, however, neutrality *did* prove to be disturbing. They attacked it from several angles. Some supposed that by not expressing a personal view in the discussion teachers might be perceived by pupils as not caring about the issues. This is a misconception, for it is important to discuss with pupils why the teacher is adopting a procedural neutrality. Indeed, it is precisely because teachers do have strong personal commitments on the issues under discussion and recognise that pupils have a right to develop similar commitments that they might wish to adopt the convention of the neutral chairperson during classroom discussion. Other teachers felt that they were failing students and parents if pupils were not given positive advice – even though they might disagree among themselves as to what advice should be given:

Students are looking, sometimes with desperation, for a lead and if it is not given, will only reflect the views of the society of which they are a part ... a good teacher, like a good parent, must be loving, devoted, and anything but neutral.[9]

Teachers who took this line assumed that a consensus existed among the wise and the good – ie all teachers and all parents – but this is empirically not so except at the level of fundamental values such as respect for life, care of the frail, and so on. Some teachers also felt that they were distancing themselves from their pupils if they did not join in the discussion and offer their views. Interestingly, evidence from the evaluation of the work suggests that most pupils, once they understand why teachers act as neutral chairperson, are more inclined to view them sympathetically; they find that their teachers are, perhaps for the first time in their school lives, giving them time to think aloud and listening to what they have to say. Moreover, some pupils know a teacher's position from his or her actions in other contexts. They may say: 'She actually believes such and such – but she doesn't let her view get in the way of our discussion'. The adoption of a procedural neutrality is a way of emphasising that in the context of handling controversial issues the teacher's commitment is to education and not to his or her own views.

Of course, the case for neutrality is diminished if the teacher is convinced that his or her view, if expressed, will be subjected to the same critical scrutiny as any other evidence available to the group. This argument is put well by Brameld:

(The teacher) owes it to the group to indicate his (sic) preferences frankly and clearly, while yet making apparent that these preferences are continually subject to reconsideration, modification or even disapproval ... the ethical leader does everything he can to provide opportunity for expression of feeling and opinion by those who differ with him.[10]

What Brameld underestimates, I think, is the pupil's readiness (see earlier, p. 8) to question the teacher, as well as the teacher's readiness to have his or her 'right to be sure' undermined. As Elliott notes:

Since in practice it is difficult for students to disassociate a teacher's authority position from his or her 'personal knowledge', neutrality will normally involve refraining from expressing his or her views in person – at least in the early stages of the work.[11]

Charlotte Epstein also sees the dilemma. Her aspirations were close to ours:

We can educate the next generation to solve many of our problems if we are courageous enough to free them from our own prejudices and anxieties.[12]

She would like teachers to express their values so that pupils 'may know the roots of our teaching' but she admits that it is 'a very difficult part of the teacher's job to make her values explicit without coercing her students to adopt those values'. Her response is to work out her own version of classroom neutrality.

To sum up, in devising our teaching strategy we believed:
1 that the fundamental educational values of rationality, imagination, sensitivity, readiness to listen to the views of others, and so forth, should be built into the principles of procedure;
2 that the pattern of teaching should renounce the authority of the teacher as an 'expert' capable of solving value issues, since this authority cannot be justified either epistemologically or politically. In short, the teacher must aspire to be neutral on controversial issues;
3 that the teaching strategy should maintain the procedural authority of the teacher in the classroom, but should contain it within rules which can be justified in terms of the need for responsiveness, sensitivity and rigour in helping pupils to a deeper understanding;
4 that the strategy should be such as to satisfy parents and pupils that every possible effort is being made to avoid the use of the teacher's authority position to indoctrinate pupils with his or her own views;
5 that the procedure should help pupils to understand how different people can learn constructively together through discussion and shared activities: in particular, that minority opinions deserve to be critically examined and not merely ridiculed or ignored;
6 that above all, the aim should be understanding. Pupils should not feel any pressure to reach a firm opinion or a premature commitment. The object is that the pupil should come to understand the nature and implications of his or her point of view, grow to adult responsibility by adopting it in his or her own person, and assume accountability for it – while being prepared to reconsider it in the light of further evidence or experience.[13]

Problems in practice

In practice, the teacher, acting as neutral chairperson, would work with a stable group of 12 to 15 pupils for several sessions a week, helping the group to identify issues within topic areas that they want to discuss, and making available to the group evidence to help them focus, deepen and extend their inquiries. In the approach, simple and straightforward as it seems in summary, teachers have to take on board a number of challenges: they have to think about the technique of group work – in particular about helping children to free themselves from the role-determining labels that they carry over from other areas of school work; they have to think about ways of building continuity from one session to the next in order to avoid the dismissive complaint: 'Oh, we did 'War' last week'; they have to think about the way that different kinds of evidence (photographs, cartoons, poems, newspaper articles, paintings) can be valued and criticised; they have to legitimise the pupils' right to be uncertain and the group's right to be thoughtful; they have to think about the nature of understanding and how it can be assessed if the work is to be examined; and they have to think how to monitor their own performance as an aspiring neutral chairperson.

As the work progressed in schools we were able to document the difficulties that teachers and pupils met in attempting to handle controversial issues through discussion.[14] For example, in relation to the technique of group work, experienced teachers drew up a list of common problems that inhibited the development of discussion. This meant that teachers embarking on the work could at least be alerted to the likely pitfalls. These were the common problems identified:

- pupils' tendency to depend on the teacher rather than to take initiatives themselves or be prepared to learn from each other;
- dominant pupils;
- individual pupils who are used by the group as a scapegoat or who become the object of ridicule;
- silent pupils;
- isolates;
- polarisation of male/female views;
- acceptance of an over-easy consensus;
- escape – ie attempts to avoid facing difficult issues;
- use of the group, by a pupil, for personal ends;
- attention-seeking, usually through the adoption of bizarre roles;
- conflict rather than cooperation.

In a guide prepared by experienced teachers, each problem was presented as vividly as possible to help other teachers recognise the dimensions of the situations that they might find themselves in. For example, Figure 1 shows how they presented the first and last problems on the list.[15]

Figure 1

Dependence (on teacher)

Symptoms:
- eyes on teacher, even when others are speaking
- statements addressed to the teacher
- 'What do you think, sir?'
- attempts to engage the teacher in dialogue

How pupils and teachers talk about the problem:

'Introducing discussion to this group was rather like jerking the carpet from under their feet – the carpet being the teacher – and certainly initially they were at a loss, many of them. They expected Sir to give them orders – and Sir didn't.'
(A teacher)

'The group find it impossible to listen to each other's views and are constantly looking, visibly sometimes, to the chairman for approval or comments. When they find that this is not forthcoming they find this very disconcerting.'*(A teacher)*

'He kept saying "This is not a lesson. You mustn't think of me as teacher." But you can't help. . . . I mean, after you've been thinking of him as a teacher for about five years, you can't help thinking of him as a teacher.' *(A pupil)*

'I say something and I know no one else will talk back at me, so I just talk straight to the teacher.' *(A pupil)*

Conflict

Symptoms:
- angry pairing
- very fast pace of discusson
- responses immediate, with minimal reflection

How teachers talk about the problem:

'One thing I noticed was the tendency of a youngster to sort of jump at somebody on some point they've raised, and sort of argue back at him. . . .' *(A teacher)*

'A rowdy argument is exciting – the group always seems to enjoy it. I always feel that I've failed when his happens.' *(A teacher)*

'There's an unwillingness to go beyond the first superficial reaction to any problem. The occasional flare-ups of dispute are not sustained beyond the "you should . . ." "no you shouldn't . . ." routine.' *(A teacher)*

'Problems of authority arise when confrontations in a group arise and abrupt affirmations are fired across camps, without any effort to explore the opposing stand.' *(A teacher)*

Teachers were also given help with the task of self-monitoring: they were encouraged to tape record discussions and listen to them, bearing the following points in mind:

1   To what extent do you interrupt students while they are speaking? Why and to what effect?

2   Reflective discussion can often be slow-paced and contain sustained silences. What proportion of these silences are interrupted by you? Is your interruption ever simply a matter of breaking under the strain or is it a real contribution to the task of the group?

3   Are you consistent and reliable in chairing? Are all the students treated with equal respect, and are all views, including those with which you sympathise, critically examined?

4   Do you habitually rephrase and repeat students' contributions? If so, what is the effect of this?

5   Do you press towards consensus? For example, 'Do we all agree?' If so, what is the effect of this type of question? Compare this with the effect of: 'What do other people think?', 'Does anyone disagree with that?', 'Can anyone see another possible view or interpretation?'.

6   To what extent do you confirm? Do you, for example, say: 'Yes' or 'No' or 'An interesting point' or 'Well done' or 'That's interesting'? What is the effect of this on the group? Is there any trace of students looking for rewards to you rather than to the task?

7   To what extent do you ask questions to which you think you know the answer? What is the effect of such questions on the group? What is the effect of questions to which you do not know the answer?

8   Do you attempt to transmit, through eliciting questions, your own interpretation of the meaning of a piece of evidence such as a poem or a picture?[16]

Helping pupils to understand the approach

There are two stages in the development of this approach to handling controversial issues with which teachers seem to need particular help. First, there is the task of introducing the approach to pupils; second, there is the task of identifying, within the pupil group, the issues that the group members want to explore so that they have a sense of ownership of the discussion. Problems arise at both stages, largely, it seems, as a result of assumptions about the school's right to impose work patterns on pupils; there is no tradition of justifying and explaining new curriculum content and learning styles to pupils. Pupils are usually pawns in the curriculum games played by others. Nor is there any tradition of negotiating an agenda for learning with the learners. This is a responsibility that teachers have not generally paid a lot of attention to. Some might not even recognise it as a responsibility.

First, let us look at the task of introducing innovation to pupils. The difficulty of the task will vary according to the 'novelty' of the change that the teachers have in mind. Some changes might more aptly be called 'developments', in that the framework of values and practices remains essentially the same and the proposal can be accommodated without significant disorientation or dislocation of habit. But other changes represent a sharp break with the habits and values of past practice and the pupils and teachers involved have inevitably to exorcise the spirit of ·past practice in order to make possible a new way of working and of perceiving work.[17]

In situations where fairly radical change is proposed, teachers are seen as needing help with the transition, and opportunities are sought for exploratory dialogue with colleagues who will be affected by the change. There may even be specially-designed induction courses to ease the passage from one way of working to another way of working. Pupils are not usually offered such planned transition experiences[18] and yet they, like teachers, can be trapped by past habits and patterns of expectation. It is not surprising therefore if, faced with unexplained and bewildering new demands, pupils resist and act, unwittingly, as a conservative force. It is, for them, more comfortable to cling to the familiar than to build up new securities through the mastery of new routines. The experience of innovation is different for teachers in another way: teachers may have an educational ideology or vision which helps them to tolerate the ambiguities and discomforts of change, but rarely are those values and visions shared with pupils as a way of motivating them to join their teachers in effecting a welcome change of practice.

In our work on the handling of controversial issues, we found it difficult to see how to communicate the principles of discussion-based enquiry to pupils who were used to the norms of instructional teaching. By the time they are 15, pupils have strong images of what teachers are and what teaching is. Explanations at the level of principle have little impact: either pupils simply do not understand what the implications for their action are, or they do not believe that the teacher actually intends to engage in the bizarre practices that he or she is outlining. We found that images were more powerful than words in communicating to pupils the meaning of a proposed change of practice. Video-tapes of other groups engaged in the discussion of controversial issues gave pupils a common reference point for interpreting the new language of learning, which included terms like 'chairperson', 'neutrality', 'evidence', 'discussion'. In a group which was making no progress with discussion-based enquiry one boy said, after seeing a video-tape of other pupils working in this way:

Miss is talking too much and getting too interested in the group. As chairman she shouldn't talk, you know, as much, leaving it to the group to argue between themselves. Well, not sort of argue – to talk between themselves and have more discussion between themselves than with the teacher because you are you know sort of being the chairman and not the teacher . . . Oi you lot, instead of talking to Miss, talk between us lot. Whatever you say you say to Miss. Why don't you talk between us lot?

Here, in his own way, the boy sums up for the group the transitions they have to make if they are to develop a way of learning through discussion.[19] The video-tapes helped pupils to translate their tentative and partial understanding of the innovation into action. They also served to legitimise the approach: to many pupils, schools are places which hire teachers to tell them what they should know. The roles and procedures that our discussion-based approach required looked like deviant behaviour to pupils. Seeing other pupils and other teachers indulging in these odd classroom behaviours as though they were normal was reassuring.

Once the teacher has found a way of building a shared understanding, however embryonic, of what the innovation might look like in action and why the group might benefit from trying it out, there comes the task of negotiating with pupils the agenda that, as a group, they want to pursue in their enquiry into controversial issues.

Teachers with whom we worked experimented with various ways of identifying issues within a broad content area. Films, photographs, case studies and visits proved to be powerful stimuli for starting an enquiry; from the general reactions that such materials or events provoke, teachers can often recognise, and help the group to recognise, a provisional agenda for enquiry. For instance, during an initial explora-tory session on 'war and society' pupils selected photographs from a large number that were made available in multiple copies and then explained why they had made their choices. They were also encouraged to question each other about the basis for choice. The teacher, as chairperson, had an important role to play in offering a model for courteous and unthreatening questioning – asking questions which the pupils and *not* the teacher had the answer to! The teacher, as chairperson, also had a responsibility to offer back to the group a summary of the questions that seemed to emerge from the exchanges. The group's task was then to decide whether the list had significant omissions, whether the questions were worded in a way that conveyed the meaning that a pupil had intended, and which issues they wanted to start on in their discussions. These were the 'starter' questions that one group's opening activity threw up: 'In war, is killing murder?', 'Why do people kill in wartime?', 'Should children be involved in war?', 'Should women be soldiers?', 'Is war ever just?', 'Should the atom bomb ever have been dropped?', 'Why do people demonstrate about war?'.

By taking seriously the task of setting an agenda – which must, of course, be flexible and reflect developments in the group's concerns – the teacher helps the pupils to feel that they own the issues and that the agenda is not something that has been determined, for them, by teachers.

A capacity to handle controversial issues is, now perhaps more than at any time, something which schooling should offer young people. Many new content areas which are bidding for space in the secondary curriculum are rooted in controversy and have as their aim the development of personal understanding. I am thinking, for instance, of peace studies, multicultural studies, gender studies and economic awareness programmes. The strategy developed by the Humanities Project team and outlined above is worth reviewing in the present climate. It offers a framework for handling controversial issues which will protect the teacher who works conscientiously within it from the charge of indoctrination.

Not all teachers are fully aware of the difficulty of supporting fair and open inquiry into controversial issues with pupils for whom the principles of evidence-based discussion are unfamiliar. The task can be very demanding. Whatever teaching strategy is adopted must be ethically and intellectually justifiable. It must meet the criterion of integrity and it must meet the criterion of engagement. The issues are too challenging to be handled superficially and too humanly significant to risk pupils being bored by them. In the new curriculum of secondary schools the 'real' world is increasingly annexed to the 'limbo' world of school through direct sorties such as work experience, residential trips and so forth. Classroom-based courses that offer pupils insight into the complex social issues that give everyday life its textures and tensions are another way of locking into realities. One doesn't *always* have to go out of the classroom to achieve respect and meaning in the secondary curriculum. But one has to get the teaching strategy right, as well as the content.

Notes and references

1 'On teaching independence' J Rae, in *New Statesman* 21 May 1973.
2 'Curriculum and the quality of schooling' L Stenhouse, a paper given at Goldsmiths College Annual Conference, printed in the conference proceedings, 1982.
3 *Ideology, culture and the process of schooling* H Giroux (Falmer Press, 1981).
4 This study was reported in *The sixth form and libraries: problems of access to knowledge* J Rudduck and D Hopkins (Library and Information Research Report 24, British Library, 1984).
5 'Recent trends in research on learning in schools and universities' N Entwistle, in *Scottish Educational Review* 1981, Vol 13, pp 112–21.
6 *Forms of intellectual and ethical development in the college years: a scheme* W G Perry (Holt, Rinehart and Winston, 1970).
7 See *The Humanities Project: an Introduction* (Heinemann, 1970) revised by

J Rudduck (School of Education publications, University of East Anglia, 1983).

8 Adapted from the *HCP Handbook*, 1983 edition, p 8 (see note 7).

9 *Learning to teach through discussion* J Rudduck (ed) (CARE publications, University of East Anglia, 1979) p 17.

10 'Ethics of leadership' T Brameld, in *Adult Leadership* 1955, Vol 4, pp 5–8.

11 'A curriculum for the study of human affairs: the contribution of Lawrence Stenhouse' J Elliott, in *Journal of Curriculum Studies* 1983, Vol 15, No 2, pp 105–23.

12 *Affective subjects in the classroom: exploring race, drugs and sex* C Epstein (Scranton, Pennsylvania: Intext Educational Publishers, 1972).

13 Adapted from 'The Humanities Project and the problem of motivation' L Stenhouse (1970) reprinted in *Authority, Education and Emancipation* L Stenhouse (Heinemann, 1983) pp 110–32.

14 See, for instance, the *Humanities Project Handbook* (see note 7) and *Learning to teach through discussion* (see note 9).

15 *Learning to teach through discussion* (see note 9) p 53 and 55.

16 Adapted from the *HCP Handbook* 1983 edition (see note 7) pp 30–1.

17 See 'Pupil strategies and the open classroom' M Denscombe, in *Pupil Strategies: Explorations in the Sociology of the School* P Woods (ed) (Croom Helm, 1980); 'In-service courses for pupils as a basis for implementing curriculum development' J Rudduck, in *British Journal of In-Service Education* 1983, Vol 10, No 1, pp 32–42; 'Curriculum change, management or meaning?' J Rudduck, in *School Organization* (1986, Vol 6, No 1, pp 107–14).

18 *The effects of systematic induction courses for pupils on pupils' perception of an innovation* C Hull and J Rudduck (Final Report to the SSRC, HR 6848/1, 1981).

19 See 'Introducing innovation to pupils' J Rudduck, in *Alternative Perspectives on School Improvement* D Hopkins and M Wideen (eds) (Falmer Press, 1984) pp 53–66.

Chapter 2

Dealing with controversy in the curriculum: A philosophical perspective[1]

David Bridges

Controversiality and the curriculum

There are controversies in all areas of human thought – in science, in history, in literary criticism, in economics, in theology, in politics, in philosophy, in engineering, in art, in medicine – but when it comes to representing any of these areas of thought in the school curriculum we are not entirely consistent in the attention which we are ready to give to their controversial nature or matter.

In some areas teachers are ready to present the subject matter as controversial in its very nature, and the public is by and large ready to allow this. This is perhaps best illustrated in the arts. Children are widely encouraged to be individual in their production of art in its various forms and to respond to others' art individually. At a more advanced stage they are invited to consider the varied and competing interpretations of a portrait, a poem, a play or a piece of music, which have been offered by different critics and interpreters. Arguments about the merits of alternative interpretations or evaluations are the very stuff of classroom discussion, essays and even examinations – even if the point of argument is sometimes lost in a woolly-minded subscription to a naively subjectivist view of aesthetic judgement.

Science provides a different but interesting example. Few science teachers would deny that science is a field of controversy (and I mean *scientific* controversy, not just controversy about the moral or social implications of science) and many would recognise, in Popperian fashion, that it proceeds and develops out of the conjecture and speculation which is fed by controversy.[2] Yet the vast proportion of school science is selected as, or presented as, uncontroversial – the well-established findings of science rather than its living activity, the ashes rather than the fire. There are exceptions to this. Nick Selley, for example, has argued for the place of 'alternative models' in school science:

The view that scientific theories/models are not absolutely true, but only *relatively* fruitful as schemes for systematizing observations, gives the teacher a new freedom to deal with more than one model in a given area of science. It also places importance on our reasons for preferring one model to another, since it can no longer be maintained simply that one is true and the others false. This pluralistic approach could bring science education more into line with other areas of the curriculum, such as English, religious education and the humanities, in which pupils' personal opinions are given some respect, and in which the discussion, clarification and criticism of such opinions is encouraged.[3]

On the whole, however, scientific controversy has little place in school classrooms. This is not, I think, because of particular fear of public disapproval. Rather it stems from a combination of a somewhat restricted view of the nature or philosophy of science; a narrowly instrumental view of the purposes of science teaching; and/or a simple conviction that to present science as controversial is too difficult or too confusing for most pupils.

The teaching of history provides a different and revealing example. Here, curriculum development programmes like the Schools Council Project on History 13–16 have made a serious attempt to shift the paradigm of history teaching from the teaching of 'established fact' to the teaching of ongoing disputes. On this model different and conflicting interpretations of historical events and characters are presented through contemporary and later historiography, and pupils are themselves invited to explore through discussion, role play and writing their own evaluations of the sources and their own interpretations of history. In this way, arguably, classroom history more closely resembles history as an activity practised by historians. At least, the status of historical 'knowledge' is more faithfully represented.

The examples that I have taken so far illustrate a number of points which it may be useful to clarify as a preliminary to subsequent discussion. The first is that controversy in the form of argument and counter-argument, variety of opinion and conflict of interpretation is a central and dynamic feature of many of the subjects (eg the arts, history and science) which traditionally feature in the school curriculum. Indeed, one cannot properly or fully understand or engage in the subject without understanding and engaging in at least some of its controversies. The second is that to a greater or lesser extent (this varies both between and within subject areas) teachers will already reflect the controversial nature of their subject matter in their selection of material and in the way in which it is taught in schools. Third, we might add that there is (so far at least) little evidence of public objection to these developments, except perhaps where they are accompanied by a perceived failure to teach 'the basics'. On the whole however (with the possible exception of the arts) controversy in these fields lies very largely with academics rather than with a broader 'lay' population. The role of the Star Chamber may have divided Tudor politicians and even 20th century historians, but its teaching is hardly the stuff to inflame the correspondence columns of national or local newspapers in the 1980s.

In general it is not the teaching of historical, scientific or even aesthetic controversy which is the focus of wider public and political concern and debate but moral, social and political controversy – issues to do with racism, sexism, peace and nuclear disarmament, unemployment, strikes, Northern Ireland, law and order, poverty, sexual ethics, the political economy . . . It is the way schools handle these kinds of issue (or the way they fail to handle them) which most provokes statements from political platforms, angry pamphleteering and letters to the newspaper or to the headteacher. It will be with these kinds of controversial issue that I shall be primarily concerned in this chapter.

There are certain epistemological features of the moral, social and political domains of belief which go to explain both the controversy about their handling in schools and the heatedness of that controversy. The bitter controversies about belief are not resolvable by reference to more factual information or more evidence. Nor will they ever be so, for they are rooted in personal or social values. Controversy may arise because:

- people are attached to different values;
- people attach different priority to the same values (compare, for example, socialist and liberal priorities in relation to the values of freedom and justice);
- people give different interpretations to the same value (eg 'peace' can be seen on the one hand as the absence of conflict, and on the other as the absence of oppression; 'equality' can mean treating all the same, or treating people differently according to relevant differences.)

One of the distinctive features of controversy in this area is that it typically (though not invariably) runs through several levels at which the issue may be considered. Thus, to give an over-simple example, people may debate whether or not the use of violence in the battle against apartheid in South Africa can be justified (level 1). This may develop into an argument about the priority which should be given, on the one hand, to values to do with peaceableness and non-violence and on the other, to values to do with justice, human rights, etc (level 2). If any of the protagonists are at all philosophically inclined, this in turn may develop into an argument to do with how you might *justify* any of the fundamental principles referred to – or indeed whether they are in any sense rationally justifiable (level 3). Are such values simply socially relative? Purely subjective? God-given? Intuitively knowable? Rationally defensible? These questions too are plainly controversial and contested at a level where even philosophers who have every respect for the intellectual calibre and philosophical understanding of each other can disagree fundamentally. Controversy in the area of moral, social and political issues thus runs much deeper than that in science or history, where there is a relatively well-established consensus about *how* questions might be resolved, even if there is dispute – at level 1 – as to the resolution which should be given to a particular question.

A second distinctive feature of controversies in this field of moral, social and political issues is that they tend to engage the emotions and passions as well as the intellect. Arguably at least (and I am not going into the argument in this context) the connection between 'valuing' and 'feeling' is not a purely contingent one. Feeling is logically entailed by the notion of valuing, so that to value freedom or justice or order is to have one's feelings engaged in a way which is quite different from having a belief about the causes of the Civil War or transmutations in a particular species of moth. This is not to say that historical or scientific controversy may not engage the passions of the protagonists, but it is to hold that there is a special logical or epistemological connection between beliefs and feeling in the field of moral, social and political values. Francis Dunlop argues, for example, that:

> moral reasons and principles . . . become available to us, or manifest themselves as relevant through feeling and emotion. If we did not experience feelings of horror and disgust at gratuitous cruelty we would not know – except in an 'empty', 'formal' and completely unmotivating way (*morally* unmotivating, that is) that, for example, cruelty was morally wrong, apart from being merely unpleasant to those who are its victims.[4]

Further, and still considering epistemological features of this domain, moral, social and political controversy is not just descriptive – about what is right, what ought to be the case and what ought to be done.[5] Beliefs in this field, if at all seriously held, affect how we *act* towards each other – and they do so in a way which is quite unlike beliefs which fall squarely in the domains of science, history, maths, geography or even literary criticism. What people believe thus has public as well as private consequences – it matters socially. The population of a school classroom does not sensibly view with equanimity the convictions of one of their number that blacks should be 'repatriated' or that only the fittest should survive – and nor should those who have an interest in their welfare.

So I have suggested that controversies in the field of moral, social and political issues are distinctive epistemologically in four respects:

- the centrality to them of disputes about values;
- the several levels at which controversy takes place;
- the particular connection in this field between belief and feeling;
- the particular connection between belief and action.

It is not surprising, therefore, that whether and how such issues should be handled in the school curriculum is a matter of considerable professional and public interest and indeed controversy. As Robert Stradling suggests, in his excellent study of the teaching of controversial issues, 'It is this kind of issue, arising out of a conflict of values, which confronts the teacher with the most fundamental pedagogic problems'.[6]

In practice, of course, schools cannot help but introduce some social and political teaching, though it may be very largely part of the hidden rather than the visible curriculum. Schools will represent moral, social and political values to their pupils through their own daily life and practice – their system of rules, rewards and punishments; their own hierarchical or non-hierarchical structures; the emphasis they place on competition and cooperation; the way they resolve conflict; the way they treat the weak or the slow; the hidden messages of racism or sexism in school readers or subject texts; explicit discrimination between boys and girls, black and white children, etc. All this gives powerful enough opportunity, one might think, for moral, social and political education or miseducation.

Moral, social and political values will also enter into the curriculum in connection with traditional subjects of which they are not a necessary or central feature. The teaching of literature is (almost) inseparable from consideration of the myriad of moral and social insights which is its very substance. Can one really study history without entering into the working out of particular social and political principles in given historical settings or (albeit with scholarly reserve) entering into some evaluation of 12th century feudalism, 16th century monarchy, 18th century revolutions, 19th century capitalism, 20th century fascism or the experience of war through the ages? Scientists, also, are naturally and responsibly drawn into exploring with their students social issues related to scientific and technological developments – issues to do with, for example, pollution, conservation of natural resources and ecological balance. Many geography teachers, having flirted somewhat unenthusiastically with approaches based on statistical modelling, have now embraced whole-heartedly the social and political dimensions of their subject. A brochure for the recently launched journal *Contemporary Issues in Geography and Education* promised forthcoming issues which would deal with (I quote selectively): 'Education for peace: what does it mean?'; 'Theoretical frameworks: an analysis of ideology in geography'; 'Colonialism and new colonialism: multinationals in the classroom'; 'Sexism and anti-sexism: of what relevance in a geography course?'.

Scruton and his colleagues, in *Education and Indoctrination* sought to exclude reference to these kinds of social and political issues in the traditional school subjects. They went to the extent of proposing a draft amendment to the 1944 Education Act which would exclude by law 'the introduction of contentious political attitudes into the presentation of material that could be as well taught without reference to such attitudes'.[7] Scruton's case, however, seems to be built upon the most extreme instances his reading and imagination can muster. It fails to address the modest, responsible and educationally well-grounded concerns of, for example, scientists as well as teachers of science, that students should understand the social consequences of scientific advance and should recognise that their practice of science does not release them from moral and social responsibility for the consequences of that practice. This concern to combat the tendency of the traditional school and university curriculum to insulate one area of thought and learning from another is entirely defensible on educational grounds as well as being a prerequisite of moral responsibility. It does not lead us as far as the kind of politicisation of the curriculum which Scruton caricatures, but it certainly does allow the introduction into the curriculum of 'contentious political attitudes' which he seeks comprehensively to exclude.

What, then, of the explicit handling of 'controversial issues' in the classroom? The school curriculum has tended to take two steps forward and then one and a half steps back over the last 20 years or so in introducing moral, social and/or political education as explicit and clearly-identified ingredients of the curriculum, sometimes (but not always) choosing to address directly central controversies. Among the most challenging and significant initiatives was the Schools Council/ Nuffield *Humanities Curriculum Project*, published in 1970.[8] This had a whole agenda of issues: war; education; the family; relations between the sexes; poverty; people at work; living in cities; law and order; and, to begin with at least, race. Its expectation, however, that teachers should test out the strategy of procedural neutrality proved to be more than any except the most patient, skilful and committed could sustain.

A few years later, in 1976, Robin Richardson managed to harness some very disparate educational pressure groups (concerned, variously, with world peace, human rights, poverty and oppression, racism, ecological balance and social justice) in a World Studies Project[9] whose publications envisaged not merely the good-tempered discussion of such issues but role play, experiential learning and indeed learning aimed at helping youngsters to take direct political action. Again it is perhaps only a small minority of teachers who will have the stomach (or whatever else it requires) not merely to give new status to their students' opinions (as did HCP) but to support that with political empowerment. But curriculum development projects like these challenge us to place moral, social and political controversies firmly in the school curriculum and require us to consider what ethical, professional and practical principles should determine our ways of handling these issues in the classroom.

I believe we should accept this challenge, and in what follows I propose to identify and discuss four different strategies which we might adopt, and which indeed some teachers have adopted: proselytisation and indoctrination; neutrality; reason and impartiality; and 'oppressive tolerance' and counter-indoctrination.

Proselytisation and indoctrination

It would be surprising if among those teachers who wish to introduce controversial moral, social or political issues into the curriculum there were not many who have themselves strong moral, social or political commitments. Naively, perhaps, many people have been drawn to teaching through some sense of wanting to help a disadvantaged section of society, or some notion that by the influence they exercise over their pupils they might contribute to the shaping of a more honest, a more open, a more caring, a more just and a better-informed society in the future. 'Since wars begin in the minds of men,' said Clement Attlee, 'it is in the minds of men that we must construct the defences of peace.' (Perhaps if he had spoken today he would not have thought it necessary to express his proposition in terms of 'men and women'!) Why not? Teachers have a precious opportunity, if not a responsibility, to shape the opinions of the young, of the new generation who (and this has been the aspiration of successive generations) may grow up to create a better world than our own generation has so far succeeded in doing. Why should teachers not advocate, proselytise, argue, persuade with all the skill at their command to uphold the convictions which they themselves believe to be so important? If some want to call such an approach indoctrinatory, let us not be put off by their disapproval, but seek plainly and expertly to secure in children's consciousness principles which we believe to be for the ultimate good of themselves and of the community.

I do not want to get too entangled among different styles of advocacy and indoctrination or to examine whether all advocacy is indoctrinatory. What I want to characterise is an energetic teaching approach in which ethical and educational considerations to do with *how* beliefs or attitudes may be inculcated are sacrificed or subordinated to a determined effort at their successful inculcation. What are we to make of this approach to the handling of moral, social and political issues which a teacher might nevertheless acknowledge to be controversial socially (though no doubt only because of the ignorance, over-complacency, greed or stubbornness of those who contest the passionately-held opinion)? More particularly, what objections, if any, can be presented against it?

I think there are at least three closely-related arguments which might well dissuade some teachers from this stance. The first is not necessarily a counter-argument, but a consistency test. For a teacher consciously to choose to indoctrinate in moral, social or political values which she or he acknowledges to be socially controversial is itself to offend against some such values or principles. For example, it appears at least to offend against most notions of respect for other people and their opinions. It appears to conflict with social values to do with personal autonomy, which in the educational context often seem to require that pupils come to understand the choices open to them and to make these choices freely, intelligently and authentically for themselves.[10] If the teachers who espouse indoctrinatory procedures do not value these things, they may at least, thus far, preserve their consistency. However, it is difficult to see how teachers whose moral purpose and enthusiasm includes the cultivation of personal autonomy and respect for persons could reconcile this with indoctrinatory procedures.

My second argument represents a more comprehensive objection to indoctrinatory procedures or benevolent proselytisation. It relates to what I wrote earlier in this section on the several layers of contest about opinion on moral and social values. My point is that it is simply dishonest to present as true anything which cannot in any ordinary way (by reference to evidence or argument) be established as true. The passion of one's own conviction is no substitute for 'publicly' demonstrable reasons, evidence and argument. Equally, it is dishonest to present a belief as the only one deserving serious attention when there are, in fact, other beliefs subscribed to by those whose judgement, in different areas, one might acknowledge to be worthy of respect.

This consideration seems quite compelling, but I would have to acknowledge that for, say, a teacher whose vision of the right or the good was a matter of some kind of divine revelation, my argument would not carry much weight. To those to whom God has revealed 'the truth' other people's scratching around for publicly testable reasons, evidence and argument must seem a rather pathetic, or indeed perverse, occupation. Honesty nevertheless requires that true believers acknowledge the efforts some make to scratch for the truth in the dust – just as the dust-scratchers, the measurers and the testers must acknowledge that others believe they have found it in the heavens.

Third, it seems to me that it does and should matter to teachers not only *what* children come to believe but *how* they hold those beliefs. More explicitly, we achieve relatively little if we simply replace one dogma, one prejudice, one unintelligent and irrational belief or one closed mind by another. Are we entitled to assume that our generation has at last got all the right answers to the ancient problems of human life and can foresee how they can be applied in the rapidly changing decades ahead? Whatever wisdom we have acquired must surely include the realisation that new generations of people will test and criticise our beliefs and adapt our knowledge to the changing circumstances of their own age. If our pupils are to be able to handle our ideas in this way, they have to receive them not as categorical truth or dogma but with a full appreciation of the strength and weakness of the evidence and thinking which underlie them, and of the ideas which contend with them for credence. Apart from anything else, if beliefs are, as those involved in social and political education generally hope them to be, a springboard to action, they need to be held as something more than received wisdom. As John Stuart Mill warned:

However unwillingly a person who has a strong opinion may admit the possibility that his opinion may be false, he ought to be moved by the consideration that, however true it may be, if it is not fully, frequently and fearlessly discussed, it will be held as a dead dogma, not a living truth.[11]

Neutrality

The rejection of proselytising and indoctrination, or the fear of either, leads people to urge on teachers working in obviously controversial areas like moral, social and political education, a concern for 'balance' in their presentation. They maintain that the teacher should either put both sides of an argument with equal enthusiasm or perhaps refrain from presenting either.

These kinds of concern are illustrated in the responses which a group of teachers from Groby Community College in Leicestershire received when they circulated for comment a new World Studies syllabus which they were proposing to introduce. The first comment comes from a local MP:

While I am sure that this course is well intentioned, there seems to me a very real risk that it might turn out to resemble indoctrination rather than education, to present matters of opinion and controversy as if they were matters of fact, and to contain an excessively political content. I trust, therefore, that you will do everything you can to guard against these risks and in particular to enable those taking the course to develop their critical faculties by presenting them, in the fairest way possible, with a critique of the arguments and views set out in the syllabus. If this should prove impossible, I think it would be better not to offer this type of course at all.[12]

A slightly more sophisticated comment came from one school Geography department but the notion of balance expressed is I think very much the same:

The syllabus seems to have a distinct bias towards the view that the 'First' World (however defined) exploits the 'Third' World (however defined). This is not an established fact overall and it is important in schools to give a full range of facts and opinions. Again to present ourselves and the rest of the 'First' World as heartless exploiters is unhelpful: the real world situation is far more complicated than that. Clearly a balance has to be struck between saying nothing and giving too simplistic a picture to immature pupils. The exploitation of the so-called Socialist countries of Eastern Europe by the Soviet Union (and of Cuba) should be mentioned alongside criticisms of say the Western oil companies. Always, a full, balanced view should surely be our aim. It will always be hard to achieve.[12]

What seems to be called for in these statements and, I think, in a long tradition of scholarly teaching, is a style of pedagogy in which teachers present to their pupils as many sides of a controversy as possible without, at least initially, indicating by the manner of presentation which they personally support. I shall refer to this style as 'affirmative neutrality'.

There are a number of drawbacks associated with this approach. It pushes the teacher into a role which involves the transmission of a rather large amount of information in a form which may mitigate against reflective criticism by pupils. It is particularly difficult for the teacher to be at one and the same time the source of so much opinion and the chairman of a discussion. In practice, of course, it is extraordinarily difficult to present a range of opinions without this presentation being coloured or at least limited by the teacher's own views.

These were among the considerations which led those responsible for the Schools Council/Nuffield Humanities Curriculum Project (HCP) to define and explore a somewhat different teaching strategy which they referred to as 'procedural neutrality'. The HCP was faced with a very similar problem to that which I have presented in this paper: what role should the teacher adopt in the classroom in relation to subject-matter which (in this case by definition) is controversial? The role that the HCP invited teachers to explore was that of the neutral chairman of a classroom discussion. It was not imagined for one moment that teachers were in fact neutral in relation to the issues under discussion or that they would pretend to be. Teachers would simply enter into an explicit role clearly explicated to their pupils, in which they would refrain from supporting one or other position in the controversy under discussion. To support them in this role and assist them in maintaining the position as procedural chairmen, information about the controversy and different points of view relating to it would be available in the form of packs of material – newspaper cuttings, poems, letters, photos, cartoons, etc. – in HCP terminology the 'evidence' for the discussion[13] [the notion of 'procedural neutrality' is discussed fully in Jean Rudduck's paper in Chapter 1].

A body of literature now exists about HCP in general and the notion of procedural neutrality in particular. At the risk of over-simplification, I want to pluck out of this three arguments which I have come to regard as the most significant ones in support of the stance of neutrality.

The main argument in support of procedural neutrality starts from the HCP's decision to have as its teaching aim the *understanding* of certain controversies. As Lawrence Stenhouse, the Project Director, has suggested: 'given a dispute in society about the truth of a matter, the teacher might wish to teach the dispute rather than the truth as he knows it'.[14] What HCP chose to do was to teach the dispute and to try to get young people to appreciate the range of different perspectives available socially – and indeed among themselves – on the issues under discussion. This implied valuing and protecting a divergence of opinion rather than seeking consensus. It also implied restricting teachers from intentionally, or quite contrarily to their intentions, giving their authoritative legitimation to one particular view.

This brings us to the second major consideration underlying HCP's support for procedural neutrality, what one might refer to as its empirical base. Time and time again in the research team's observation of classroom discussion and interviews with 'students', the HCP was faced with the power and pervasiveness of pupils' expectations that in any school setting there was a right answer to a question, and that right answer was the one which the teacher indicated was his or her answer to the question. The pupils' task was to discern, learn and return that right answer. Other answers were of little or no relevance in the school context. I paraphrase, but I think I represent fairly the gist of the experience of the HCP. Expressed in these terms the problem of authority is not just that of the teachers' intentions but also of their pupils' expectations. Teachers may not intend to use the authority of their position to support a particular opinion but this lack of intent is not sufficient to prevent this from being precisely what happens in practice. According to Elliot:

Years of educational conditioning may make it extremely difficult for students to understand and accept the teacher's renunciation of the role of 'expert' so ingrained is the notion by their past educational experiences . . . (The teacher) can so easily deceive himself into believing that students are not ascribing authority to his views, when in fact they are.[15]

The only way out, at least 'at this stage of education' is for the teacher to refrain altogether from supporting any side in the controversy.

The third argument underlying the advocacy of procedural neutrality takes us into the logical or epistemological status of the value judgements which underlie the kind of controversial issues handled by HCP. This argument rests on the observation or premise which I have already offered that reason, argument and evidence marshalled according to 'publicly' recognised procedures can take you only so far in ethical argument – for example, ruling out certain empirical claims as contrary to observation and certain arguments as internally inconsistent. There comes a point in such argument where fundamental differences of view remain which cannot be resolved by reference to those same publicly recognised standards of reason, or at least, to be more precise, where the question as to whether reason can resolve these differences of view is itself controversial even at (or especially at) the most sophisticated level of ethical or meta-ethical argument. This being the case, it would be quite improper (dishonest) for a teacher to present as objectively correct an opinion which must essentially rest upon a foundation of what one might regard as nonrational or criterionless choice.

This notion of 'the neutral teacher' received a predictable bombardment of criticism in the educational press. The change of role proposed fundamentally challenged many assumptions about teaching. It was certainly not easy to implement in practice, and many teachers found the struggle out of proportion to the gain. Some simply realised that, when the chips were down, they cared more about promoting certain substantive opinions than encouraging the exploration of divergent opinion in group discussion. (The National Union of Teachers' representatives on the HCP's steering committee, for example, effectively prevented the HCP from extending its neutral teacher approach to the issue of race relations.) The Schools Council Moral Education Project directed by Peter McPhail objected to the neutral chairman role on the grounds of children's interest in and right to know the teacher's own opinions.[16]

These responses I shall leave without further comment. There are, however, two other lines of argument about this teaching strategy which I would like to explore a little more fully.

The first concerns the question 'what are the values of the neutral teacher?' Or more especially 'what values is the teacher promoting through his or her neutrality?' This sounds paradoxical but it is not. The HCP never imagined that the neutral teacher was in fact value-free. Teachers refrain from taking a stance on the substantive issues under discussion precisely in order to promote other qualities of learning and learning outcomes which they consider desirable – including, for example, the values associated with the activity of discussion itself, respect for the opinions of others, concern for evidence, a sense of the worth of one's own judgement and an increasing reliance on that judgement as a basis for one's opinion. The 'neutral' teacher is not without commitment. Rather, as the HCP introductory booklet put it: 'The teacher's commitment is to education, not to his own views'.[17] However, if the social values that teachers wanted to promote were in fact of a roughly liberal democratic order, they might well discover that their ends were better served through the so-to-speak 'hidden curriculum' of procedural neutrality than through any explicit attempt at their promotion. A particularly interesting case of this phenomenon occurred in connection with the HCP's trials with its (subsequently censored) Race materials. The evaluation study suggested that marginally, but by a statistically significant degree, teachers who adopted the stance of procedural neutrality were more likely to encourage tolerant interracial attitudes than those who sought actively to promote such attitudes.[18] The authors of the study have since had occasion to qualify the validity of the initial research and to extend their study into wider comparisons,[19] but its general force is still supported and offers intriguing possibilities to the teacher who shares the kinds of values which I have indicated.

The second important question raised about the strategy of procedural neutrality concerns the attitude of the teacher towards rational argument and the place of rational argument in the discussion of value questions. I will discuss this question in the context of my comments on the next teaching stance – that of rational and impartial leadership.

Reason and impartiality

I take the term neutrality to imply a strategy through which one either supports alternative points of view equally (affirmative neutrality) or withholds support from any point of view (negative or procedural neutrality). Impartiality differs from neutrality in that it allows or even requires differential support to opinion, provided that the different level of support is related to objective merits rather than any other consideration to do with, for example, one's personal interest, advantage or feeling.

That all is subject to argument, that no person counts for more than his argument counts, even the teacher, and that all statements are subject to rational criticism – all this is part of the rational commitment and is picked out in the conception of impartiality . . . To be impartial is to consider views and interests in the light of all possible criticisms and counter-claim, and to ignore any kind of special pleading, whether from authority or whatever, from myself or whomsoever.[20]

Charles Bailey, who defined impartiality in these terms, argued that this principle, rather than that of neutrality, should guide the teacher in handling controversial value issues in the classroom. The classroom discussion in his view should have the objective not just of expressing an interesting range of opinion but of employing rational criticism to try to establish the truth of the matter.

In another attack on the idea of neutrality Mary Warnock[21] offered a rather more didactic version of the teacher's role, but again one that emphasised the responsibility for teaching pupils 'how to draw rational conclusions rationally':

Unless the teacher comes out into the open, and says in what direction he believes that the evidence points he will have failed in his duty as a teacher. For what his pupils have to learn is not only, in an abstract way, what counts as evidence, but how people draw conclusions from evidence . . . Thus the teacher must if he is to teach his pupils to assess evidence fairly, give them actual examples of how he does this himself. His pupils may disagree with him. The more adult they become, and the better their earlier experience of arguments, the more capable they will be of weighing the probabilities differently. But unless they see before them the spectacle of a rational man drawing conclusions rationally, they will never learn what rational probabilities are.

Support for this kind of position came from no less an authority than Sir Keith Joseph when as Secretary of State he addressed a conference called by the National Council of Women of Great Britain on Peace Education:

His (the teacher's) presentation needs to be as objective as he can make it, in the sense that he ensures that what is offered as a fact is indeed true; that the selection of facts gives a picture which is neither unbalanced nor superficial; that facts and opinions are clearly separated; and that pupils are encouraged to weigh evidence and argument so as to arrive at rational judgements.[22]

It would be difficult to deny the general desirability of helping children to respect reasons and argument and to come to hold their opinions on the basis of reasons and argument. From this point of view impartiality would seem to be preferable to both indoctrination, which bypasses the activities of rational deliberation, and neutrality, which even if it does not offend against rationality on the face of it stops short in its support for it.

There are, however, two important reservations to this conclusion both of which arise out of arguments I have already indicated in support of the strategy of negative or procedural neutrality.

The first of these reservations concerns children's ability to separate the authority of a teacher's social position in the classroom (and the examination hall) from the authority of reasons, evidence or argument which the teacher may adduce in support of an opinion he or she holds. The teacher may sincerely and earnestly urge pupils to treat his or her opinion just like any other and to judge it by reference to the evidence which supports it, not the authority or otherwise of its source. But when pupils are accustomed to accepting no better reason than 'because I say so' and when, institutionally, teacher's opinion coincides so universally with right opinion, the transition to the impartial assessment of evidence is psychologically not an easy one. As I have argued elsewhere,[23] for the teacher to adopt the stance of negative neutrality and withhold his or her opinions from discussion altogether for a time may be a useful transitionary stage in weaning pupils from dependence on his or her authority.

The second reservation takes us into more profound problems of moral philosophy or meta-ethics. The critical question here is to what extent ethical questions or questions of moral value are amenable to rational argument as against a rational preference. I have already indicated that members of the HCP took the view either that such questions were not ultimately resolvable by reference to reason or that whether or not they were was itself a controversial question. This view underlay at least one form of the argument in favour of neutrality. By contrast, Charles Bailey suggests that there are indeed good reasons for preferring some moral positions to others and that more specifically a commitment to rationality itself entails a commitment to a range of substantive and important values. This view underlies his argument in favour of impartiality.

The significant point for teachers is that they need perhaps to be a little clearer and more consistent as to where they stand on this meta-ethical question about values and about the implications of their stance. Are values essentially and logically controversial – or are they so simply because some people have not followed the argument correctly? The confident assertion of values by, for example, some teachers working on World Studies programmes, suggests that their proponents regard these as having some objectively defensible and universal value independent of the subjective preferences of a particular proponent, independent even of his or her particular social or cultural affinities. People speak of the evil of apartheid, for example, in a manner which suggests a judgement rooted in considerations more fundamental and universal than one expressed in terms of what is right or wrong *for me* or *for our society*. At the same time, however, the allegiance of World Studies teachers to the idea of a multicultural society and their endorsement of cultural pluralism often lead them into a kind of social relativism. I am not sure that such a position can be consistently maintained. Certainly its implications would come uneasily from the lips of most World Studies teachers — 'racial apartheid is wrong unless you happen to live, for example, in South Africa where it's right'? The morality of seeking change in society becomes difficult to explain in a context in which we are supposed to derive our moral precepts, not just in fact but rightly, from those which already pervade that society.

I will not try to resolve 2000 years of moral argument in a footnote. My central point here is that the rationale for one's teaching strategy in relation to socially controversial moral, social and political values must be consistent with and rooted in a defensible view of the logical status of those values, and in particular in some judgement on the extent to which they can be rationally and objectively defended. In particular I suggest that the issue between those who defend neutrality and those who argue for impartiality is related to a difference of perspective on this meta-ethical problem.

'Oppressive tolerance' and counter indoctrination

The longstanding liberal preference for openness of discussion, balanced presentation of all sides of an argument, the tolerance and even encouragement of dissent and the impartiality or neutrality of those with special authority, is based on a conviction that these are the conditions most conducive to the development of knowledge and understanding at the personal and at the social level. John Stuart Mill's essay *On Liberty* is a classic source for this opinion:

In the case of any person whose judgment is really deserving of confidence, how has it become so?

Because he has kept his mind open to criticism of his opinions and conduct. Because it has been his practice to listen to all that could be said against him; to profit by as much of it as was just, and expound to himself, and upon occasion to others, the fallacy of what was fallacious. Because he felt that the only way in which a human being can make some approach to knowing the whole of a subject is by hearing what can be said about it by persons of every variety of opinion, and studying all modes in which it can be looked at by every character of mind. No wise man ever acquired wisdom in any mode but this; nor is it in the nature of human intellect to become wise in any other.[24]

The same tradition of thought was expressed by Voltaire 'We should tolerate each other because we are all weak, inconsistent, subject to mutability and to error'[25] and by John Milton:

Where there is much desire to learn there of necessity will be much arguing, much writing, many opinions; for opinion in good men is but knowledge in the making. Under these fantastic terrors of sect and schism, we wrong the earnest and zealous thirst after knowledge and understanding which God hath stirred up in this city ... So Truth be in the field, we do injuriously, by licensing and prohibiting, to misdoubt her strength. Let her and falsehood grapple; whoever knew Truth put to the worse, in a free and open encounter? Her confuting is the best and surest suppressing.[26]

What these extracts illustrate are three central ingredients of what I would refer to as the liberal epistemological tradition:
- the importance of the ready availability of the full range of opinion on an issue (a free market in ideas);
- an acknowledgement of the fallibility of opinion including our own;
- a confidence in the free competition of ideas as a condition for the emergence of a true or, given our second consideration, the best opinion available.

This kind of view enjoys considerable popularity in liberal/progressive educational circles. It has not, however, passed unchallenged. One form of challenge has, I think, particular relevance to approaches to political education. I refer to the radical critique of the liberal theory of free discussion and more especially to Herbert Marcuse's important and seminal essay *Repressive Tolerance*. I am not sure that I can do anything like justice to Marcuse's argument in a short space, but let me try to give enough indication of it to prompt the interested reader to pursue it at source.

The first stage in the argument is to make the point that the merits of tolerance, impartiality and free discussion presuppose the existence of conditions which, however, do *not* exist even in so-called democratic societies, notably the equal availability and expression of alternative opinions. The dice, claims Marcuse, are heavily loaded in favour of those opinions which support the status quo:

The antagonistic structure of society rigs the rules of the game. Those who stand against the established system are *a priori* at a disadvantage, which is not removed by the toleration of their ideas, speeches and newspapers.

Similarly the liberal position presupposes the rationality, autonomy and open-mindedness of those who attend the expression of alternative opinion. Instead, in reality, we are faced with manipulated and indoctrinated individuals who parrot, as their own, the opinions of their masters. From this Marcuse concludes that the actual effect of the indiscriminate toleration of opinion oppressive and liberationist, regressive and progressive is simply to reinforce the forces of oppression and conservatism – all the more perhaps by allowing them the appearance of being tolerant of dissent and open to criticism.

The active, official tolerance granted to the Right as well as to the Left, to movements of aggression as well as to movements of peace, to the party of hate as well as to that of humanity. I call this non-partisan tolerance 'abstract' or 'pure' inasmuch as it refrains from taking sides – but in doing so it actually protects the already established machinery of discrimination.

Accordingly, says Marcuse, if people are to become truly autonomous and freed from the prevailing indoctrination we would need to take apparently undemocratic measures:

They would include the withdrawal of toleration of speech and assembly from groups and movements which promote aggressive policies, armament, chauvinism, discrimination on grounds of race and religion, or which oppose the extension of public services, social security, medical care etc. Moreover, the restoration of freedom of thought may necessitate new and rigid restrictions on teachings and practices in educational institutions which, by their very methods and concepts, serve to enclose the mind within the established universe of discourse and behaviour . . . (Indeed) the trend would have to be reversed; they would have to get information slanted in the opposite direction.

This policy of selective tolerance and the deliberate slanting of opinion of course requires judgement by some person or persons as to what precisely are the progressive and liberating opinions as distinct from the regressive and oppressive ones. For someone who is so acute in his criticism of other people's presuppositions Marcuse seems to have a startlingly simplistic confidence in the self-evidence of these distinctions. He is also relatively unforthcoming on the identification of those who will somehow make such distinctions on behalf of the blinkered masses:

everyone 'in the maturity of his faculties' as a human being, everyone who has learned to think rationally and autonomously. The answer to Plato's educational dictatorship is *the democratic educational dictatorship of free men* [my italics].

At this point Marcuse's position gets particularly contorted. He appears to want to avoid the idea of a kind of Platonic educational élite, sorting out the ignorant or misguided masses. At the same time he has to concede that on his own analysis of society the mass of the people must be unable to make the kind of discrimination he is after. (If they can, his analysis of society breaks down.) So the educational revolution has to be imposed on the majority by a minority. The new enlightenment, the new way of perceiving the world, justice and injustice, oppression and liberation, will be one which, if anything, is the product of closer, more restrictive (and why not more oppressive?) intellectual management than that which it replaces. It is difficult to see why one should suppose the post-revolutionary thinker to be any less restricted intellectually than the thinker whose place he or she has taken.

On my reading, Marcuse's position founders on the problematic nature of judgements about social progress and regression and on the contradiction between his concern to combat totalitarianism and oppression and his need to re-establish it as his own instrument of change. I think, too, that he may exaggerate the power and potency of the indoctrinatory processes at work in a democratic society (though others have no doubt underestimated them). It is, after all, immensely difficult to distinguish the extent to which anyone's ideas, beliefs or values are the result of indoctrination or autonomous reflection. It would be interesting to have Marcuse's own account or to explore for ourselves the educational or social conditions which enabled Marcuse and other like-minded critics of the 'oppressive' society to develop the intellectual equipment which they use so forcefully to analyse the structure and weaknesses of that society. Perhaps if we could extend to more people the advantages of *their* upbringing we might establish that democracy of free human beings to which Marcuse aspires without taking to expedients which would seem to fly in the face of its aspirations.

If I find it difficult to accept some of Marcuse's conclusions I believe nevertheless that teachers can study his criticism to advantage. In particular those who want their pupils to be able to consider a full range of alternative opinions will have to be alert to the social and psychological barriers which will inhibit access or the giving of serious attention to ideas which challenge the deep-seated orthodoxies of their own assumptions or of society. This is indeed a key practical question for teachers, though not for them alone. I do not however believe that it is answered by attempts to replace one sort of indoctrination, one sort of oppression, one sort of one-sidedness, one sort of myopia by another.

Conclusion

Where does all this leave us? I do not ask this question rhetorically or purely for effect. It is a question which has nagged at me for many years, since I first addressed social and political controversy in school myself. However, let me try and pull out of my previous discussion the positive principles which underlie my comments. They include, most importantly I think, the following:

1 A respect for persons, which I take to include respect for children's and parents' rights to hold opinions which differ from our own and a readiness to understand these opinions ourselves.

2 A concern to cultivate and develop the personal autonomy of young people – including in that the understanding and self-confidence which are conditions of free choice.

3 An honest acknowledgement of the true state and status of opinion – including in that an open recognition of the uncertainty, the provisionality, the controversiality of judgement and recognition of the albeit problematic distinction between fact and value.

4 A readiness on behalf of teachers to detach from their opinions as far

as is possible the authority which belongs to their social role or personal charisma and to rest it instead on the authority of reason alone.

5 A concern that pupils as far as possible grasp, along with any opinion that we teach, the reasons, evidence and argument underlying that opinion.

6 A concern to teach the controversy and not just one person's view of the proper conclusion of the controversy.

7 A concern to cultivate in our pupils and ourselves a constant alertness to, and ruthless criticism of, those beliefs which we take most for granted.

Such principles are intended to support rather than inhibit the introduction of moral, social and political controversy in the classroom. I return to the view that I expressed in my introduction that controversy is the dynamic, the growth point of any area of knowledge. Any intellectual domain which fails to generate it must soon atrophy and die; and any educational system which seeks simultaneously to initiate its young into the life of the intellect and to debar them from intellectual controversy must condemn their minds to the same paralysis.

Notes and references

1 This chapter is based on a paper previously published under the title ‘“So truth be in the field . . ?” Approaches to controversy in World Studies teaching’ in *Teaching World Studies* D Hicks and C Townley (eds) (Longman, 1982). It appears here in substantially revised form by kind permission of the publishers.

2 *Conjectures and Refutations: The Growth of Scientific Knowledge* K R Popper (Routledge and Kegan Paul, 1963).

3 ‘The place of alternative models in school science’ N Selley, in *School Science Review*, December 1981.

4 *The place of feeling in the moral life* F Dunlop, paper read to the Cambridge branch of the Philosophy of Education Society of Great Britain.

5 *The Language of Morals* R M Hare (The Clarendon Press, 1952).

6 *Teaching Controversial Issues* R Stradling, M Noctor, B Baines (Edward Arnold, 1984).

7 *Education and Indoctrination* R Scruton, A Ellis-Jones and D O’Keefe (Education Research Centre, 1985).

8 *The Humanities Project: an Introduction* Schools Council/Nuffield Humanities Project (Heinemann, 1970).

9 *Learning for Change in World Society* R Richardson (ed) (World Studies Project, 1976).

10 *Beyond the Present and the Particular: A Theory of Liberal Education* C H Bailey (Routledge and Kegan Paul, 1984).

11 ‘On Liberty’ J S Mill, in *Three Essays by John Stuart Mill* (Oxford University Press, 1971).

12 ‘World Studies on the runway: one year’s progress towards a core

curriculum' J Aucott, H Cox, A Dodds and D Selby, in *The New Era* 1979, 60, 60, pp 212–29.

13 *The Humanities Project: an Introduction* (see note 8).

14 *An introduction to curriculum research and development* L Stenhouse (Heinemann, 1975).

15 'The values of the neutral teacher' J Elliott, in *Values and Authority in Schools* D Bridges and P Scrimshaw (eds) (Hodder and Stoughton, 1975).

16 *Moral Education in the Secondary School* P McPhail, J R Ungoed-Thomas and H Chapman (Longman, 1972).

17 *The Humanities Project: an Introduction* (see note 8).

18 'Teaching race in schools: some effects on the attitudinal and sociometric patterns of adolescents' G Verma and C Bagley in *Race* 1971, Vol 13, No 2, pp 187–202.

19 'Teaching styles and race relations: some effects on white teenagers' G Verma and C Bagley, in *The New Era* (London World Education Fellowship, 1978) Vol 59, No 2, pp 53–7.

20 'Neutrality and rationality in teaching' C H Bailey, in *Values and Authority in Schools* D Bridges and P Scrimshaw (eds) (Hodder and Stoughton, 1975).

21 'The neutral teacher' M Warnock, in *Philosophers Discuss Education* S C Brown (ed) (Macmillan, 1975).

22 Sir Keith Joseph: speech to the National Council of Women of Great Britain conference, published in *Educating People for Peace* (National Council of Women of Great Britain, 1984).

23 *Education Democracy and Discussion* D Bridges (NFER/Nelson, 1979).

24 See note 11.

25 *Philosophical Dictionary* P Voltaire, trans J Betterman (Penguin, 1971 edn.).

26 'Areopagitica' J Milton, in *Prose Writings* (Dent, 1985 edn.).

27 'Repressive tolerance' H Marcuse, in *Critical Sociology* P Connerton (ed) (Penguin, 1976).

Chapter 3
Global education

Graham Pike and David Selby

Global education: response to a systemic world

Consider the view of the world held by a British teenager growing up in the last quarter of the 20th century. She may never stray far from her home or community, and yet she is constantly building up an intricate picture of the wider world. In the foreground, probably, is the world of material goods: the family car, television set and washing machine all clearly display evidence of their origins in the major industrial nations (she doesn't yet know that the picture is even more complex, that 'made in Britain' can simply denote the final place of assembly for a global cocktail of manufactured parts and raw materials). Her clothes and food feature centrally in the global mosaic. The weekly supermarket expedition reveals fresh fruits and vegetables from Mediterranean climes, tea and coffee from barely heard of places in Africa, Asia and South America; in surveying the shelves, she is reminded of a recent news report about people not buying produce from South Africa. The last pair of shoes she bought came from Israel, her favourite jumper was made in Mauritius while the shop window in front of which she frequently lingers displays the young fashions of Paris, Milan and New York.

That television set, of course, contributes much to the background of her world picture, a world characterised, according to news and fictional programmes, by violence, disaster and misfortune. She knows that modern technology enables her to witness events on the other side of the globe as they happen, just as the telephone permits her to speak with distant relatives at Christmas. She accepts such phenomena, unthinkable to her grandparents when they were her age, as quite commonplace components of *her* world.

Almost all of us are caught up in a network of links, interactions and relationships that encircle the planet like a giant and intricate spider's web. The wider world is a pervasive and ubiquitous element in the routines of our everyday life. The term 'global interdependence' is often used to describe this reality. Whilst not a purely contemporary phenomenon (there have been trading links and migrations of peoples between nations for many centuries), the interdependence of the modern world is markedly different in its *degree of frequency*, its *depth* and its *scope*.[1] An analysis of major events which have shaped history over the past five centuries reveals an increasing trend, the nearer one gets to the present day, towards events which have carried significance for many nations, rather than just one.[2] Whereas in the past the impact of global interdependence was relatively limited, there are today almost no people and very few human activities or concerns not affected, in some part at least, by the interdependent nature of the world.

Global interdependencies have become operationally immediate. They affect the purity of the air we breathe and the water we drink; the levels of employment and inflation; the price of tea; the level of taxation; fuel costs; the survival prospects of wildlife; the availability and subject matter of the books and newspapers we read; the changing roles of men and women in society; our relative peacefulness or unpeacefulness of mind and our image of the future. As we gallop towards the 21st century, we are witnessing a relatively advanced stage in the continuing and quickening transformation of the world from a *collection* of many lands and peoples to a *system* of many lands and peoples.

The world is becoming increasingly characterised by its systemic quality. To touch any part of the spider's web is to trigger vibrations in many – sometimes all – other parts. A distant political struggle is a luggage search for plane passengers at Manchester Airport. An upheaval in Iran is a lowered thermostat in Buenos Aires. An assassination in India sparks off demonstrations in South London. The uranium requirement of French nuclear power stations is the desecration of sacred homelands in Queensland. A sneeze in Hong Kong becomes an epidemic in the Outer Hebrides. Insights from General Systems Theory help us to comprehend the nature of the emergent global system. According to Systems Theory, nothing can be fully understood in isolation but must be seen as part of a dynamic, multi-layered system. Relationship is everything; the activity of the system comprises the simultaneous and interdependent interaction of its many component parts, the nature of the system is always more than the mere sum total of the separate parts.

Global education is a response to the need, in the contemporary world, to understand the emergent global system. Students may accept the ramifications of global interdependence as unremarkable features in their daily lives, but mere acceptance is insufficient if they are to make sense of the world in which they live. The news pictures which flash nightly on to the television screen present, at best, a truncated, distorted image of the world. The simple 'made in . . . ' statements on manufactured goods cover a complex web of trading relationships incorporating financial deals, political allegiances and the personal lives and fortunes of thousands of people around the globe. Major problems of our time, such as unemployment, environmental pollution and urban violence, cannot be adequately explained within a purely local or national context.

Seemingly 'domestic' events are often manifestations of global interactions and proceed, themselves, to impact on the global stage; so-called 'foreign' events can have profound domestic repercussions.

To what extent does formal schooling facilitate the process of global understanding? To what extent does it equip students with the capacities and skills for effective participation in a fast-changing systemic world? To what extent does it encourage students to embrace other cultural viewpoints, to seek out divergent solutions to problems, to envision alternative futures? To what extent does the curriculum reflect the global interdependence which is the reality of the students who study it? The answer to such questions in the majority of British primary and secondary schools would be 'not at all' or, at best, 'to a limited extent'. Thus, children at school find themselves in a paradoxical situation: inextricably bound up in the web of global connections, yet receiving an education which all too often fails to acknowledge this fact. They are buffeted daily by news of personal, national and global crises, yet rarely encouraged to develop the skills and understanding necessary to seek out solutions; bombarded by the multifarious impact of new technology, yet not equipped with the skills and attitudes to cope with the rapid change it will inevitably precipitate.

Global education is an attempt to resolve this paradox, to help students attain a profounder understanding of the world of which they are a part. Such understanding often demands a process of self-awareness: many people who have made voyages of discovery have found that they learn as much about themselves as about the new landscape they enter. The outward journey is also the inward journey. The two journeys are complementary and mutually illuminating. A student brought face to face with new perspectives, new ways of seeing the world, alternative visions of the future . . . and learning that her life is inextricably bound up with the problems and prospects of people thousands of miles away, will almost inevitably begin to critically examine her own perspectives, attitudes and patterns of behaviour. Many writers[3] have cogently argued that the needs of the person and the needs of the planet are inextricably interrelated. They suggest that the well-being of the global environment is dependent upon the achievement of full and authentic personhood. Jean Houston warns us of the dangers inherent in the imbalance of our present lop-sided process of development:

We find ourselves in a time in which extremely limited consciousness has the powers once accorded to the gods. Extremely limited consciousness can launch a nuclear holocaust with the single push of a button. Extremely limited consciousness can and does intervene directly in the genetic code, interferes with the complex patterns of life in the sea, and pours its wastes into the protective ozone layers that encircle the earth. Extremely limited consciousness is about to create a whole new energy base linking together computers, electronics, new materials from outer space, biofacture and genetic engineering, which in turn will release a flood of innovation and external power unlike anything seen before in human history. In short, extremely limited consciousness is accruing to itself the powers of Second Genesis. And this with an ethic that is more Faustian than Godlike.[4]

We have argued that schools, in failing to provide a global perspective, leave students insufficiently prepared to understand or to participate constructively in the global system. What, in summary, are the aims of global education? Below we offer five aims which together constitute the irreducible global perspective. If any of the five are not met, then the school is failing in part to address and prepare students for contemporary reality.

1   *Systems consciousness* Students should acquire the ability to think in a systems mode, abandoning simple dualities such as cause/effect, problem/solution, local/global. This mode of thought should enable them to acquire an understanding of the systemic nature of the world, and a holistic conception of their own capacities and potential.

2   *Perspective consciousness* Students should recognise that they have a world view that is not universally shared and that there are dangers in using their own framework of thought and perception as a yardstick for interpreting and judging the values, lifestyles and world view of others. They should also develop receptivity to other perspectives.

3   *Health of planet awareness* Students should acquire an awareness and understanding of the global condition and of global trends and developments (eg wealth distribution, types of development, environmental impact of human activity). They should develop an informed understanding of the concepts of justice, human rights and responsibilities and be able to apply that understanding to the global condition. In considering the health of the planet, students should also develop the capacity for future projection.

4   *Involvement consciousness and preparedness* Students should become aware that the choices they make and the actions they take, individually and collectively, have repercussions for the global present and the global future. They should develop the social and political action skills necessary for becoming effective participants in democratic decision-making at a variety of levels, grass-roots to global.

5   *Process-mindedness* Students should understand that learning and personal development are continuous journeys with no fixed or final destination; and that new ways of seeing the world are revitalising but risky. New vision may bring some things into focus but obscure others and it will, in any case, become obsolete in time.

Schools as dustbins of human potential

The thrust of the argument so far has been that schools fail in two of their most basic functions: to enable students to make sense of the world in which they live, and to endow them with the skills and insights necessary for effective participation in a democratic society. Schools do not sufficiently facilitate the 'journey outwards'. Nor, we submit, do they adequately promote the 'journey inwards', the process of attaining a profound understanding of one's own capacities so as to develop the globality of one's potential. There is plenty of evidence to support Charles Handy's description of schooling as a 'disabling system'.

Raw material is passed from work station to work station, there to be stamped or worked on by a different specialist, graded at the end and sorted into appropriate categories for distribution . . . That so many come through it, smiling, grateful and grown up, is a tribute to the dedication of many teachers who impose their humanity and personality on those huge processing plants. But many do not come through as well. They leave alienated by an institution that seems to them oppressive, irrelevant and dismissive of their possible contribution to the world.[5]

Such a process represents an enormous and damaging waste of human potential, a failure to recognise that

this is what all of us bring into life and to school: a wholly unexplored, radically unpredictable identity. To educate is to unfold that identity – to unfold it with the utmost delicacy, recognizing that it is the most precious resource of our species, the true wealth of the human nation.[6]

'Alone among creatures', writes Theodore Roszak, 'we can fail to become what we were born to become.' We are 'the unfinished animal'.[7] The capacity to express ourselves creatively – one of the characteristics of humankind which sets us apart from the rest of the animal world – has been stifled in all but a few individuals whose exceptional talent has enabled them to break free from the oppressive influence of 'extremely limited consciousness'. What are the manifestations of this myopic condition in schools, turning many institutions into overflowing dustbins of human potential? They would surely include:

- compartmentalisation of mental and physical activity, with a higher value placed on the development of the mind in isolation;
- an emphasis on learning through abstract concepts, rather than through actual experience;
- little value given, or time allocated, to the development of sensory awareness (save for the first few years of primary school);
- a pervading atmosphere of individualistic competition, thereby fostering selfishness, self-importance and aggression;
- little attention paid to an exploration of personal attitudes and values, and the development of positive feelings towards others;
- failure to recognise and nurture the richness and diversity of each individual's talents;
- little contact with the community, thereby underlining the isolated unreal nature of schooling.

If a fundamental aim of education is to 'unfold the identity' of every child then we need to develop a much broader consciousness within schools. In addition to curriculum changes to promote understanding of the global system, a re-appraisal of the quality of inter-personal relationships amongst teachers and students is also required. We need a commitment to creative, open and co-operative approaches to teaching and learning: an examination of the implicit messages of the 'hidden curriculum'; and the development of open and constructive school-community links.

Global education or global indoctrination?

Much of the inspiration for global education has emerged from the United States. The educational implications of viewing the world as an interdependent system have been explored by educators such as Lee Anderson, James Becker and Robert Hanvey. Revolutionary new insights from the convergent findings of physics, mathematics and parapsychology have been added by scientists and writers like Fritjof Capra, Jean Houston, Marilyn Ferguson and Theodore Roszak. Apposite teaching and learning approaches owe their origins to a long lineage of humanistic educators including John Dewey and Carl Rogers.[8]

The focus of global education initiatives in England and Wales over the last decade has been world studies, launched initially by the *World Studies Project* of the One World Trust, further developed by the Schools' Council *World Studies 8–13 Project* and now operational, to varying degrees, in some 45 local education authorities.[9] World studies, too, has drawn much inspiration from American writers and educators, but also from internationalists such as U Thant, Robert Macnamara, Willi Brandt and Barbara Ward. Furthermore, the area has close links and shares many overlapping interests with the related fields of development education, environmental education, human rights education, multicultural/anti-racist/anti-sexist education, and education for peace and international understanding. Through its association with these fields, world studies has been able to draw upon the insights of educators such as Paolo Freire, Johan Galtung and Ian Lister.[10]

World studies has been attacked by writers from far right and far left positions. Of the former, Roger Scruton's pamphlet *World studies: education or indoctrination?* is the most prominent, though by no means thorough, critical account; the paucity of its academic base has been thoroughly exposed.[11] From a far-left viewpoint, Chris Mullard has accused world studies of failing to adequately consider the issues of power and inequality in our society, with particular regard to the life chances of members of ethnic minorities.[12] Richard Hatcher has argued that the world studies classroom excludes radical critiques of world capitalism and, by so doing, helps to perpetuate inequality.[13] Such criticisms have served to remind practitioners that the educational principles on which world studies is based are not universally shared. The media coverage given to the far-right position has also clearly indicated the alarming degree of misconception about the basic aims and methods of world studies. It may be useful, then, to explore some of the more serious (as opposed to the merely spurious) reservations about the place of world studies/global education in the curriculum.

World Studies deals with political issues

There are schools of thought which hold that political issues should be kept out of the classroom on the grounds that students' immature minds are susceptible to wilful indoctrination on the part of teachers. 'Politically contentious subjects', writes John Marks, 'should normally form no part of the curriculum for pupils below the age of 16 and should be rigorously excluded from primary schools.'[14] Such a view ignores the fact that students themselves are caught up in the global system: non-involvement is not an available option. The workings of that system raise crucial questions concerning human rights, justice, equality and peaceful/conflictual relationships. For education to be a relevant preparation for life in the 21st century, those issues need to be thoroughly considered and relevant skills for constructive democratic participation developed.

Scruton repudiates Marks' stance. 'It is undeniable', he writes, 'that there is massive inequality between the richer and poorer countries of the world . . . and that a process of education that ignores this fact ignores one of the most salient features of the modern world.'[15] It also has to be remembered that schooling only forms part of education. Children of primary school age are exposed daily to political issues on BBC television's John Craven's *Newsround*. A small-scale survey undertaken by the Centre for Global Education revealed that between eight and twenty per cent of children in top junior and first year secondary classes in a range of English schools watched the 1984 BBC late evening television drama-documentary, *Threads*, on the subject of a nuclear attack on Sheffield. Schools, we would submit, have a responsibility to ensure that any possible media bias is countered by the sensitive and professional examination of such topics within the classroom. It smacks of dangerous élitism to suggest that only those able and prepared to continue education beyond 16 should have the opportunity to reach an informed understanding of key global issues. As Sir Keith Joseph has recognised, politically controversial issues have to be tackled in schools in the interests of good education. 'How this is best done for pupils and students of varying maturity and understanding,' he argues, 'is a matter of professional judgement and calls for the exercise of professional responsibility.'[16]

World Studies is concerned with attitudes, values and feelings

Education, some argue, is and should be value-free and should avoid learning approaches which touch upon attitudes and feelings.[17] Objectives of world studies such as the development of students' respect for the rights, feelings and essential worth of other people and their appreciation of the diversity and riches of other cultures, inevitably reveal underpinning values and involve learning in affective as well as cognitive domains. But what process of education, we need to ask, is *not* concerned with attitudes, values and feelings? The very choice of what knowledge, skills and culture to transmit in the classroom – and the choice of mode of transmission – involves moral and political judgements, based on a certain set of values and assumptions. Is it not also a purpose of education to help students develop a personal morality and civic consciousness (the nature of which we may need to constantly re-define, given the increasingly systemic quality of the contemporary world)?

Learning in the affective domain is central to global education, as it is to good education generally. Understanding others' perspectives can often be efficaciously achieved by confronting one's own perspective and the beliefs and assumptions which have shaped it. Furthermore, breaking out of what Jean Houston calls the 'extremely limited consciousness' of our time requires the full awakening of human potential. New research indicates that such an awakening will only come about through holistic approaches to learning, harmonising the complementary capacities of mind and body, reason and emotion, analysis and intuition, logicality and imagination.[18] The cognitive learning of the traditional classroom may be oriented towards the suppression of one's emotional self, but that too carries significant, albeit hidden, messages for personal development.

World Studies is destructive of national culture and values

During the process of the world's evolution from a collection of lands and peoples to a system of lands and peoples, the concept of nationhood has undergone a profound change. Whereas in the past it may have been possible to generalise, with some degree of accuracy, about a 'British' person, 'British' culture, or 'British' interests, it has now become increasingly difficult. A working-class family in the north of England, for instance, may well have a very different view of British culture and British interests from that of a middle-class family from the London stockbroker belt. Ethnic minority families, although British, often identify more readily with the culture and values of communities in other parts of the world. The movement and resettlement of peoples has helped create a complex web of transnational ties, loyalties and sentiments within and between national communities. What are the definitive characteristics of 'Britishness' which adequately sum up Britain today?

Would they focus upon place of birth, citizenship and voting rights? Upon family lineage and length of residence? Upon respect for British parliamentary democracy and involvement in the local community? Or even, perhaps, upon the more intangible, subjective attributes such as humour, sociability and degree of emotional disclosure? To define Britishness by any one, or any combination, of such characteristics would be tantamount to an act of exclusion of large groups of people, of diverse cultures, classes and creeds, currently living in Britain. It would not, therefore, reflect the plurality of British culture and society.

In an interdependent global system, national culture and values can only be understood within a global context. A culture is neither monolithic nor static; it is susceptible to constant adaptation from myriad influences from both within and outside itself. The term 'national' is, in this context, misleading, in that it refers to a polymorphic and changeable collection of assumptions, perspectives and patterns of behaviour, many of which originate from outside the national boundaries but many of which, on the other hand, have been transported to other parts of the global system.

World Studies is oriented towards change and action

Many writers have argued that one of the most salient features of the modern world is the degree and pace of change: change itself has changed.[19] Humankind has reached the stage where change occurs so swiftly that it would appear essential that we continuously re-assess our values, beliefs and patterns of behaviour, if we are to avoid 'future shock' – the psychological disease afflicting many who are unable to cope with the velocity and pervasiveness of change.[20]

Preparedness for change necessitates the development and practice of action-oriented skills, such as decision making and problem solving, creative thinking and future projection, as well as those which facilitate participation in group processes. If a primary function of schooling is to prepare young people for the future – a future which is likely to be characterised by the new, the unexpected and the uncertain – then development of the capacity to deal constructively with change at all levels, personal to global, must necessarily figure prominently in the curriculum.

The aim of developing involvement consciousness and preparedness (which encompasses the development of social and political action skills) is central to global education. Only rarely, however, have world studies proponents confronted the ramifications and practical implications of what has been called 'education for involvement'. If the aim is to promote 'involvement literacy', is it sufficient to consider the issues from within the closed confines of the classroom? Can the exploration of avenues and techniques for participation in contemporary society ever be much more than a barren exercise if treated in an abstract, sedentary manner? What would an inventory of world studies action/involvement skills look like (we still await the first)? Should they be coached, for 'skills are best (and probably only) acquired by *practising* them'?[21] How would student involvement be monitored outside the classroom? How would assessment and evaluation take place? What is encompassed by 'involvement literacy'? These – and other closely-related questions – must inevitably be faced if talk of developing participation skills is to go beyond the rhetorical.

The potential dangers for the teacher and the school in promoting involvement are always just below the surface and need to be recognised. What if a 'Community against the Bomb' group, antipathetic to most things military, chooses to enter into debate with, or demonstrate against, visiting Army careers officers? What if a group of students, fired by concern for the environment, take some form of action against council plans to pipe and thus destroy life in a local stream? Can and should the school permit such activities? At what point will even a sympathetic executive be forced to say 'enough is enough'? For the most part, these questions remain purely hypothetical, but it is well within the bounds of possibility that cases will occur where teachers embarking upon involvement programmes will actually have to face them.

The other area of danger, for some schools, is that students coached in action skills may direct those skills against aspects of the institution in which they find themselves.[22] Clearly, the world studies teacher wishing to promote involvement and develop action skills is riding a tiger but it is a tiger which may well have to be ridden if proponents really mean what they say about education for participation. What is now needed is for teachers working in the field to give a full and professional airing to the issues raised, so that involvement as a facet of the school experience can be approached with more confidence and surety of purpose.

Global education in practice: implications for classroom and school

Perhaps the most controversial aspect of global education concerns the implications of its philosophical and conceptual base for the structure of the school, the climate of the classroom and the organisation of the learning process. Both the journey outwards, towards a greater understanding of the global system, and the journey inwards, towards profounder self-awareness and realisation of one's potential, suggest a certain style and process of teaching and learning which is none too evident, in any consistent form, in the average school. As Johan Galtung, reflecting on peace education, puts it: 'We should structure schooling much more in the way we would like the world to look. This means quite a lot of concrete things: decentralisation, horizontal education, emphasis on dialogue between pupils and between teachers.'[23] There remains, for instance, something essentially 'unpeaceful' about the teacher who lectures on peace issues from the front of the class. However worthy the topic, the teacher's credibility is undermined through the format in which she chooses to operate. Peace education, Galtung argues, has to avoid the 'structural violence of one-way communication'. The learning environment should encourage an information/opinion flow between all participants (ie 'horizontal education'). Co-operation, dialogue and participation should be the hallmarks of the classroom.

In global education, likewise, the medium is of crucial importance because it is directly related to the message of the topic, indeed the medium *is* the message. How can one teach about respect for the rights and essential worth and dignity of others in a classroom or school in which a lack of such respect is patently evident? Can one realistically expect students to grasp the concept of global interdependence and the need for co-operation between peoples and nations in a climate which fosters competition and extols individual endeavour? As Robin Richardson writes:

Certainly it seems idle to promote 'a world community' or 'a democratic and participatory multiracial society' without seeking to bring these concepts alive – these concepts of community, democracy, participation, equality – in each classroom, and without enhancing teachers' images and expectations of their pupils.[24]

Attainment of the five aims comprising the irreducible global perspective requires a shift away from dependence upon cognitive learning and a movement towards holistic approaches to learning, in which the complementary capacities of reason and emotion, intellect and imagination are harmonised. 'Perspective consciousness', for example, necessitates the student taking an imaginative leap outside her own cultural framework, assuming, in her mind, a 'fly on the wall' position. Such a position is unlikely to be reached through cognitive reasoning alone, which itself helps to construct the limited framework; it requires a constant interplay between cognitive and affective learning. The emotional 'slap on the face' which so often accompanies the sudden self-awareness of one's limited world view is a powerful tool for learning, a deep-felt dawning which can stimulate the intellect into accommodating the new horizons glimpsed. Both 'systems consciousness' and 'process-mindedness' demand a rejection of the simplistic 'right-answer syndrome' which characterises so much of examination-oriented schooling. Students are encouraged to see that solutions to problems – personal to global – are, at best, helpful adjustments within the system. They are helped to realise that decisions and judgements they reach are, by their nature, impermanent – they are stills taken from a life-long moving picture. New information and new perspectives will help them to see things in different ways.

The global education classroom, then, places considerable emphasis on experiential and co-operative learning, on active participation by individuals and groups in the initiation, direction and evaluation of what is learnt, and on creative, imaginative and divergent thought and action. The classroom climate, too, is significant: such learning is unlikely to take place unless an affirmative atmosphere and environment prevails – one in which the integral worth and experience of each individual is cherished and their self-concept enhanced. In practice, students will often be involved in structured small group activity, which encourages communication, co-operation, negotiation and decision making. Role-play, simulation games and experiential activities (short activities designed to stimulate an intense learning experience through employing the emotions and/or the senses) will also feature prominently, enabling students to explore their own perspectives and attitudes and to consider other viewpoints and feelings. The controlled use of fantasy and visualisation is becoming recognised as an effective means to activate creative and problem-solving processes.[25]

It would be erroneous to suggest that global education eschews class discussion and teacher input altogether. Activity and experiential approaches often generate a thirst to know more. This may be fulfilled by a talk by the teacher or visiting speaker, film or television programme input or research from books and other printed materials. There is a quintessential difference, however, between input that arises from students having some control over and stake in the classroom process, and imposed input. Talks, films and study can also be so structured as to harmonise with a participatory classroom climate.[26] Nor would it be correct to imagine that the learning approaches advocated in global education are employed at the expense of high levels of cognitive attainment; that global education, in other words, is no good for passing examinations. There is a substantial body of research evidence which shows that co-operative learning, an affirmative classroom environment, and the development of open, trusting and empathetic relationships among teachers and students, all lead to higher levels of cognitive attainment, for both able and less able students, than in classrooms where the emphasis is on individualistic work and competitive personal relationships.[27] Co-operative learning has been found to be more efficacious the greater the degree of conceptual learning required; additionally, higher cognitive learning will result from co-operative situations in which the task undertaken generates controversy or conflict of ideas, opinions and theories (as compared with individualistic study of controversy, or a group task based on a non-controversial issue).[28] Such conclusions would seem to be of great significance not only for global education but also for the choice of teaching and learning styles in other areas of education which tend to be concerned with complex concepts and controversial issues.

What of the role of the teacher in the co-operative, participatory classroom? 'Teaching', says Carl Rogers, 'is a vastly over-rated function.' By this he means that the process of imparting knowledge and information is no longer relevant in the contemporary world: 'We are, in my view, faced with an entirely new situation in education where the goal of education, if we are to survive, is the *facilitation of change and learning.*'[29] Perhaps the term 'facilitator' would be more appropriate than 'teacher', implying that the adult in the classroom is using her skill and experience to draw out and advise upon a process of change and development which is innate in every student. Let us not imagine that this is, in any sense, an easy task. The art of facilitation is like the fine tuning of a sensitive musical instrument; the capability for creating harmonious sound is always present within the instrument but is dependent upon the tuning skills of the musician. Once the instrument is finely tuned – and it will need periodic adjustment – the capacity for creating music is limitless. Effective facilitation not only demands consummate sensitivity and skill, it also requires a transference of power from the 'teacher' to the students. The teacher as instructor in the traditional classroom uses her power to override the students' autonomy, to manipulate and limit their personal power; the teacher as facilitator in the co-operative, participatory classroom encourages the constructive use of that power, thereby limiting her own.

This shift in the locus of power and decision-making in the classroom is both difficult and risky. The teacher no longer has 'all the answers' and cannot expect to be respected or obeyed *solely* on the basis of her status. Above all the teacher must be, and be seen to be, a genuine human being, with strengths and weaknesses, wisdom and ignorance, emotions, prejudices and integrity. Through devolving power, however, the facilitative teacher helps to safeguard against the indoctrination or manipulation of credulous minds. Indoctrination – the instruction of a doctrine – becomes less feasible in co-operative, participatory learning situations where decision-making is shared among all those involved. One should be aware, of course, of the persuasive power of the group to stifle or subvert the nonconformist individual opinion; the teacher's role here is to ensure that such opinions are listened to and seriously considered.

What, finally, are the implications of global education for the structure and management of the school? As in the classroom, the medium is the message. The development of co-operative, affirmative attitudes among students is largely dependent upon teachers and ancillary staff displaying these same attitudes – whether in the staffroom, on the playing fields or in the dining hall. A respect for the intrinsic worth and rights of other people must be enshrined in school regulations, disciplinary and compaints procedures. The encouragement of students to actively participate in their own learning and development needs to be supported through opportunities to share responsibility for the management and direction of the school. A commitment to experiential learning can be positively expressed through sending students out into the local community, to learn from its expertise and to contribute to its growth. A respect for, and appreciation of, diversity and creativity should be reflected in the curricular and extra-curricular opportunities open to students.

A global perspective should infuse the curriculum. While the establishment of a single subject or interdisciplinary core course might be the most viable means of introducing such a perspective and developing staff expertise, the credibility of this perspective may well be undermined unless it is reinforced across the curriculum. Recently, the most exciting innovations in global education have taken place in the primary school and in areas of the secondary school curriculum such as science, maths, home economics, religious education and literature.[30] Such developments raise important questions about the present rigid compartmentalisation of knowledge within the curriculum and mechanisms for achieving interdisciplinarity – and about the training of teachers so they can handle issues which lie outside their traditional areas of expertise.

Notes and references

1 *Schooling and citizenship in a global age* L F Anderson (Bloomington, Indiana: Mid-America Program for Global Perspectives in Education, 1979) pp 78–83.
2 *ibid* p 81.
3 See *The turning point* F Capra (Flamingo/Fontana, 1983); *The Aquarian Conspiracy* M Ferguson (Granada, 1982); *The possible human* J Houston (Los Angeles: Tarcher, 1982); *Person/planet* T Roszak (Granada, 1981).
4 *The possible human* J Houston (Tarcher, 1982) p 213.
5 *The future of work* C Handy (Basil Blackwell, 1984) pp 136–7.
6 *Person/planet* T Roszak (Granada, 1981) p 186.
7 *Unfinished animal* T Roszak (Faber, 1976) pp 84–5.
8 'The world studies story: projects, people, places' R Richardson, in *PEP Talk* (Journal of the Peace Education Project) Winter 1985, No 8, pp 4–16; *Freedom to learn for the 80s* C Rogers (Ohio: Merrill, 1983).
9 R Richardson, *ibid*.
10 See *The pedagogy of the oppressed* P Freire (Penguin, 1972); 'Peace education: problems and conflicts' J Galtung, in *Education for peace: reflection and action* M Haavelsrud (ed) (IPC Science and Technology Press, 1976); *Teaching and learning about human rights* I Lister (Council of Europe, 1984).
11 *World studies; education or indoctrination?* R Scruton (Institute for

European Defence and Strategic Studies, 1985); 'Scrutinising Scruton' G Pike and D E Selby, in *Times Educational Supplement* 11 April 1986, p 24.

12 'The problem of world studies in a multicultural society' C Mullard, in *World Studies Journal* Autumn 1984, Vol 4, No 1, pp 13–17.

13 'The construction of world studies' R Hatcher, in *Multiracial Education* Winter 1983, Vol 11, No 1, pp 23–6.

14 *'Peace studies' in our schools. Propaganda for defencelessness* J Marks (Women and Families for Defence, 1984) p 1.

15 R Scruton, *op cit* p 13.

16 'The treatment of politically controversial issues in schools and colleges' Sir Keith Joseph, issued on 4 February 1986 in conjunction with DES News Circular 32/86 *How to approach politically controversial issues when teaching.*

17 See, for instance, R Scruton *op cit* p 27, 35, 53.

18 See, for instance *The possible human* J Houston (Tarcher, 1982) and *Teaching for the two-sided mind* L V Williams (Prentice-Hall, 1983).

19 *Teaching as a subversive activity* N Postman and C Weingartner (Penguin, 1983) pp 22–3.

20 *Future shock* A Toffler (Pan, 1971).

21 *Issues in teaching and learning about human rights* I Lister (University of York Political Education Research Unit, Document No 32, 1981).

22 *ibid.*

23 J Galtung, *op cit.*

24 'Talking about equality: the use and importance of discussion in multi-cultural education' R Richardson, in *Cambridge Journal of Education* 1982, Vol 12, No 2, pp 101–14.

25 See, for instance, J Houston *op cit*; L V Williams *op cit* and *The centering book* G Hendricks and R Wills (Prentice-Hall, 1975).

26 See 'Education, world studies and films' P Whitaker, in *World Studies Journal* Spring 1980, Vol 1, No 1, pp 28–34 and *Justice and equality in the classroom – the design of lessons and courses* R Richardson (Centre for Global Education, document No 7, 1983).

27 See, for instance, the research findings of Aspy and Roebuck and Tausch and Tausch in C Rogers *op cit*, pp 197–224 and *Circles of Learning* D W Johnson, R Johnson, E J Holubec and P Roy (Alexandria: Association for Supervision and Curriculum Development, 1984).

28 'The socialization and achievement crisis: are cooperative learning experiences the solution?' D W Johnson and R T Johnson, in *Applied social psychology annual 4* L Bickman (ed) (Beverly Hills: Sage Publications, 1983) pp 145–7.

29 C Rogers *op cit* pp 119–20.

30 See, for instance, 'Language and literature for understanding and transforming the world' *World Studies Journal* 1984/5, Vol 5, No 3 and 'Global pi' *World Studies Journal* 1985, Vol 5, No 4.

Suggestions for initial reading

Capra, F *The turning point* (Flamingo, 1983).

Ferguson, M *The aquarian conspiracy* (Granada, 1982).

Fisher, S and Hicks, D *World studies 8–13: a teacher's handbook* (Oliver & Boyd, 1985).

Heater, D *World studies* (Harrap, 1980).

Hicks, D and Townley, C (eds) *Teaching world studies: an introduction to global perspectives in the curriculum* (Longman, 1982).

Houston, J *The possible human* (Tarcher, Los Angeles, 1982).

Pike, G and Selby D E *Global teacher, global learner* (Hodder & Stoughton, 1987).

Rogers, C *Freedom to learn for the '80s* (Charles Merrill, Ohio, 1983).

Roszak, T *Person/planet* (Granada, 1981).

Selby, D E *World studies: towards a global perspective in the school curriculum*, being the Association for the Teaching of The Social Sciences' Briefings, No 37, a pull-out supplement in *The Social Science Teacher*, Spring 1984, Vol 13, No 2, 8 pp.

Some suggestions for further reading (see also references above)

Anderson, L F *Schooling and citizenship in a global age* (Bloomington, Indiana: Mid-America Program for Global Perspectives in Education, 1979).

Becker, J M *Schooling for a global age* (McGraw-Hill, 1979).

Bridges, D 'World studies in a multicultural society: some questions', *World Studies Journal* Autumn 1982, Vol 4, No 1, pp 7–9.

Brown C 'National identity and world studies', *Educational Review* June 1984, Vol 36, No 2, pp 149–156.

Cogan, J *Developing a global perspective in the school curriculum* (Global education documentation service, Centre for Global Education, University of York, Document No 13).

Cogan, J (ed) *The global classroom. An annotated bibliography for elementary and secondary teachers* (Global Education Centre, University of Minnesota, 1984).

Crum, M J (ed) *The global yellow pages. A resource directory* (Global Perspectives in Education, 1981). Available from GPE at 218 East 18th St., New York, NY 10003.

Hanvey, R G *An attainable global perspective* (Global Perspectives in Education, 1982).

Pike, G (ed) *World studies resource guide* (Council for Education in World Citizenship, 1984).

Selby, D E *World studies, the participatory classroom, the open school* (Global education documentation service, Centre for Global Education, Document No 10).

Handbooks/articles on interactive learning techniques for global education

Brandes, D and Phillips, H *Gamesters' handbook* (Hutchinson, 1977).

Borba, M and C *Self-esteem: a classroom affair* (Minneapolis, Winston Press, 1978).

Canfield, J and Wells, H C *100 ways to enhance self-concept in the classroom* (Prentice-Hall, 1976).

Coover, V *et al Resource manual for a living revolution* (Philadelphia, New Society: 1978).

Hendricks, G *The centered teacher* (Prentice-Hall, 1981).

Hendricks, G and Wills R *The centering book* (Prentice-Hall, 1975).

Hendricks, G and Roberts, T *The second centering book* (Prentice-Hall, 1977).

Judson, S *et al A manual on non-violence and children* (Philadelphia Yearly Meeting of the Religious Society of Friends, 1977).

Kinghorn, J R and Shaw, W P *Handbook for global education: a working manual* (Charles F Kettering Foundation, 1977) available from CFKF at 5335 Far Hills Avenue, Dayton, Ohio 45429.

Liebmann, M *Art games and structures for groups* (Bristol Art Therapy Group, 1982).

Prutzman, P, Burger, M L, Bodenhamer, G and Stern, L *The friendly classroom for a small planet* (Avery, 1978).

Richardson, R *Justice and equality in the classroom – the design of lessons and courses* (Global education documentation service, Centre for Global Education, Document No 7).

Richardson, R *Learning for change in world society* (World Studies Project, 1979).

Richardson, R 'Talking about equality: the use and importance of discussion in multi-cultural education, *Cambridge Journal of Education*, 1982, Vol 12, No 2, pp 101–114.

Richardson, R, Flood, M and Fisher, S *Debate and decision: schools in a world of change* (World Studies Project, 1980).

Schniedewind, N and Davidson, E *Open minds to equality: a sourcebook of learning activities to promote race, sex, class and age equity* (Prentice-Hall, 1983).

Selby, D E 'The purple armband experiment: an experiential unit in discrimination', *The New Era*, November/December 1980, Vol 61, No 6, pp 218–221.

Wolsk, D *An experience-centred curriculum* (UNESCO educational studies and documents No 17, 1975).

'World studies. The learning process', *World Studies Journal*, 1984, Vol 5, No 2, (available from Centre for Global Education, University of York).

Appendix

In recent years there has been a move towards legislation enabling parents to withdraw children from lessons or activities which do not comply with their religious or philosophical opinions. The following list indicates some of the implications of such a law.

1   *Assembly*
    Daniel's parents, members of Christian CND and pacifists, object to the militaristic overtones of hymns such as 'Onward Christian Soldiers', 'Fight the Good Fight'. Withdraw him.
2   Rowena's parents object to the headmaster's talk about the proposed new school appeal, to raise money for sports equipment, on the grounds that essential equipment should be provided by the state not voluntary effort.
3   *Lesson 1: Geography: Lesson on plantation farming*
    Jason's parents object that learning about black teaworkers won't teach him anything about British industry and won't help him get a job.
4   Wayne's parents, local Oxfam organisers, object because the content of the lesson ignores the rights, denials and injustices involved in a plantation economy.
5   James's parents object to him drawing and writing about black workers when they've contributed so much to unemployment and urban violence.
6   *Lesson 2: Maths*
    Graham and Stefanie's parents object to the stereotypical images of men and women in the Maths textbook. Men are always portrayed in activity and responsibility roles whilst women, if portrayed, are passive and supportive.
7   Benjamin's parents object to the atmosphere of individualised competition in the Maths class, calling for the introduction of co-operative and problem-solving techniques.
8   *Lesson 3: P.E.*
    Claire's parents want her to play football but, for organisational purposes, permission is refused. She is withdrawn.
9   Darryl's parents object to him being forced to play Rugby because it teaches aggression and can be physically harmful, especially to adolescents.
10 *Lesson 4: History*
    Elizabeth's and William's parents object to the history course as being nothing but a succession of battles and wars ignoring the social, cultural and aesthetic developments of the period.
11 Tracey's parents object to history because of its concentration on kings and queens, arguing that children should not be indoctrinated into acceptance of royalist sympathies.
12 Henry's parents object to the Eurocentric bias of the history course. Their son has learnt little about the world beyond Britain and Western Europe.
13 John's parents object to the fact that the people learnt about in history are upper class; the contribution of ordinary folk is by and large ignored.

14 Samantha's mother objects to the history course ignoring the role and achievements of women with predictable regularity.

15 *Lesson 5: Biology*
Charlene's parents object to learning about reproduction in the classroom divorced from moral and social considerations.

16 Sarah's parents object to her learning about reproductive organs and activity outside the home.

17 Andrew's parents, animal rights sympathisers, object to their son having to dissect a frog.

18 Lindsay's parents object to the textbook pictures of black people used to illustrate the world's most common diseases given the total absence of reference to and pictures of some of the diseases of affluence, such as obesity, heart attack and cancer.

19 *Lesson 6: English*
Rowena and Rachel's parents withdraw their daughters on the grounds that all the set O-level texts are by male authors who do not adequately represent women's perspectives.

20 Daniel and Louise's parents withdraw their children on the grounds that the course includes works by D.H. Lawrence which offend their views on sexual morality. Lawrence, they maintain, has done more than any author to promote the permissive society.

21 Sean's parents object that no Irish authors are included in the curriculum and yet some of the best – if not the best – twentieth-century literature has been Irish, e.g. James Joyce, Brendan Behan, William Butler Yeats, Synge, Edna O'Brien, Sean O'Faolain.

22 *Lesson 7: Home Economics* – Cooking Sausage Rolls
David's parents object to his presence in a classroom where there is meat that is not kosher.

23 Eileen's and Rebecca's parents, vegetarians, object to their presence at and involvement in a lesson involving the cooking of meat.

24 Sharon's mother, a dietician, objects to the lack of information about the poor nutrition value of and harmful additives contained in the ingredients of sausage meat.

25 Darren's father objects to his having to take compulsory home economics, particularly cooking which is a women's role in life.

26 Matthew and Lisa were absent.

Chapter 4

Gender bias in schools: the controversial issues

Judith Byrne Whyte

The burgeoning literature and corresponding activity on gender in education was launched in the late 1970s, largely by feminists. Within the critique of schooling as gender biased there can already be discerned two distinct directions with rather different implications for school and classroom practice.

At the turn of the century and earlier, feminist campaigns fought for girls' *access* to the broader range of educational experience and qualifications. In the mid-1960s, before the emergence of the new feminism, a Labour government promoted coeducational comprehensive schooling, in the belief that it would increase the opportunities available to all children. At that time, the question of supreme importance was how to improve the chances for working class children. It was assumed that coeducation would benefit girls because they would have *access* to exactly the same curriculum as boys. In consequence, the majority of British schoolchildren now experience coeducation. Even the independent sector, long the bastion of single sex education, is beginning to see certain benefits in educating boys and girls together.[1] Yet equality of access as practised in mixed schools has clearly failed to bring about equality of outcome between the sexes.

The 'new' feminism is, in one of its aspects, merely a continuation of the original struggle to give girls and boys the same educational benefits. There are two issues which exemplify this trend: efforts to bring more girls into science and technology; and, more recently, campaigns to bring more women teachers into senior management posts in the educational world. Both can be seen as attempts to widen access to benefits enjoyed disproportionately by the male sex, although as we shall see that is not the whole story.

The other approach has focused not so much on access as on the *content* of the curriculum, and on its *process*: the way the curriculum is delivered. Analysis of children's reading books and school texts has shown how women and girls are stereotyped, ignored or undervalued.

There are many descriptions of male domination of classrooms and schools which emphasise the different *experience* of schooling on the part of girls and boys. In this approach, the characteristic strength of the women's movement's emphasis on consciousness-raising, shared experience and recognition of the collective rather than individual nature of discrimination against females is evident: *'the personal is political'*.

Both types of feminist critique challenge the assumption that merely educating girls and boys under the same roof is any guarantee that they will receive equal educational benefits. Many local education authorities are now implementing equal opportunity *policies*. This chapter considers the issue of gender in schooling, and the controversies associated with access, content and process, and policy.

Equal opportunity approaches

Girls' access to science and technology

The argument here is not parallel to the issue of class. Although working class children are still *under*-achieving in school, almost the reverse is true of girls. Their school achievement surpasses boys' at 11 plus (as it has for a long time) and recently they have been gaining, on average, more passes at 'O' level. As table 1 shows, the trend during the 1970s was for more pupils to gain school-leaving qualifications, and the number gained by girls increased even more than by boys.[2]

Table 1 Attainment of school leavers as a % of relevant population, UK

	1970–71		1980–81	
	Boys	Girls	Boys	Girls
1 or more 'A' levels	18	15	17	17
5 or more 'O' levels	6	8	8	10
1–4 'O' levels (A–C)	16	17	23	27
1 or more 'O' levels (D–E)	11	9	31	30
No GCE/SCE qualification	44	44	16	12

There is nothing extraordinary about girls doing well at school. As a look at other countries shows, girls' achievements are frequently superior to boys. In France and Hungary, to mention two, girls achieve better results than boys right up to university level. In France there is growing concern that women are coming to dominate humanities subjects in higher education, and in Hungary differential entry requirements to university for the two sexes have been introduced to ensure that males have a 'fair' share of university places.

In England and Wales, the major and most publicised issue is that schoolgirls' qualifications and prospects on leaving school are inferior to boys', despite the high level of their academic achievement. While boys get qualifications in maths, the physical sciences, technology and computer studies, girls typically leave with a group of exam passes in arts, languages, and subjects like religious studies, art and home economics. These are not the sorts of subjects which lead into well-paid employment, nor, in the current context of a shortage of university places, do they offer many routes into higher education. A number of studies, here and in the US, have shown that able girls achieve much lower status in the labour market than comparable males after they have left school and a study of the impact of teacher training cuts in this country shows that this has had a considerable effect on female entry to higher education.[3] Girls of average ability have even more circumscribed prospects.

Under the educational provisions of the Sex Discrimination Act (1975) it is illegal for a mixed school to offer different curricular provision for boys and girls. It is at school that children make subject choices which determine to a large extent their occupational futures, so a lot of interest has focused on girls' 'failure' to take up the options of physical science and technology when these are available in mixed comprehensives. The problem was initially seen as one of girls' motivation, a perspective which has been criticised for presenting girls as deficient males or 'blaming the victim': 'if only girls would see the advantages of taking science and technology as boys do, they could achieve much more'. The GIST (*Girls Into Science and Technology*) project, among others, has shown the factors at work which make it unlikely that girls in coeducational schools will pursue the same curriculum as boys. The teaching of the subjects is geared to masculine interests; teachers expect boys to take physics and technology and are more doubtful about girls who want to make the same choice; boys define science and technology as *their* area; and the options system and staffing norms are built on the assumption of a sex segregated curriculum.[4] Three GIST booklets offer practical ideas for the classroom teacher.[5]

Teacher attitudes are significant; it appears that the subject taught may be a better guide to teachers' beliefs about equal opportunities than their sex. Teachers of traditionally masculine or feminine subjects like Craft, Design and Technology, Home Economics, Maths and the Physical Sciences appear to be least in favour of equal opportunities. Those who teach English, Humanities or Social Studies are more willing to accept the arguments about male bias.[6] London teachers are noticeably more 'liberated' about the gender issue, either because those who gravitate to the metropolis have different attitudes, or perhaps because ILEA has promoted equal opportunities longer than authorities elsewhere.[7]

Solutions to the girls and science/technology problem have been proposed by the GIST team, by GATE (*Girls and Technology Education*) and others. Teachers need in-service training to alert them to the factors which discourage girls or make them feel unwelcome in the science lab or craft workshop.[8] The way subject options are presented to third year pupils is important, and positive efforts have to be made if schools wish to reverse the usual pattern of sex stereotyped choices. This is not, as sometimes objected, an interference with children's free choices: the evidence is that boys, in particular, are choosing science less because they enjoy it or are good at it than because it is the expected choice. Girls seem to be more influenced by whether they find the subject interesting.[9] Both sexes perceive the relevance of subjects for future jobs as being very important. This is why careful pre-options counselling and broad based non-sexist careers education are generally advocated.[10]

In every area of life, even where females predominate numerically, men are to be found in positions of power and responsibility, with women in subordinate roles. There has been very little change indeed in the sexual segregation of labour, with women clustered in a small range of familiar feminine occupations where status and pay are relatively low. The division of the curriculum into 'feminine' arts subjects and 'masculine' science subjects reconstructs and reinforces the sexual division of labour which is a major source of sex inequality.

Women teachers

The sexual division of labour is almost perfectly reflected in staff common rooms. In the primary sector, where 77% of teachers are women, only 44% are heads, and that includes many infant heads. Junior schools are frequently headed by two male Chiefs and staffed by many female Indians. In secondary schools, the only women heads of department are likely to be in charge of Home Economics, Religious Education or Languages. Most of those teaching physical science will be men, and CDT departments are generally all-male enclaves. Women's share of senior management posts in secondary schools has actually declined over the last two decades,[11] in part because of the move towards larger coeducational comprehensives, and the prejudiced assumption that it is preferable to have men leading large mixed schools.

The reasons usually adduced for this state of affairs are that women are less well qualified, that they have less experience than men of the same age because of a career break to have children, that they are less committed to the job because of domestic responsibilities and/or that they are just less ambitious. There have been several studies to establish the validity or otherwise of these explanations. They reached similar conclusions: women are no less qualified on entry to the profession than men,[12] but when they apply for secondment for in-service training, a characteristic preliminary to promotion, they are less likely to be given it.[13] The ILEA study found differences in length of experience between men and women of the same age, mainly due to the career break, but it was insufficient, particularly among primary teachers, to account for the imbalance in senior posts held. On average, women teachers take about 5 years out of teaching to build a family, a relatively short time within a career of up to 35 years, and there is recent evidence that younger teachers are taking only the statutory maternity leave rather than sacrifice their place on the promotion ladder.[14] Analyses of male and female absences from school and 'commitment' to the job do not support the notion that women are less committed. And as Sandra Acker has pointed out:

Writers get tangled up trying to equate 'commitment' with what men do. 'Lack of commitment' turns out to mean interruptions for childrearing; 'commitment' to mean furthering one's own career, especially by moving out of classroom teaching.[15]

Her favourite finding (from an American study) is:

that the small number of male primary teachers in the sample had low commitment and low interest in their work. Nevertheless, they all hoped to be principals (heads) within five years.

The ILEA study found, significantly, that one reason women gave for *not* seeking further promotion was that they had no desire to move out of the classroom into purely administrative work. This should not necessarily be interpreted as a lack of ambition. Women are aware of the attitudes of appointing panels[16] and their unwillingness to apply for senior posts may arise from well-founded doubts about women's realistic chances of promotion. More than one study has remarked on the double standard at the root of the assumption that married men with families need/deserve promotion, while women with families are considered unsuitable.

Initiatives to bring more girls into science and technology and more women into senior posts are both addressing the under-representation of women in important areas of social life. There have been criticisms of this approach. As Madeleine Arnot has argued,[17] the equal opportunity strategy is more adaptable for policy makers; it fits into the prevailing professional rhetoric, and is consistent with 'more centralized control and compulsion (eg getting girls to do science)'. It is a strategy aimed at joining the male power structure rather than changing or challenging it.

The feminist challenge to the process and content of education

Curriculum content

A number of feminist teachers and researchers have analysed primary school materials, in particular, reading books, for gender bias[18] and more recently, teachers have begun to do the same while researching into their own classrooms.[19] They find that central characters are overwhelmingly masculine, and that women and girls, when they do appear, are weak, soppy creatures bearing little resemblance to real live females. Myers (1985) reports work in a secondary school where a young teacher followed a class round for the day, simply looking at the images of women and girls presented in textbooks and worksheets.[20] Women either appeared in stereotyped roles – wearing an apron, cooking, looking after children – or else there was an absence of human beings altogether, as in some scientific and technical books. (The latter point is important; we know that girls become more enthused about these subjects when human implications and social applications are introduced, see Kelly.[21])

It may seem curious that girls nevertheless turn out to be better readers, in the sense that they prefer longer books than boys, and have fewer problems with learning to read. The problem with biased content lies not in the possible interference with learning, for it seems that girls adapt to male-centred materials, but in the subliminal message implying the inferiority of women. Both sexes are imbibing a cultural norm of women as wives and homekeepers, considerably at odds with reality in a country where a larger proportion of women are employed outside the home than anywhere else in Western Europe. Teachers of young children in Brent found several ways of beginning to counteract negative images of women and girls, including an interesting, and apparently successful piece of assertiveness training for infants in the reception class![22]

Male domination of the classroom

The tendency of teachers in mixed classes to give more time and attention to boys is well proven by research (for a summary, see Sears and Feldman[23]). Boys receive more teacher-initiated contacts, are asked more questions and contribute more to classroom discussion. They receive more criticism from teachers, but also more attention. A study of secondary teachers in Birmingham found they actually preferred teaching males because they are more active, outspoken, and willing to exchange ideas.[24] Michelle Stanworth, also in a secondary school, found that the teachers frequently had difficulty remembering girls' names, even when they had learned the boys'.[25]

Efforts to change the situation have met with some success under action research conditions, but only when the teachers were highly motivated.[26] The changes teachers make can be quite small, for instance a maths teacher realized that her unwritten hands-up rule was favouring a few of the more extrovert boys. When she took the trouble to distribute questions evenly, by posing them to individuals by name, participation increased.

In the last three or four years, several writers (eg Sarah, Scott and Spender, 1980,[27] Shaw, 1984[28]) have advocated separating boys and girls as the only way to ensure that girls can participate fully in the classroom, have their needs and interests fairly catered for, and feel genuinely free to opt for non-traditional subjects:

The major . . . educational value of separate schooling for girls . . . is the *subversive potential of women learning from one another*, rather than from men whose authority and power is reinforced in the process. In a crucial sense it is this characteristic which defines the *feminist* response to patriarchy.[29]

The single sex debate

In single-sex schools it may be that girls benefit in confidence and self esteem from being educated separately from boys. Set against that is the admitted artificiality of single sex environments, and the rather neglected question of what happens to boys and men if they are educated apart from the female sex. Arnot (1984) in one of the few articles about the non-sexist education of boys comes down in favour of mixed schooling because she believes the single sex debate is irrelevant to the question of how we educate boys in a way which does not lead them to expect power and privilege in society. Men who have received a single sex education may become even less likely to respect feminine rights or appreciate feminine and feminist values.[30]

Jan Harding studied girls' take-up of physics and biology in comparable mixed and single sex schools.[31] It was clear that girls in girls' schools were significantly more likely to take physics, while biology choices were more or less the same in all types of school. A difficulty facing researchers in this area is that single sex schools tend to recruit more able and more middle-class pupils, so that girls' better performance in the physical sciences may only reflect the class and ability bias of the schools. In a comprehensive review of the evidence Bone found that girls' academic achievements were conditioned far more by the type of school they attended – comprehensive, grammar, modern or independent – and the *style* of school – traditional or otherwise – than by whether the school was single sex or mixed.[32] Another study based on longitudinal data from the National Child Development Study[32] concluded that differences in examination results between mixed and girls' only schools are markedly reduced once differences in initial attainment and home background are allowed for. Moreover, all the results in Steedman's study showed that the advantages which did exist applied to the most able girls, and that the majority of girls would not stand to gain at all from single sex schools. Middle-class parents of able girls should deduce that their offspring will benefit from single sex schooling, and on the whole the girls' schools which have been most innovative in providing facilities for their pupils to study traditional boys' subjects are the girls' grammar and independent schools. They certainly have more money to buy the extra facilities of laboratories or workshops, or special teachers of self-defence as in one London girls' independent school.

For the mass of girls, comprehensivisation has offered the main if not the only chance of access to subjects previously denied them, and the evidence does not inspire confidence in a national policy of return to sex segregated schooling. In countries where it is, or has been until recently, the norm for girls and boys to be educated separately (eg Austria, the Netherlands) it is usually the case that the education offered to girls is limited. They are taught arts, humanities and domestic accomplishments, while boys are taught a wider range of subjects, more explicitly linked to jobs in the labour market. Before coeducation became so widespread in this country, girls' schools offered a sexually-slanted curriculum, with emphasis on the arts and home-making skills, and in many cases no study of physics at all. The earliest girls' public schools taught geography as the only science, perhaps on the grounds that it has no masculine associations. By most criteria, the educational provision for girls was second rate, and the sexual division of labour was even more rigorously recreated than is the case today. Even if agreement could be won on a return to single sex schooling to promote girls' interests, future administrations could only too easily revert to the provision of poorer facilities and curricular offerings for girls.

Reversing the whole trend towards coeducation seems even more daunting than trying to change mixed schools so that they reflect to a much greater degree the needs and interests of girls and women. Pragmatically, this has led to suggestions for forming single sex groups within mixed schools.

At Stamford Park School in Tameside, the Deputy Head became concerned about the very poor attainment of girls in mathematics, and instituted quite a long running and well controlled experiment in single sex grouping. Matched single sex and mixed groups who received instruction from the same teachers – as far as that was possible over a five-year period – were compared. In the early stages, it looked as if girls in the girls' groups were going to do markedly better than their peers who were working with boys, and there was some evidence of improvement in maths and science performance for girls in the single sex sets.[34] However, the final analysis was disappointing in its results, with no clear benefit to girls in maths performance.

Smith has not yet published his final results, but there are several reasons why his experiment cannot be taken as conclusive. There were special conditions at the school. At the time when staff began to notice maths results, the school had been mixed for a relatively short period, indeed it was still frequently referred to in the neighbourhood as Stamford Park Boys' School. It had been a merger of two unequal schools, girls' achievement in the former girls' school being considerably lower than average. Smith retired from the school before the experiment was complete, and there were no moves to extend the experiment, far less the concern with gender equality, to other areas of the curriculum or school practice beyond science and maths. Male domination of school activities continued unabated elsewhere, and teachers in other departments took little or no notice of the Smith experiment. Finally, it is important to remember, as Smith reports (1984) that the girls enthusiastically proclaimed their preference for working in single sex groups, at least in the maths and science departments. They said that they had benefited from the experience, because it was easier to get the teacher's attention, and their confidence increased when the boys were not around to tease or inhibit them.

Some other schools in the same authority experimented with single sex science as part of the Tameside Girls and Science Initiative. Despite objective evidence that girls' performance improved while that of the boys was not significantly affected, teachers felt they were somehow disadvantaging the boys, and in several schools the experiment had to be abandoned. Teachers also complained of discipline problems with both girls' and boys' groups. In contrast, a similar experiment in one of the GIST schools continued beyond the end of the active phase of the project, and appears to have been successful. Significantly more girls opted for physics, the girls were keener on the subject and enjoyed the freedom from the constraining influence of boys. Some of the boys disliked or resented the new arrangement, but the teachers continued to believe in it, and were convinced by the evidence that boys were not suffering academically.[35] It is difficult to assess these different results, and more research and experimentation is needed. Success may depend on teacher commitment and the 'right' climate in the school.

While much of the above depends very firmly on academic research findings, there is also an important source of evidence from the experience of women themselves, stressing the commonality rather than individual nature of the oppression or discrimination women and girls face in schools, as in other organizations. A recent book edited by Gaby Weiner emphasizes female personal experience of schooling and perceptions of the need for change from girls and women themselves.[36] One report from the book describes how a school's women's group initially seemed to have had some success in altering the practice of addressing and referring to women staff by their marital status: Miss or Mrs. But some time later they found that only those women perceived as feminists were listed and referred to as Ms., intentionally or otherwise setting them apart from other women teachers. Another chapter shows how differently males and females may perceive the same event. A boy had painted a picture of a dismembered woman's body surrounded, significantly, by stiletto darts. Some female staff and pupils protested when the picture was hung in the entrance hall that they found it objectionable and offensive to women, but their protest was pooh-poohed by the male staff, who refused to have the picture taken down on the grounds that it was an artistic expression and not necessarily degrading.

Sexual harassment

Sexual harassment in school is not an easy subject to tackle, for two reasons: the perceptions of men and women about what *constitutes* sexual harassment often differ, and discussion of the topic naturally leads on to issues of control and discipline within the school. A conference about 'Equal Opportunities and Boys' used a series of vignettes about school as a focus for teachers' discussion. This was one item:

A young woman teacher is deliberately 'touched up' in a crowded corridor. The two 13-year-old culprits are identified by their form teacher, who hears them brag about it.
He and the male head of year tell them off and make them apologise. Other teachers, especially women, say "What about our policy on assault? They should have been sent home and then interviewed with their parents." But many argue that this would be over-reacting to a 'natural' if offensive prank. Heard in the staffroom later: "With that tight skirt and those legs, she was asking for it. I told 'em, we aren't allowed to touch, and nor can they!"[37]

The more staff see physical sexual differences as important, the more their attitude is likely to transfer to pupils. In the context of controlling and disciplining disruptive pupils it is not infrequently assumed that men will do the task better, with the underlying implication that, ultimately, physical force may need to be brought into play. This may not necessarily imply corporal punishment. When teachers say that men can obtain better discipline because of their lower, gruffer voices, the unconscious idea is that men *qua* men have greater authority. This is to underestimate the power of moral authority on which teachers of both sexes can call. Cunnison describes an incident in which a group of boys made ribald comments outside a class where girls in leotards were taking a dance lesson. The female teacher automatically frogmarched the boys down to the male Deputy Head's office because that was the way of the school. The office was empty, and she was thrown back on her own resources. Instead of relying on the threat of male authority, she decided to insist that the boys apologise directly, there and then, to the class of girls. Not only was her action immediately effective, but it avoided the possibility of trivialisation of the incident by the Deputy Head, and confirmed her status and authority as a member of staff. More often, one must assume, teachers unthinkingly accept the dictum that only men can deal with difficult boys, a social rule which has sexual harassment as one of its indirect consequences.

Policy on gender

National governmental policy, as expressed in documents and circulars from the Department of Education and Science, broadly favours equality of opportunity.[38] But it tends to be seen within a framework of general recommendations rather than specific requirements laid upon local education authorities or training institutions. Despite this rather luke-warm encouragement, a growing number of local authorities have introduced guidelines on gender equality, run in-service courses for staff, or started other initiatives. They include Brent, Cleveland, Clwyd, Derbyshire, Devon, Humberside, ILEA, Leicestershire, Manchester, Norfolk, Rochdale, Sheffield, Shropshire, Stockport, Tameside and Wigan. This is still smaller than the number which have explicit policies and associated appointments for multicultural education.

It is unfortunate when policies for race and gender equality appear to be in conflict with one another, but the reason is frequently traceable to fundamental stereotyping both about girls and boys, and about ethnic minorities. Brent's adviser, Hazel Taylor has very succinctly summarised and taken apart this kind of defensive reaction.[39] She quotes an imaginary Head who refuses to introduce gender equality policies because he 'doesn't want to upset my Asian parents'. As Taylor points out, the assumptions behind this refusal are highly questionable. It is not necessarily easier to persuade white parents of the need for gender equality, nor is it a mistake to assume that the subordination of women is an issue in non-Western cultures: the point is rather to ensure that ways of perceiving and addressing the problem are centred upon the experiences and outlook of girls and women from different sub-cultures. The Head's approach also seems to gloss over real and important differences between people from a vast sub-continent, and to imply a picture of the demure, passive, subservient Asian girl which is itself a stereotype. Taylor recommends more positive approaches to parents of ethnic minorities, and more ethnic minority teachers to help decide the best content of a non-sexist multicultural curriculum.

There is considerable unevenness about the way policies are being implemented at school and local authority level. A growing number of local authorities now state in their job advertisements that they are 'equal opportunity employers', but this may mean little more than a paper commitment to equality. When the claim is backed up by appointments, as in Brent and Inner London which are the only authorities to have funded appointments at adviser level specifically for the promotion of gender equality, the results have been visible and well reported. In Brent, for instance, all headteachers and groups of subject teachers have been offered in-service training.[40] Groups of teachers have also carried out their own action research into patterns of gender inequality at school. In ILEA, there have been similar in-service training activities[41] and a number of impressively glossy, but practically focused documents to help schools evaluate their own progress towards greater equality.[42] Other authorities have appointed at a lower advisory teacher level, or seconded teacher fellows to carry out investigations into subject options or girls' take-up of science. Tameside have run a Girls and Science Initiative for some years, and reports have been published describing special career talks for girls, single sex teaching and other interventions. Wigan has two advisory teachers. Sheffield has one, whose brief is to concentrate on careers education. All these authorities are going considerably further than simply publishing guidelines to good practice, which appears to be the first and most minimal stage of activity.

There has been some dissatisfaction with the minimal approach, on the grounds that it is merely a way of accommodating the feminist critique without actually doing anything to improve or change the female experience of schooling, far less confronting uncomfortable issues like the interaction of race and sex prejudice.[43] These critics tend to polarise strategies for change as either *equal opportunities oriented*, ie wishy-washy, liberal and ultimately ineffective, or *feminist*, boldly addressing issues of male power, such as male domination of scarce resources or sexual harassment in school.

In practice, once working parties, advisory teachers or advisers have been appointed to investigate and take action, both 'safe' issues like the shortfall of girls in science and technology, and more difficult ones like sexual harassment are likely to be raised by women teachers and girl pupils.

The two approaches have been separated in this chapter, but are not, of course, mutually exclusive. Nor is it likely that only one sort of strategy will be used in particular instances. More probably, the radical feminist and equal opportunity directions will be pursued alongside one another, with different groups of teachers and policy-makers favouring one emphasis or the other. The trouble with both is that the criteria for success are far from clear. If the aim is more girls choosing science and technology, how long is it reasonable to wait until 50% of engineers are female, and is that the important criterion? If the goal is a broader one of transforming educational institutions so that they no longer reflect the patriarchal structures of power, can it realistically be achieved before society itself is transformed? Reports of what has been done already tend to be descriptive, and sometimes optimistic, as if the fact that teachers are *talking* about the need for gender equality will ensure that the female experience of schooling and the outcomes for the two sexes, will beneficially change. Many teachers striving to implement non-sexist schooling feel isolated. There is a lack of clarity about how we are to measure the steps forward towards the ultimate goal of what Yates has termed the *sexually inclusive curriculum*.[44] Evaluation of change is not very easy to plan, and can sometimes be disappointing when compared with the original goals. On the other hand, women (and it is mostly women) who have been working so long for a de-gendered or feminist education could do with some yardstick to measure their achievements so far.

Notes and references

1 'Girls in boys schools: a prelude to further research' G Walford, in *British Journal of Sociology of Education* 1983, Vol 4, No 1, pp 39–54.
2 'The writing on the wall: beginning or end of a girl's career?' J White, paper presented at *Girl Friendly Schooling* conference, Manchester Polytechnic, September 1984.
3 'The effects on women's opportunities of teacher training cuts' A Bone, in *Women and Teaching – the Way Ahead* Conference Report, (Equal Opportunities Commission, 1982).
4 *Girls into Science and Technology: Final Report* A Kelly, J Whyte and B Smail, Manchester University, 1984; *Girls Into Science and Technology: The Story of a Project* J Whyte (Routledge and Kegan Paul, 1986).
5 See: *Ways and Means: Girls in Craft, Design and Technology* J Catton (Longman, for the Schools Council, 1985); *Girl Friendly Science: Avoiding Sex Bias in the Curriculum* B Smail (Longman, for the Schools Council, 1984); *Gender, Science and Technology: In-service Handbook* J Whyte (Longman, for the SCDC, 1985).
6 'The attitudes of teachers' J Pratt, and 'Teachers' attitudes towards girls and technology' M G Spear, in *Girl Friendly Schooling* J Whyte *et al* (eds) (Methuen, 1985).
7 'Traditionalists and trendies: teachers' attitudes to educational issues' A Kelly *et al* in *British Educational Research Journal* 1985, Vol 11, No 2, pp 91–104.
8 B Smail (1984) *op cit*; J Whyte (1985) *op cit.*
9 J Whyte (1986) *op cit.*
10 'Combating sex stereotyping through careers education' C Avent in *School Organisation* 1985, Vol 5, No 1, pp 53–57.
11 'A question of judgment' L Kant, in *Girl Friendly Schooling* J Whyte *et al* (eds) (Methuen, 1985).
12 'Women's careers in teaching: a survey of teachers' views' R Martini *et al* Research and Statistics Report RS 921/84 (ILEA Research and Statistics Branch, January 1984);
13 H Davidson *op cit.*
14 'The life cycle of the teacher' P Sikes, in *Teachers' Lives and Careers* Ball and Goodson (eds) (Falmer Press, 1985) pp 27–61.
15 'Women and teaching: a semi-detached sociology of a semi-profession' S Acker, in *Gender, Class and Education* Walker and Barton (eds) (Falmer Press, 1983).
16 L Kant *op cit.*
17 'Current developments in the sociology of women's education: Review Essay' M Arnot, in *British Journal of Sociology of Education* 1985, Vol 6, No 1, pp 123–30.
18 'The influence of the school on sex role stereotyping' G Lobban, in *The Sex Role System* Chetwynd and Hartnett (eds) (Routledge and Kegan Paul,

1978); *Pour out the cocoa, Janet: Sexism in Children's Books* R Stones (Longman, for the Schools Council, 1983).

19 *Sex Stereotyping in the Early Years of Schooling* N May and J Rudduck (School of Education Publications 1, University of East Anglia, 1983).

20 'Beware of the backlash' K Myers, in *School Organization* January/March 1985, Vol 5, No 1 (special issue on Sexism in the School).

21 *The Missing Half: Girls and Science Education* A Kelly (ed) (Manchester University Press, 1981).

22 'It Ain't Necessarily So: Studies in Schools' Constructions of Female Gender Roles' H Taylor (ed) CDSU, London Borough of Brent Education Department, 1986.

23 'Teacher interactions with boys and girls' P S Sears and D H Feldman, in *And Jill Came Tumbling After: Sexism in American Education* Stacey *et al* (eds) (Dell Publishing, 1974).

24 'A review of schooling and sex roles, with particular reference to the experience of girls in secondary schools' L Davies and R Meighan, in *Educational Review* 1975, Vol 27, No 3, pp 165–78.

25 *Gender and schooling* M Stanworth (Hutchinson, 1983).

26 'Observing sex stereotypes and interactions in the school lab and workshop' J Whyte, in *Educational Review*, 1984, Vol 36, No 1.

27 'The education of feminists: the case for single sex schools' E Sarah, M Scott and D Spender, in *Learning to Lose: Sexism and Education* D Spender and E Sarah (eds) (Women's Press, 1980).

28 'The politics of single-sex schools' J Shaw, in *Co-education Reconsidered* R Deem (ed) (Open University Press, 1984).

29 Sarah, Scott and Spender *op cit.*

30 'How shall we educate our sons?' M Arnot, in *Co-education Reconsidered* R Deem (ed) (Open Univerity Press, 1984).

31 'Sex differences in science examinations' J Harding, in *The Missing Half: Girls and Science Education* A Kelly (ed) (Manchester University Press, 1981).

32 *Girls and Girls Only Schools: A Review of the Evidence* A Bone (Equal Opportunities Commission, 1983).

33 *Examination Results in Mixed and Single Sex Schools: Findings from the National Child Development Study* J Steedman (Equal Opportunities Commission, 1983).

34 'Single sex setting' S Smith, in R Deem *op cit.*

35 (in press) D Bowes, in *Action Research in Classrooms and Schools* D Hustler (ed) (Allen and Unwin, 1986).

36 *Just a Bunch of Girls* G Weiner (Open University Press, 1985).

37 'Equal Opportunities: What's in it for Boys?' Conference Report (ILEA/ Schools Council, 1983).

38 'Sex bias in schools; national perspectives' P Orr, in *Girl Friendly Schooling* J Whyte *et al* (eds) (Methuen, 1985).

39 'Sexism and racism; partners in oppression' H Taylor, in *Cassoe Newsletter* May/June 1983, pp 5–9, published by CASSOE, 7 Pickwick Court, London SE9 4SA.

40 'Inset for equal opportunities in the London Borough of Brent' H Taylor, in *Girl Friendly Schooling* J Whyte *et al* (eds) (Methuen, 1985).

41 'Teacher attitudes towards issues of sex equality' C Adams, in *Girl Friendly Schooling* J Whyte *et al* (Methuen, 1985).
42 *Implementing the ILEA's Anti-sexist Policy: a guide for schools* C Adams (ILEA, 1985).
43 G Weiner *op cit.*
44 'Is girl friendly schooling really what girls need?' L Yates, in *Girl Friendly Schooling* J Whyte *et al* (eds) (Methuen, 1985).

Chapter 5
Multicultural teaching

Alma Craft

Controversial issues are those problems and disputes which divide society and for which significant groups within society offer conflicting explanations and solutions based on alternative values.[1]

Controversial issues are matters on which there is no social consensus. Controversy may range from local issues such as the routing of a by-pass around a village or the privatisation of the local bus service, to national issues such as unemployment, or the conflict in Northern Ireland. They also include matters of international significance such as nuclear weapons and Third World development, as well as changing social attitudes to gender, race and class. In a period of rapid social change, there are likely to be many sources of controversy; numerous interest groups in society may differ in their analysis of a situation and its underlying causes, and intergenerational disagreement will be widespread. There may be conflicting views about appropriate solutions and disagreement about the means to any particular end, but in an egalitarian society there will be consensus about the right of individuals to hold and express their own opinions.

During the second half of the 20th century one major change in Britain has been a marked increase in cultural heterogeneity. Britain has always been multicultural, encompassing Celts, Romans, Anglo-Saxons, Normans, Huguenots, Jews, and the Irish. However the recent migration and settlement here of large numbers of British West Indians, and British Asians, and the presence of a sizeable migrant workforce from the European community has focused attention on the extent of cultural diversity. The needs and opportunities presented by a multiracial, multilingual and multifaith population have become key issues in all aspects of social policy, including education.

Why is multicultural education controversial?

Education involves socialising young people for adult life. During the last

This paper draws heavily on the *Agenda for Multicultural Teaching* prepared for the school Curriculum Development Committee by Alma Craft and Gillian Klein (Longman for SDC, 1986)

decade, there has been much discussion, debate and controversy about the role of the school in preparing pupils for life in and for a society which is multicultural. There are several discrete strands to the debate.

1 Assimilation vs cultural pluralism

Alongside other Western democracies, Britain subscribes to the notion of equality of opportunity for all. Early educational responses to cultural diversity emphasised assimilation to the British 'norm' as the best way forward. Schools concentrated on teaching English language and customs to ethnic minority pupils, so that they could be quickly absorbed into the host community and compete on equal terms with their peers. There are many who still hold such views. Others, however, have called assimilation policies into question. They point to the continued low achievement of some ethnic minority pupils, and to the extent of intercultural prejudice and hostility inside and outside the school, which presents serious obstacles to the absorption of new communities. There has also been increasing recognition of the right to maintain a cultural heritage; although some individuals of ethnic minority origin may be keen to assimilate, others are very reluctant to abandon their cultural roots and draw great strengths from their ethnicity.

Newer approaches view cultural diversity as a positive asset, and seek to improve educational opportunity by building on pupils' cultural background rather than ignoring or disapproving of cultural difference. Bilingualism and biculturalism are beginning to be seen as advantages rather than handicaps.[2] Many teachers are supporting the language and culture of their ethnic minority pupils *in addition* to developing full competence in standard English.

2 Cohesion vs diversity

The assimilation *versus* cultural pluralism debate links closely with discussions about the limits of diversity. There are some who argue that social stability may be endangered if young people are encouraged to maintain and develop diverse language, culture and belief systems. If taken to extremes, they feel, this could result in social and even political separatism. Focusing on similarities between cultures and stressing common core values unites individuals, groups and nations and can help avoid such schisms, although an excessive concern for homogeneity seems inappropriate in a social democracy. The delicate balance between education for cohesion and education for diversity has been extensively explored by philosophers and sociologists. In other words,

educationalists have to decide at what point the acculturation necessary for full participation in society becomes a repressive assimilation; and at what point the celebration of diversity ceases to enrich and becomes potentially divisive.[3]

3 Particular needs vs education for all

Whether the societal goal is perceived as assimilation or cultural pluralism, cohesion or diversity, many people still believe that such educational issues relate only to pupils of ethnic minority origin. Much has been written about their particular needs: research has sought to identify the extent and causes of ethnic underachievement and the needs of bilingual learners; curriculum development has investigated strategies for reducing intercultural prejudice and for creating effective liaison between school and community; resources and assessment procedures have been reviewed for bias and teachers have been urged to extend their understanding of and respect for the cultural backgrounds of their pupils.[4]

In the last decade, the focus of attention has shifted away from particular needs towards the crucial importance of preparing *all* pupils for life in a culturally diverse society. Teachers are increasingly recognising the vital importance of educating their pupils to have open and positive attitudes towards people who look, speak or behave differently from themselves. In a global context, this echoes long-established concerns for international understanding and for world citizenship. Ignorance is likely to breed intercultural hostility as well as prejudiced attitudes and discriminatory practices against ethnic minority groups – now frequently referred to as racism. Schools can help prepare future citizens who accept and appreciate cultural diversity and who are alert, and opposed, to intended and unintended racism in employment, housing policy, police practice, media reporting and elsewhere. In addition it is argued that efforts to meet the particular needs and to improve the life chances of ethnic minority pupils are much more likely to succeed within an overall educational framework which has an explicitly non-racist stance towards religious, linguistic, cultural and racial diversity.

4 Multiculturalism vs anti-racism

Even amongst those who fully accept that this is an issue which concerns all teachers and all pupils, there is disagreement and controversy. Those who focus on cultural diversity have become described as 'multicultural-ists': they seek to engender a less ethnocentric perspective by enriching the curriculum with studies of and particular examples from other cultures, and by drawing on the particular skills of ethnic minority pupils. Others, often termed 'anti-racists', emphasise the need to reveal and combat racist attitudes and practices which disadvantage and discriminate against some minority groups, and which result in an unequal distribution of opportunities, wealth and power.

Multiculturalists thus stress the value of diversity, anti-racists stress the quest for equality. However, these are *not* polar opposites; they share a complex interrelationship. On the one hand, the celebration of diversity is no more than patronising tokenism unless it is accompanied by a fundamental belief in the equality of individuals from every background: a multicultural approach must embrace an anti-racist one. On the other hand, anti-racist strategies alone are unlikely to be successful in attaining equality of outcome unless the educational system is permeated with a real and fundamental sensitivity to diversity and ensures a formal curriculum response. The multicultural and anti-racist approaches are therefore not *alternatives*, but interlocking parts of one whole; each is essential, but neither is sufficient on its own. The composite approach has also to take account of the need to develop among pupils a core of shared values which contributes to societal cohesion.

Implications for schools

There is by no means universal resolution of the controversies briefly outlined above, but policy and practice are evolving. Many LEAs have agreed formal policy statements on the aims of multicultural education, and are providing advice, staffing, resources and in-service courses to help schools review their own practice (eg Berkshire, Bradford, ILEA, Leicestershire). Elsewhere, individual schools are preparing their own policy documents with the active involvement of all school staff and of governors and parents, and with formal procedures to coordinate and evaluate implementation. Most of these policies stress that education in and for a multicultural society involves all aspects of school life, and note that the librarian, the caretaker, the catering, administrative and clerical support staff all have a significant role to play, as well as the head and the whole teaching staff.

Arguments about emphasis and approach continue, and specific controversies (such as the Honeyford affair in Bradford) attract media attention and publicity. At national level, the 'Swann Report', *Education for All*[5] attempted a detailed review of opinion, research, policy and practice. It addressed the controversies outlined earlier, and sought to provide guidelines for educational action in a plural society. The very title of the Report – *Education for All* – emphasised that multicultural education concerns *all* teachers and *all* pupils. It recommends the permeation of the formal and hidden curriculum with a multicultural perspective, from nursery schools through to higher education. Its central messages are that schooling in a plural society must take account of:
- the particular needs of pupils of ethnic minority origin;
- the need for *all* pupils to develop a positive approach to cultural diversity;
- the need for strategies to combat attitudes, behaviour and practices

which discriminate against individuals and groups who are culturally, linguistically, religiously or racially different.

Attacked by the Right for being too liberal[6] and by the Left for being too conservative[7] the Swann Report has itself been controversial. Nevertheless, it is fast becoming the current 'orthodoxy' on teaching in a culturally diverse society. Some of the practical implications of Swann's recommendations for whole school matters and for the curriculum are explored below.

Whole school matters

Many schools are now recognising the importance of clear procedures for dealing immediately with racist badges, graffiti, leaflets, racially-based threats and physical assaults. All schools, whether monocultural or multicultural, agree that racially prejudiced remarks and behaviour cannot be tolerated under any circumstances and many are developing a formal policy for such incidents.

The school environment itself can signal a school's positive response to pluralism, through the use of corridor, library and classroom displays and visuals which draw on a variety of cultures, and by the presence of staff and visitors of ethnic minority origin. The Swann Report stressed the urgency of increasing the numbers of teachers of ethnic minority in training and in post. Allowing for current problems of supply, LEAs are beginning to make special efforts to recruit staff from ethnic minorities, and are developing codes of practice to help ensure there is no unconscious bias on racial, cultural or religious grounds.

Many 'all-white' schools use assemblies to introduce and explain some of the religious beliefs, practices and festivals of the range of faiths of our fellow citizens. Topic and project work offers plenty of opportunities to draw on the diversity in multilingual and multicultural Britain. Library resources and classroom materials are being developed which avoid presenting a solely Anglocentric view of the world and of knowledge. Teachers and pupils are learning together about the culture and background of the ethnic groups now present in British society.

In schools which are multiethnic in composition, there is much good practice to emulate. School assemblies, catering and timetabling policies are becoming much more sensitive to the needs of ethnic minority pupils. Bilingual communications to parents, home visits, consultation with community leaders, and making school premises available for community supplementary schools, are all improving the extent and quality of home-school and school-community liaison. In many multilingual schools, there is now timetable provision for mother tongue teaching at primary level and for heritage languages at secondary level, as well as classroom support for bilingualism, bidialectalism and English language development.

Ethnic monitoring of pupil performance, banding and streaming is increasingly advocated to help schools identify any unintentional stereotyping or racism which may be denying some pupils full access to their educational opportunities. Pastoral care staff have a vital role in identifying and countering any specific disadvantages or difficulties related to cultural difference. Careers staff are equally crucial in helping ethnic minority pupils maximise their educational and vocational chances in a society where discrimination against the employment of pupils of ethnic minority origin regrettably remains a statistical reality.[8]

Curricular content

A school context which values cultural diversity enhances and is enhanced by what happens in individual classrooms. In every curriculum area there can be initiatives and approaches that pay particular attention to the needs of ethnic minority pupils.

Where pupils of other cultures and faiths are present in the classroom, pluralist education is a natural development of a pupil-centred approach. For example, subject-specific projects can allow ethnic minority pupils to pursue in-depth studies of their culture of origin, if they so wish; the inclusion of literature, folk-songs, recipes and examplars from ethnic minority cultures provides relevance and motivation. Appropriate classroom materials are now widely available and pupils (and parents) of ethnic minority origin can be an additional valuable resource – although some may not feel ready to share their own experiences, perhaps from understandable fears of arousing the hostility of their peers. Teacher sensitivity is vital here. Teachers must also be aware of particular cultural constraints, eg Muslim attitudes to the representation of human figures in art lessons, or, in home economics lessons, religious restrictions and customs about handling or eating certain foods.

As mentioned earlier, supporting the English language development of pupils whose first language or dialect is not English remains a priority, but withdrawal classes are giving way to work which builds on the pupils' interaction with the teacher and their peers as part of the normal curriculum within the mainstream primary and secondary classroom. A number of LEAs are providing mother tongue teaching as part of the primary school curriculum, and secondary school syllabuses in community languages such as Urdu, Panjabi and modern Greek are gaining momentum.

These strategies are largely concerned with education *in* a multicultural society and aim to improve the quality of schooling experienced by pupils of ethnic minority origin. But subject specialists are also reviewing how they can best educate *all* pupils *for* a multicultural society. They are enriching their courses by including examples drawn from other cultures, and they are identifying topics within their courses which may help challenge racist attitudes and stereotypes. They are finding that the process of permeating the curriculum (and its assessment) with a multicultural and anti-racist perspective is providing an opportunity to improve the quality and integrity of their subject courses and materials.

Social science and social studies teachers made an early start in trying to introduce their pupils to other cultures. Their lessons can provide a rational framework for discussion of the causes and effects of intercultural tension, and for critical analysis of the 'facts' of racism and discrimination. Religious education has broadened to include the study of world faiths and offers opportunities to consider the moral basis of race relations legislation. Courses in personal and social education include similar material.

Teachers of the arts have traditionally used examples from many European cultures and are beginning to extend the range further afield; they are also able to draw pupils' attention to the stereotyped views of other cultures portrayed in some literature and art, and the part these can play in generating prejudiced views and attitudes. The content of literature and drama provides a rich source of material for classroom discussion of other lifestyles and of racial and religious prejudices; studies of media representation can help pupils discern racist images in printed and audio-visual material. Studying another language (and its literature) can help pupils understand and appreciate a culture and a world view other than their own.

Good history teaching involves the development of pupils' analytical skills so that they examine the evidence and seek to view historical 'facts' from several points of view. For example, in teaching about the 'voyages of discovery' or the spread of colonialism, historians can encourage their pupils to consider the viewpoints of the countries 'discovered' or colonised; historical study of racism in Nazi Germany and South Africa and the civil rights struggle in America provides a way of dealing with important but controversial issues at some distance from the current British situation. Human and social geography has always explored the relationships between the physical environment and human lifestyles and can help to develop pupils' appreciation of cultural diversity, and their understanding of national and international migration. Geography (and world studies) teachers also seek to promote understanding of global inequalities, and to counter stereotyped and racist images of people in other parts of the world.

Biology has a key role in challenging pseudoscientific theories of 'race', through careful investigation of the role of inheritance and environment in 'racial' characteristics. Science and mathematics teachers can ensure that pupils fully realise the substantial contributions of other cultures to the knowledge base in these subjects. Home economics teachers are realising their extensive opportunities to build on the international differences and similarities in cookery, dress, home-making and child-rearing.

Such subject-specific developments try to incorporate anti-racist teaching as a central feature of an eclectic multicultural education programme. However, direct teaching about race and racism as a specific curriculum topic or course remains a controversial matter. This is partly because it is difficult; teachers have found that it can be explosive and may be counterproductive. It has also become associated with Marxist perspectives on inequality and thus part of the larger controversy relating to political education in schools. Yet there are bound to be occasions when race-related issues are raised spontaneously in the classroom, arising from local, national and international events, or from racist incidents in school. Teachers must be ready to respond, and it is more likely that ensuing classroom discussions will be rational and constructive where they have already adopted a multicultural and anti-racist approach to daily curricular practice. The issues may be highly controversial, but ignoring them offers no solution. The classroom is one of the most appropriate places for a sensitive and informed exploration of such vital matters.

Conclusion

This chapter has reviewed the controversies associated with multicultural education in British schools and the current strategies designed to meet the particular needs of ethnic minority pupils and to prepare all pupils for a culturally diverse world. It has suggested that educationalists increasingly feel that these should be integrated across the curriculum and should be part of a school framework that affirms cultural, linguistic, religious and racial diversity.

Provision will, of course, vary according to the cultural composition of the school. Clearly, the views of parents must always be considered. Where many pupils are of West Indian origin, parents may be anxious about achievement levels, and about the possibility that some teachers have negative stereotypes and low expectations of their children. Schools with pupils of Asian or European background may need to give particular attention to English as a second language, mother tongue provision and support for home cultures and religion. The precise formulation of the multicultural curriculum is often controversial, as schools strive to maintain a balance between parents' wishes, pupils' needs and education for society. The particular needs of minority communities (eg for mother tongue teaching and culture maintenance, even to the extent of pleas for separate schools) have always to be weighed against the need to educate pupils for the wider society where they will need to be bicultural and (in some cases) bilingual. 'All-white' communities may regard multicultural teaching as an unnecessary and unwelcome intrusion, but teachers have a professional responsibility to prepare their pupils for a world which is both multicultural and multiracial. As the Swann Report indicates, teachers need to probe their own and their pupils' attitudes to cultural difference, and make every effort to counter stereotypes and challenge racist views, however controversial this may be in some regions and localities.

Teachers have a central role in preparing future citizens who accept and respect cultural difference, and who will challenge prejudice and discrimination wherever it occurs. The multicultural curriculum is a powerful tool for putting these ideas into practice, and fuller descriptions of ideas, resources and strategies can be found in the references below. The very extent of current developments at national, local and school level suggests that multicultural teaching is becoming far less of a controversial issue, but is increasingly perceived as an integral part of good educational practice.

Notes and references

1 *Teaching controversial issues* R Stradling *et al* (Edward Arnold, 1984).
2 *Supporting Children's Bilingualism* D Houlton and R Willey (Longman, 1983).
3 *Education and Cultural Pluralism* M Craft (ed) (Brighton: Falmer Press, 1984).
4 See: 'Curriculum for a multicultural society' A Craft, in *School-based Curriculum Development* M Skilbeck (ed) (Harper and Row, 1984); *The Educational and Vocational Experiences of 15–18 Year Old Members of Ethnic Minority Groups* J Eggleston *et al* Report to the DES, 1985; *Reading into Racism* G Klein (Routledge and Kegan Paul, 1985); *Assessment in a Multicultural Society* (Series of 8 subject-specific reports) Schools Council (Longman, 1983/4); *Caught Between: A Review of Research Into the Education of Pupils of West Indian Origin* M Taylor (NFER/Nelson, 1981); *The Best of Both Worlds: a Review of Research into the Education of Pupils of South Asian Origin* M Taylor with S Hegarty (NFER/Nelson, 1985).
5 *Education for All* (The Swann Report) Department of Education and Science (HMSO, 1985).
6 *Education in the Multiracial Society* S Pearce, (Monday Club Policy Paper, 1985).
7 *NAME on Swann* (National Anti-Racist Movement in Education, 1985).
8 *Racial Disadvantage Seventeen Years After the Act* (Policy Studies Institute Report 646, 1985).

Resources and further reading

The following books provide useful introductory reading and include practical examples of school and classroom approaches.

Arora, R and Duncan, C (eds) *Multicultural Education: towards good practice* (Routledge, 1986).

Cohen, L and Manion, L *Multicultural Classrooms* (Croom Helm, 1983).

Craft, A and Bardell, G (eds) *Curriculum Opportunities in a Multicultural Society* (Harper and Row, 1984).

Craft, A and Klein, G *Agenda for Multicultural Teaching* (Longman for School Curriculum Development Committee, 1986).

Houlton, D *Cultural Diversity in the Primary School* (Batsford, 1986).

Klein, G *Resources for Multicultural Education: an introduction* (Longman for Schools Council, revised edition, 1984).

Lynch, J *Teaching in the Multicultural School* (Ward Lock Educational, 1981).

Nixon, J *A Teacher's Guide to Multicultural Education* (Basil Blackwell, 1985).

Straker-Welds, M (ed) *Education for a Multicultural Society: case studies in LEA schools* (Bell and Hyman, 1984).

Twitchin, J and Demuth, C *Multicultural Education* (BBC Publications, extended edition, 1985).

Chapter 6

Education for employment and unemployment: is this the age of the trained?

Rob Fiddy

A fundamental decision we have to make about education is whether it should transform the mind so as to equip us for independent judgement and rational action, or whether it should be directed towards practical skills for particular ends. This is the distinction between liberal education – education for freedom, for tackling problems as yet unknown – and schooling as training, for instrumental tasks as they are currently perceived.[1]

Thus Maurice Holt began his article on 'Vocationalism: the new threat to universal education'. By so doing he took the continuing Great Debate a further step and at the same time began a small debate of his own within the ensuing issues of *Forum*. Holt's article was published in the Summer '83 edition of the journal – a few weeks before the advent of the *Technical and Vocational Education Initiative* (TVEI) in its first round of fourteen LEAs.[2] Contributors to subsequent editions of *Forum* picked up Holt's argument and related it directly to the ongoing experience of TVEI, for TVEI embodies the nub of the controversy surrounding liberal education *versus* schooling as training and much more besides.

The purpose of this paper is not only to consider the relationship between education and the world of work. It seeks also to render this relationship problematic by placing within it the notion of education for *un*employment. Trainers and liberal educators alike would no doubt agree that the fundamental purpose of education is to equip school-leavers for the wider society. For more and more school-leavers, however, experience of that society is likely to include a period of unemployment – or of employment's surrogate, the work experience or training programme.

Teaching (or training) for unemployment smacks of a nihilism which goes beyond the pale for most educationalists. Few would argue that a curriculum which prepares pupils for a life without work has anything to offer. But before we investigate the nature of the controversy regarding education for employment or unemployment, let us consider for a moment the recent recorded experience of a group of teachers undertaking a part-time MA on a Faculty of Education evening course:

The class was split into two groups, designated 'the white group' and 'the red group'. Their task was to contemplate 'the perfect curriculum'. They were given one and a half hours for discussion and to draw up notes.

Later in the plenary session the red group fed back first. They had designed a generous liberal/humanitarian curriculum which aimed – basically – at presenting to students, of all ages from four through 70 plus, knowledge and experience of the world at large via autonomous, peer and Stenhousian 'senior learner' organisations of pedagogy. An adventurous, democratic, conscientious and concerned 'perfect curriculum'.[3]

The white group had come to the more or less agreed conclusion, at quite an early stage in their deliberations, that the notion of a 'perfect curriculum' was not to be taken lightly. 'Perfect for whom?' was the basis of their discussion – perfect for the state? For the individual? Are these two goals mutually exclusive? And so on. To summarise – fuelled with cynicism from a hard core of exhausted and committed teachers the group decided to promote the argument that 'choice = unhappiness' and that the 'perfect curriculum' might well be one which precluded choice on behalf of the individual. The group decided to present a parodic curriculum to the plenary. They knew that, as one member put it, 'the others will come up with some liberal rubbish' and they decided for the sake of controversy to counter it.

The white group's parody of a 'perfect curriculum' was this: those currently in power select, at age seven, three per cent of the school population, on the basis of IQ tests, to be educated as leaders and decision makers via a traditional public school arrangement. The others are to be contained in a 'YTS' whirlpool – whirlpool because it is not stagnant. It moves, it is added to and drawn upon as the need arises in a more and more automated world of work. Inmates in the pool are constantly trained in 'generic or transferable skills'. So, as an area of employment develops, the pool is drawn upon. As the area declines or becomes automated the labour is dripped back. This process continues indefinitely. The mass of students leave the pool only temporarily. The norm of a pool of labour waiting for work is established, legitimised and internalised by all bar the three per cent. There is no school-leaving age. No notion of choice is given on the grounds that the realisation that there are or may be alternatives will lead to unhappiness and frustration.[4]

In the plenary the two versions of the 'perfect curriculum' elicited an animated, stimulating and exciting discussion. The juxtaposition of the two curricula, whimsical and cynical as they may have been, provoked an examination of basic educational goals. However, at the end of the session, the two groups agreed *that it was the white group's 'perfect curriculum' which was nearer to the status quo and more likely to remain there.*[5]

The white group and the red group were arbitrarily self-selected from the MA course members, they did not split into trainers or liberal educators but we might assume that elements of each were contained therein. Their 'perfect curricula', however, are important as illustrations of points on the spectrum of opinion as to the purpose of education. As

Holt points out above, the controversy over vocationalism raises questions as to this very purpose. Subsumed within this question are issues to do with the relationship between education and (un)employment and how this relationship is or should be reflected in the curriculum. The red and white groups' curricula and ensuing discussion touch on many of the current concerns, some of which we will deal with later, but one overriding point can be drawn from the anecdote at this stage: it seems that one need probe only just below the surface rhetoric of either liberal educators or trainers to discover fundamental disquiet from each source as to the relationship between education and the 'reality' of life after school.

The 'reality' of life after school is itself a contentious issue. Reality is a product of perception – and perceptions are subject to circumstance. Thus the recorded reality of a Youth Training Scheme can be 'slave labour and a waste of time' or 'a useful and necessary prerequisite for employment'. Similarly, we can be presented with one perception of a very low level of unemployment among school-leavers of a particular school if membership of the Youth Training Scheme, for example, is considered as *not being unemployed*. The same figures from the same school could offer a very low level of employment among the same school-leavers if membership of the Young Training Scheme is considered as *not being employed*.

The reality of life after school can also be seen to produce some disquiet among pupils – and not only from those who have recently left. There is little doubt among some school-leavers, particularly those in areas of high unemployment, as to what the future holds. One member of a YTS course explained his situation to me:

I don't think there is much chance of me getting a job at all. Because by the time I leave here I'll be 18 plus and if I don't get a job within six months I'll be 19 – well, look at the competition for those jobs then and I still don't have any qualifications. And they'll just say 'Well, have you ever had a job?' and I'll say 'No' and they'll say 'How old are you?' and I'll say '19'. So they'll say 'Well, you have been unemployed for three years' and I'll say 'Yeah' and they'll say 'Well, you are no good. Next client, what about you?' 'Well, I am 16 and I have just left school with five 'O' levels' – 'Well, you haven't been unemployed, here is the job.'[6]

As well as expressing his pessimism about future prospects, this YTS trainee underlines his instrumental view of the purpose of education, a view reiterated in the following observation by TVEI students:

Pupil one: 'They said "TVEI's this new scheme and there's going to be some in the school". Just took my fancy.'
Interviewer: 'Did they encourage people to go on it?'
Pupil one: 'No, they said it's up to you. Your options. And it all depends what you want when you grow up. What you want to do when you grow up.'
Interviewer: 'What about your parents?'

Pupil one: 'They thought "Oh it's a good idea for you to come on computers", that's the in-coming thing isn't it?'
Pupil two: 'Businesses and that are just computers.'
Pupil one: 'If you go somewhere where someone's got a computer and you've got an 'O' level working on computers you're more likely to get that job.'[7]

This reality[8] – of the high and rising levels of youth unemployment – has increased the intensity of concern regarding the place of vocational education in the secondary curriculum – expressed by advocates and antagonists alike and among educationalists as well as pupils. Unemployment rates – particularly youth unemployment rates – are, of course, a political issue. It naturally follows that they are also a controversial issue. Their importance in the secondary curriculum is that they form the context for an increasing interest in vocational and pre-vocational education, or the 'new vocationalism' as Bates *et al* (1984) refer to it. It is no coincidence that the rise in youth unemployment rates has corresponded with growing concern about vocational education. At a Cambridge conference Barry MacDonald made the following observation:

... why, as the prospects for employment diminish, is there so much emphasis on providing work experience, work skills, work knowledge, work habits, work attitudes? Is this a form of aversion therapy? Is it a form of compensation? If so, what next, Wendy Houses for the homeless?[9]

It is when the new vocationalism is viewed from within the context of high and rising youth unemployment that the full complexity of the controversy concerning education for employment or unemployment can be seen.

Tony Watts makes the point that the high level of unemployment has had a significant influence on education in at least three identifiable areas: that it causes pupils and parents to question the effectiveness of the education system in terms of obtaining employment; that high levels of unemployment evoke for some a deficit model of schools; and that education has begun to be seen as a possible response to the problem, if only in terms of keeping unemployed youth off the streets.[10]

Elements of these three areas were reflected in former Prime Minister Callaghan's Ruskin College speech in October 1976, which introduced the Great Debate. They were also referred to in Prime Minister Thatcher's announcement of TVEI to the House of Commons in November 1982, following on from the Government White Paper, the New Training Initiative.[11]

Among the issues raised by Callaghan was the 'need to improve relations between industry and education'. Tony Watts paraphrases Callaghan's concerns in this area as follows:

He said he was troubled to find industry complaining that new recruits from schools lacked the basic skills required for some jobs, and was further troubled to discover that the best trained students from university and polytechnic had no intention of joining industry . . . While schools clearly should not aim simply to produce technically efficient robots, he said, there was no virtue in producing socially well adjusted member of society who were unemployed because they lacked skills.[12]

On 12 November 1982 Mrs Thatcher announced the TVEI to the House of Commons by declaring 'a relevant curriculum for a changing world of work'. In January 1983 David Young, then Chairman of the MSC, in a letter to all LEA Directors of Education in England and Wales, gave the general objective of the TVEI 'to widen and enrich the curriculum in a way that will help young people prepare for the world of work.'[13]

The quite overt implication in both governments' declarations is of a deficit model of education – a view often accepted by parents and pupils. Dan Finn makes the point that 'the changing needs of industry have their own direct effects on schooling . . . For school-leavers and their parents the realities of unemployment are a direct challenge to the legitimacy of schooling.'[14] This is not so far removed from the early Great Debate notions that schooling was in some way turning pupils away from industry. Moreover, these issues are clearly defined within the current TVEI thrust in promoting educational provision for the new technologies and 'a vocational awareness' amongst 14-year-olds. The recurring theme is that a lack of jobs is to do with a lack of skills and/or attitude, and lack of skills is to do with schooling. Saville Kushner defines a deficit model in the following way:

There are three stages to the development and use of a model of deficit. First a shortfall is noticed or identified in educational (or training) outcomes. (Say, standards of numeracy are falling and employers are concerned about the quality of recruits). Next, culpability is established and a culprit identified. (In this example, perhaps teachers are the focus for blame in abandoning tried and tested methods of mathematics teaching in favour of experimental curricula). Finally, a remedy is designed and legitimated with reference back to the problem. (An objectives based, mastery-learning scheme is proposed to replace modern maths syllabi under the claim that it is 'proof' against teacher modification).[15]

Kushner goes on to identify four models of deficit: student, school, curriculum and cultural. Of these it is perhaps the first three which overlap the most and are the most familiar: that unemployed school-leavers are in such a position because of their personal lack of attributes; that school-leavers are unemployed because of a shortfall in the process of schooling; that specific curricula – particularly 'experimental' or non-traditional curricula – are to blame. But it is the fourth model, cultural deficit, which may help us to highlight the current controversy over education for employment or unemployment. Kushner illustrates cultural deficit thus:

The education system has, hitherto, enjoyed a resistance to outside interventions. When the Engineering Industries Training Board (EITB) published proposals for school curriculum and examinations in 1979 and presented them at regional conferences of teachers they were met with massive and hostile resistance for what was taken to be their assertiveness. There is a sense in which the education service has been accustomed to non-educational authorities having to negotiate access to the 'insider' curriculum discourse ... But only four years after the debacle suffered by the EITB the Manpower Services Commission is welcomed by local authorities and schools. We could ... see the vocational/industrial culture as the most recent conqueror of the education system.[16]

An alternative to the deficiency model as a contributory factor in youth unemployment is to place the lack of jobs squarely in a political/ economic arena. Given this interpretation of events, the perception of vocational education in the secondary curriculum is altered. Crudely, if unemployment is not a product of lack of skills but a consequence of political acts or, more generously, of the economic climate, then what is the purpose of skills training within the education system? For some, at least currently, in terms of TVEI and similarly funded initiatives, the answer lies with centralisation of and intervention in the curriculum. Control is the goal, vocational education the means. The usefulness or not of vocational education in the real world after school becomes a side issue.[17]

Perhaps here we should return to the pages of *Forum* in order to provide a focus for the current debate. Maurice Holt, in his article mentioned at the beginning of this paper, goes on to criticise increasing vocationalism – not on the grounds of party politics, but from what might be described as a cultural perspective:

... the vocational rhetoric appeals to politicians of all parties, and with the Government's recent decision to bypass the DES and channel £7 million of MSC money into vocationalising the secondary school curriculum, all who believe that liberal education is worth defending must be ready to mount the barricades ... Despite the pervasive lack of work – and all the inevitable future changes in our concept of work in a post-industrial society – working life is to determine both the knowledge and the personal qualities addressed by the school curriculum.[18]

He goes on to draw a distinction between post-16 vocationalism (when 'the climate is different') and the 14–18 curriculum funded by the MSC in the form of TVEI, which he finds 'totally uncompelling, if our concern is education rather than short-term political convenience'. The alternative, he suggests, is a revamping of a liberal curriculum, rather than its eclipse in the wake of the new vocationalism.

Above all we must not forget that – by a rich irony – a vocationalised curriculum ill serves its pupils in precisely the respects in which it claims to be strong. For it claims to prepare them for jobs in tomorrow's society by basing a curriculum on the skills seen as necessary today. Yet the incontestable fact about tomorrow is that it will be different from today, and will present quite new problems. New problems can be solved only by those with the personal and moral autonomy to interpret our culture – by those who have enjoyed a liberal education.[19]

Two issues of *Forum* later, C J Lea, the Project Director of TVEI in Birmingham, responded to Holt's article:

As Mr Holt would have it, our roundly educated 16-year-old is to be launched into life beyond school personally and morally autonomous, with refined powers of critical judgement, with a balanced social perspective and other worthy qualities, all developed within the classroom to a standard curriculum pattern and in the face of common examination goals. I suggest that there is an ever increasing gap between this idealistic design and the reality of today's world and tomorrow's opportunities as perceived by many young people and their teachers.[20]

He goes on to promote TVEI as a 'loosening of the subject-bound curricular strait-jacket' and details the Birmingham scheme as containing the elements of a general education, rather than narrowing the aspirations of pupils. But, for C J Lea, the real value of the MSC's involvement in secondary education is in the opportunity it affords for schools to withdraw from the orientation of the ivory tower and the 'illusionary curriculum':

Maurice Holt suggests that TVEI has been propelled into action by the fuel of political expediency. I suggest that he is out of touch with the strength of feeling so widely expressed from within the profession since the Ruskin College speech acted as a trigger to our thinking. Now, the MSC has provided us with the impulse as well as the resources to escape from the vacuum generated by strong vested interests preserving the abstract curriculum model in face of the limited executive powers available to the DES, HMI and the Schools Council . . . the emphasis within the experience-based learning of our 14 to 18 curriculum is finely placed on making sense of what the student is already experiencing in their inter-personal relationships and lives; it is about doing and making; about problem-solving and making decisions that are real for the students and not the abstractions of the curriculum dream world of those who seek universality and immortality at the expense of reality.[21]

In a sense the battle lines are drawn here, if not precisely between liberal educators and trainers in a pragmatic way – there has been little evidence so far of classroom change and it is still too early for employment prospects to be altered – then certainly from an ideological perspective.

In the next issue of *Forum* Holt replied to Lea, re-affirming his position:

The truth about the TVEI is that it will secure the re-birth of the secondary modern school. But Mr Lea fails to see this, mesmerised as he is by the need to moderate 'the harsh distinction between education and training'. He should read the speeches of his mentor, the Chairman of the MSC, more carefully, for Mr

David Young nurtures no such illusions: 'Training should not be confused with education. Training is about work-related skills and is intimately connected with employment.' Quite so.[22,23]

It would be wrong to enter into the finer details of TVEI for the purposes of this paper. For one thing, the nature of the initiative is such that LEAs have been able to draw up proposals for localised interpretations under broad MSC guidelines and it would be true to say that no two schemes are identical. In fact this was the basis of subsequent articles published by *Forum* on the TVEI theme which pointed out that individual projects were re-defining or even subverting the threats imposed by the central initiative. But TVEI can be seen as the current nexus between education and the world of work, if not the world of unemployment. Still within the TVEI context, in a later edition of *Forum*, Richard Pring outlined the polarities of that debate in a section of his article he sub-headed 'Critical Concepts':

a 'liberal vs vocational' . . . many young people look for schools to be relevant to what they will eventually do, and the anxiety about a job, or about the kind of qualification and training necessary . . . colours (the) appreciation of schooling. But this concern often is unacceptable to the 'liberal educator', who sees his or her role to be initiating pupils into those different forms of knowledge which constitute the mature and developed mind . . .
b 'Education' vs 'training' . . . education indicates a relatively broad and critical understanding of things, whereas training suggests the preparation for a specific task or job.
c 'Practical' vs 'theoretical' . . . the cognitive and theoretical on the one hand and the affective and the practical on the other . . . the curriculum has often been criticised for being too academic – the response to such criticism is indeed divided and devisive – the more theoretical for the more able and emphasis upon 'learning through doing' for the others.
d 'Process' vs 'product' . . . too often, it is argued, examinations focus upon right answers – not the mental processes through which one arrives at the right answers. By contrast, so it is argued, what should be encouraged are the attitudes and the general mental abilities to engage in learning – learning how to learn.[24]

Pring describes the above categories as 'false dichotomies' in Dewey's terms,[25] and highlights how TVEI might challenge this understanding of the curriculum. He declares himself an advocate of TVEI, but with the following rider:

If we are not careful both in analysing those achievements (how we conceptualise and describe what we are doing does affect what counts as achievements and we must not be hung up on indefensible notions of 'liberal education', or of 'vocational training') and in detecting those social and political forces that might distort those achievements, then TVEI could, despite its promise and practice, be assigned a narrow and narrowing function within an impoverished vision of education.[26]

The extensive extracts from the pages of *Forum* in this paper are intended to serve as a focus for the current state of the debate concerning vocational education. Of course *Forum* is only one vehicle and the debate is handled much more frequently and extensively elsewhere. For example, during the first year of TVEI there were 46 articles concerning the initiative in the *Times Educational Supplement* alone. Additionally, TVEI itself is only one facet of vocational education.

It is a feature of controversies such as this that attitudes and positions stand in danger of becoming polarised. Education for employment or unemployment is not a simple equation, even rhetorically. Given the current political and economic realities, possible 'solutions' find even less consensus. To see the problem simply in terms of liberal education versus vocational training is as naive a view as that expressed by the MA students in the anecdote at the beginning of this paper. Yet it is still probably the most common way in which the problem is expressed – and not only in this current debate, nor in this country.[27] But the problem of education for employment or unemployment is a fundamental one. We live in a society where much more than financial independence is at stake through lack of work. Because of the continuing emphasis placed on jobs – even within the context of high and rising levels of unemployment – lack of work stands to equate with lack of individual identity.

David Hargreaves has commented that:

When employment is denied to the young school-leaver the reaction is naturally one of shock and disappointment, personal crisis and social dislocation.
Within the framework of the work ethic, then, to be denied paid employment is to be rendered not fully human.[28]

Sue Bloxham also makes a point about the 'problems' encountered by unemployed school-leavers:

. . . there is little logic in attempting to alleviate (these problems) via a course, which through its overwhelming bias towards the value of work . . . only serves to reinforce their failure and the importance of the task they have failed at.[29]

Superseding the liberal education versus schooling as training controversy is the fact that levels of unemployment for school-leavers – discounting membership of the YTS as being employed – are still rising. It is all too apparent that past efforts to rectify the situation through education *or* training have failed to secure an increase in job vacancies.

Of course work is an important part of life, and of course education must accommodate 'work' in the curriculum. During the earlier years of the Great Debate[30] there were recurring arguments concerning the teaching *of* work as opposed to teaching *about* it. Initiatives such as TVEI may well contain the capacity to be 'subverted' from the former to the latter, but there is little credence given to a place for teaching about the lack of work within such schemes. I am not talking about 'education for leisure', nor am I proposing that 'work' should not be accommodated in the curriculum. What I am suggesting is that efforts should be made to educate pupils into a critical appraisal of the past, current and possible future regarding their (un)employment prospects, and that these efforts should be formalised, overt parts of the curriculum and not left to 'subversion'.[31]

This is not to say that no attempts have been made in the past to deal with unemployment in the curriculum. Unemployment has been a feature of careers lessons, for example, for some time. But there is no doubt that the emphasis, and the preponderance of the funding, of curriculum development has been placed on obtaining employment; 'vocational chic' as Saville Kushner calls it.[32] However, handling unemployment within the curriculum is problematic, as the recorded attempts have demonstrated. Kathryn Evans and Bill Law, for instance, in their *Final Report of the Career Guidance Integration Project*[33] document the dilemmas faced by careers teachers in addressing unemployment from within a structure and climate aimed at vocationalism. Derek Kirton has also examined how six careers teachers in the Durham coalfield confronted the threat which unemployment posed for their clients.[34]

It was in the spirit of addressing youth unemployment from within the curriculum that the Further Education Unit (FEU) funded a small research project at the Centre For Applied Research in Education (CARE) of the University of East Anglia.[35] Entitled *Understanding Through Discussion: Youth Unemployment*, the project aimed at 'serving the discussion, among young people, of significant and contemporary social issues and experiences in the broad area of youth unemployment'.[36] It comprised a balanced collection of discussion support and stimulus materials, drawn from a wide range of original and published sources.

The stimulus materials pack was designed to support young people's confrontation of the 'problem' of unemployment and to 'promote a more informed understanding of their situation'. Its base-line was to place the controversial issue of youth unemployment squarely in the arena of schooling and, to a certain extent, post-school training. In this respect it followed on from (and borrowed its pedagogy from) the Humanities Curriculum Project[37] which was the first genuine attempt to bring controversial issues into the classroom.

A certain irony within the project was its attempt to reflect the aims and objectives of the FEU's *Common Core Skills for Vocational Preparation*.[38] But the 'skills' involved in the discussion of controversial issues are directly relevant to the development of personal qualities more usually associated with job preparation courses. Confronting youth unemployment within the curriculum by making it the focus of discussion did not prevent pupils developing their powers of argument or furthering their understandings. The proposal to the FEU for this project put part of the aims thus:

Young people have a language for talking *within* their culture but they do not always have command of a reflexive language which allows them to talk *about* their culture and the contexts of living . . . The intention is, then, to help young people, through the structured and supportive conventions of discussion, to articulate concerns, uncertainties and aspirations. Our experience suggests that this is best done through focussing on materials which speak to the experience of young people but which allow them, initially, the protection of talking about 'others' rather than about 'ourselves'.[39]

Care was taken, in compiling the stimulus materials, to emphasise their authenticity. Although drawn from a variety of sources, much of the material was in the form of first-hand accounts of the experience of unemployment from both young people and adults. Some of this material was taken from on-going research at CARE, more was collected specifically for the project. Draft materials packs were trialed in a variety of educational settings around the country with students between the ages of 15 and 17 and with an ability range starting from ESN(M).

Data from the trials suggested that it was the more obviously authentic materials which were the most successful in eliciting discussion. Some young people involved drew comparisons with other vocationally-orientated materials they had experience of and had rejected because of a continuing emphasis on job-search skills and interviewing techniques. This was a sentiment reflected in earlier research with Youth Opportunities Programme students on a Social and Life Skills course. One student told me his feelings about parts of the course in the following way:

We do too much of that job interviewing stuff . . . I bet there isn't one kid on this course who hasn't had plenty of practice in failing inverviews.[40]

In a similar vein, the trial packs for the project contained this interview extract:

Interviewer: 'Well, what do you want to do when you leave, in a few weeks time? Just background – like why you want to do it . . . '
Student one: 'Well, I'm gonna join the Merchant Navy. My uncle was in it. He enjoyed it.'
Student two: I'm going for an apprentice electrician. I told the Careers man that my Dad works in Fords as a sparks and he says I might as well go that road.'
Interviewer: 'Well, that's great. All you hear about here is depression and unemployment and here you are with positive ideas and something sorted out. Great.'
Student two: 'Erm . . . look . . . You don't think we're just going to *do* these things . . . ? You said what do I *want to do* so I told you. We know we're going to end up on a scheme, or the dole like everybody else . . . We *know* how hard it is.'[41]

The aspiration within the project was not to undermine the importance of obtaining employment, nor was it designed to project a necessarily negative image. A variety of issues were handled. Indeed, some of the materials dealt with entrepreneurial 'success stories'. But the basic guiding principle was to reflect a realistic version of the post-school world – to include employment *and* unemployment.

Subsequent reports from teachers who had used the trial packs suggested other ways of furthering this notion. Included were schemes which sent pupils out into the community to research for themselves the availability of jobs, thereby involving them in many of the usual social and personal development techniques, but within a realistic context. Other suggestions included writing redundancies into business simulation exercises, and one which used the 'town twinning' scheme and pen-palling to place unemployment in a global perspective.

This, then, would seem one of the more appropriate ways in which to deal with the controversial area of unemployment in the classroom: to make unemployment itself – its causes, consequences and implications both for the individual and for wider society – the focus for investigation and discussion.

Both 'liberal educators' and those who see 'schooling as training' are in the wrong if they do not, will not, or cannot accommodate unemployment as a reality for school-leavers into the curriculum. The hard fact is that unemployment in its various guises is part of the wider society. We owe it to current and future generations of school-leavers to stop perpetuating a myth, and to make it clear that generic or transferable skills, training in occupational families, or a broad-based traditional education will not provide jobs. The argument is not against vocational education *per se*. But the objection is to the implication that the acquisition of skills will, by itself, open doors to employment. So often the controversy and the ensuing debate concerns education for employment *or* unemployment, but reality demands that we focus our attention on education for employment *and* unemployment.

Notes and references

1 'Vocationalism: the new threat to universal education' M Holt, in *Forum* 1983, Vol 25, No 3, pp 84–86.

2 TVEI began in September 1983 with its first round. In September 1984, 46 other LEAs joined the scheme, and in September 1985 a third round began with another 12 authorities. For a brief breakdown of the scheme, see the *Times Educational Supplement* 3.5.85, pp 23–5. TVEI involves an extensive network of local evaluations, in addition to two major national evaluations conducted by the NFER and Leeds University. For papers on substantive areas of concern within TVEI see *TVEI Working Papers* I Stronach and R Fiddy (eds). This biannual collection of articles is available from CARE, University of East Anglia, Norwich.

3 See, for example *Personal and Social Education in the Curriculum* R Pring

(ed) (Hodder and Stoughton, 1984) and *Personal and Social Development Modules: The Scottish 16–18 Plan.*

4 The notion of 'generic' or 'transferable' skills lies at the hub of contemporary educational development. See FEU publications such as *Occupational Training Families: Their Implications for FE* R Johnson (FEU, 1984). See also CPVE notions of 'core competencies' in *The Certificate of Pre-Vocational Education* BTEC, January 1985. The under-researched and conceptually doubtful nature of 'generic' or 'transferable' skills is seldom acknowledged, but see Philip Cohen in *Schooling for the Dole* I Bates *et al* (Macmillan, 1984) and *Foundation Training Issues* C Hayes *et al* (University of Sussex, 1982).

5 Such a conclusion is also expressed in *Schooling for the Dole* (see note 4); see also *Is There Anyone Here from Education?* Wolpe and Donald (eds) (Pluto Press, 1983).

6 'YOP . . . that's Youth Off Pavements innit?' R Fiddy, in *Pupil Experience* J Schostak and T Logan (eds) (Croom Helm, 1984). For further comment see also *The Best Years?* J M Hughes (ed) (Aberdeen University Press, 1984) and chapters in *In Place of Work: Policy and Provision for the Young Unemployed* R Fiddy (ed) (Falmer Press, 1983).

7 *TVEI-Recruitment 1984* First annual report of the local, independent evaluation of TVEI in Norfolk, Suffolk and Essex. R Fiddy (CARE, University of East Anglia, 1985).

8 The realities of youth transition are under-represented. There are many reformist programmes and numerous radical critiques, but little careful research of youth in the 1980s. See, however, *Wigan Pier Revisited* B Campbell (Virago, 1984) and the writings of J Seabrook.

9 'Managing change in schools and colleges' B Macdonald, paper presented to the conference *Transition from School to Adult Life in the 1980s*, Wolfson College, Cambridge, July 1982.

10 *Education, Unemployment and the Future of Work* A G Watts (Open University Press, 1983).

11 *A New Training Initiative: A Programme for Action* HMSO; see also *Training for Jobs* Cmmd. 9135, HMSO, 1984. Critiques abound, but see *Who Controls Training* St John Brooks 1985 Fabian Tract 506, available from The Fabian Society.

12 A G Watts, *op cit.*

13 Taken from the *TVEI Operating Manual* MSC, London, which usefully contains letters from the MSC to LEAs concerning TVEI. For other interesting correspondence see *The Other Half of Our Future* Women's National Commission, 1985, Cabinet Office, London.

14 'Whose Needs? Schooling and the "Needs" of Industry' D Finn, in *Youth Unemployment and State Intervention* T Rees and P Atkinson (eds) (RKP, 1982).

15 'Vocational Chic: A Historical and Curriculum Context to the Field of Transition in England' S Kushner, in *Youth, Unemployment and Training: A Collection of National Perspectives* R Fiddy (ed) (Falmer Press, 1985).

16 *ibid.*

17 For useful updating see past and future copies of *Youth and Policy* available from 13 Hunstanton Court, Ravenswood, Gateshead.

18 'Vocationalism: the new threat to universal education' M Holt (see note 1).

19 It is interesting to note the emphasis on keyboard skills within schemes such

as TVEI as a necessary part of 'computer literacy'. Recent developments suggest that sixth generation computers will soon supersede keyboarding with oral control.

20 'Vocational Focus' C J Lea, in *Forum* 1984, Vol 1.26, No 2, pp 47–8.
21 *ibid.*
22 'The Dream and the Reality' M Holt in *Forum* 1984, Vol 26, No 3, pp 68–9.
23 *The Sunday Times* of 2 December 1985 contained a small article headed 'Technology Plan for the Young Elite'. The article detailed plans for the setting up of '16–20 technology schools in main urban centres . . . Each would take 1000 pupils, who would be specially selected and would not pay fees . . . The LEAs would not be responsible for the new schools . . . instead they would be funded directly by the taxpayer via a national education trust.
24 'In defence of TVEI' R Pring, in *Forum* 1985, Vol 27, No 1, pp 14–8.
25 *Democracy and Education* J Dewey.
26 R Pring, *op cit.*
27 See *Youth, Unemployment and Training: A Collection of National Perspectives* R Fiddy (ed) (Falmer Press, 1985).
28 'Unemployment, Leisure and Education' D Hargreaves, in *The Oxford Review of Education* 1981, Vol 7, No 3, pp 197–210.
29 'Social Behaviour and the Young Unemployed' S Bloxham in *In Place of Work: Policy and Provision for the Young Unemployed* R Fiddy (ed) (Falmer Press, 1983).
30 For useful accounts of the Great Debate see *Unpopular Education* CCCS (Hutchinson, 1981); *Schools and Industry* Jamieson and Lightfoot (Methuen, 1982); *Education, Unemployment and the Future of Work* A G Watts (Open University Press, 1983).
31 See *Schools Council Careers Education and Guidance Project* parts 1–3 (Longman, 1977).
32 S Kushner, *op cit.*
33 *Careers Guidance Integration Project* K Evans and B Law (NIEC 1984). Also see the evaluation report of this project: *Made in England* S Kushner and T Logan, CARE Occasional Publications No 14, 1984. Available from CARE, University of East Anglia, Norwich.
34 'The Impact of Mass Unemployment on Careers Guidance in the Durham Coalfield' D Kirton, in *In Place of Work: Policy and Provision for the Young Unemployed* R Fiddy (ed) (Falmer Press, 1983).
35 After trialing in various locations a final pack based on these findings was produced. This was intended to serve as a set of examples of the types of stimulus materials which worked best. Teachers who want to use the pack should update the materials in a similar style. The pack is available from the FEU, London.
36 *Understanding Through Discussion: Youth Unemployment* J Rudduck, R Fiddy and T Logan (FEU, 1984).
37 The Humanities Curriculum Project (HCP) 1962–72, was directed by Lawrence Stenhouse and funded by the Schools' Council and Nuffield Foundation. HCP investigated and provided support, stimulus and materials for teaching about controversial human issues in the secondary school. Within the pedagogy of HCP was the notion of the 'neutral chairman'.
38 *Common Core Skills for Vocational Preparation* (FEU, 1983).
39 *Ibid.*

40 'Inside the Work Introduction Course' R Fiddy in *In Place of Work: Policy and Provision for the Young Unemployed* R Fiddy (ed) (Falmer Press, 1983).
41 Included in the trials pack, this data was taken from the doctoral research of Tom Logan into *The Transition from School to Adult Life* at CARE, University of East Anglia, Norwich.

Further reading and resources

Bingham, M *et al* 1983 *Choices* A teen woman's journal for Self-awareness and Personal Planning, available from Advocacy Press, PO Box 236, Santa Barbara, CA 93102, USA.

Borrett, N W G *Education for Leisure: A Guide To the Literature* (Polytechnic of North London, 1984).

Bourne, R and Gould J *Self-Sufficiency 16–25* A report on the schemes available to help young people set up businesses of their own (Kogan Page, 1982).

Campbell, A *The Girls In The Gang* A Report From New York City. (Basil Blackwell, 1984).

Centre For Educational Research and Innovation *Education and Work: The Views of the Young* (Paris, OCDE, 1983).

COIC *Training For Versatility* pack consisting of 25 min. video and four books (Longman, 1984).

Community Projects Foundation *Sense of Direction* Exploring new prospects with unemployed young people (CPF, 1983).

Dauncey, G *The Unemployment Handbook* NEC Practical Guides, (NEC, 1981).

Dauncey, D *Nice Work If You Can Get It* How to be positive about unemployment (NEC, 1983).

Davis, E and Zelinco, M *Entrepreneurship in Voc Ed* NCRVE, (Ohio State University, 1982).

East Leeds Women's Workshop 1985 *Women and Work Video*, available from Clare Segal, 4th Floor, 18–20 Dean Street, Newcastle upon Tyne.

EC Action Programme 1985 *Transition of Young People from Education to Working Life* available from IFAPLAN, Square Ambiorix 32.B.1040 Brussels.

Fawcett, B 1985 *What Trace of Careers Education* (Longman, 1985).

The Fawcett Society, 1985 *The Class of '84* A study of girls on the first year of the YTS, available from National Joint Committee of Working Women's Organisations, 150 Walworth Rd, London.

Frith, S *The Sociology of Youth* (Causeway Books, 1984).

Frith, S *Sound Effects, Youth Leisure and Rock 'n Roll* (Constable and Co, 1983).

Gilbert, R *The Impotent Image: Reflections of Ideology in the Secondary Curriculum* (The Falmer Press, 1984).

The Grubb Institute of Behavioural Sciences 1981 *TWL Network in*

Practice Supporting young people in transition to working life, available from The Grubb Institute, Cloudesley St, London.

Handy, C *The Future of Work: a View Of The Problems and Possibilities* (St Georges House, 1983).

Hendry, L B *Growing Up and Going Out: Adolescents and Leisure 1983* (Aberdeen University Press, 1983).

Hopkins, D and Wideen, M (eds) *Alternative Perspectives in School Improvement* (The Falmer Press, 1984).

James, P *et al* 1985 *Sense of Direction* exploring new prospects with unemployed young people, Community Projects Foundation, 60 Highbury Grove, London.

McRobbie, A and Nava, M (eds) *Gender and Generation* Macmillan Youth Question Series. (Macmillan, 1985).

Murray, C *Youth Unemployment* A socio-psychological study of disadvantaged 16–19 year-olds (NFER, 1978).

NYB Youth Work Unit 1981 *Enfranchisement* An information pack for youth workers dealing with young people and the law, NYB, Leicester.

Roberts, K *Youth and Leisure* (Allen and Unwin, 1983).

ScoVO 1983 *Crossing the Threshold: Transition Learning in Vocational Preparation* available from ScoVo, 86 Southbrae Drive, Glasgow.

Smith, M 1981 *Organise!* NAYC Publications, available from 70 St Nicholas Circle, Leicester.

Smith, P W *Unemployment 1–4* (University of Durham, 1983).

Solomos, J *The Politics of Black Youth Unemployment: A Critical Analysis of Official Ideologies and Policies* SSRC Research Unit on Ethnic Relations, University of Aston, Birmingham, 1983.

THAC *Kids Moving On* resource pack available from 33 Groatmarket Newcastle upon Tyne.

TURC Video 1984 *Rights – Wot Rights* The case for Trade Union membership, available from 7 Frederick St, Birmingham.

Turkie, A (ed) *Know What I Mean*, Young men from Lewisham discuss their lives and experience (NYB, Leicester, 1982).

Varlaam, C (ed) *Rethinking Transition: Educational Innovation and the Transition to Adult Life* (The Falmer Press, 1984).

YES 1985 *Jobstart* Pamphlets, Video, Jigsaw and Card Game. Longman Resources Unit, London.

Williamson, H and P *Five Years* (NYB, Leicester, 1984).

Willis, P *Learning To Labour* (Saxon House, 1977).

Chapter 7

The facts of life: controversial medical issues in the curriculum

John Harris

It would be a scandal if any child were to leave school without knowing the facts of life. But what *are* the facts of life? Whatever they are, two things are clear. The first is that they are not what they were, and the second is that whatever they are, they are contested. If they are to discharge their obligations to help their students understand these important matters, teachers cannot help but stray into areas of controversy, and nowhere more so than where medical and biotechnological issues are concerned.

The very idea of addressing medical and biotechnological issues in the curriculum is perhaps itself controversial. For this reason I shall attempt to do two things. First, I shall review a number of the issues that seem to me to be unavoidable if school students are to be properly educated. I shall then take one particularly sensitive and intractable problem and attempt to argue towards three conclusions concerning this case: that discussion of controversial issues of the sort, and investigation of the knowledge and information relevant to their resolution, should be an important part of the school curriculum; how an adequate consideration of the various issues involved in the resolution of these problems can be arrived at; and what precisely this involves.

Problematic issues

The radical nature of the changes brought about by medical and biotechnological advance, and the rapidity of that advance mean that school students will have to face decisions, both while at school and shortly thereafter, which are complex in the extreme. If they are to be able to cope with them at all adequately, they will need to be prepared. The knowledge, information, and capacity for understanding that these decisions require are not easily obtained. For many of these students, their school or college and teachers will be the only source of the support and information that they need to help them make up their own minds. This concept of the school as a community resource centre is not, of course, new. However, the case for schools to take on this role is now more pressing than ever, in view of the problems thrown up by medical and biotechnological advance. Some examples will help to make clear what I mean.

In the now notorious 'Gillick Case'[1] the House of Lords decided that the courts were not compelled to 'hold that a girl under 16 lacked the legal capacity to consent to contraceptive advice' and that in certain circumstances this advice could be given without her parents' knowledge or consent. The implications of this case and the social practices which gave rise to it are clearly of immense interest and importance for school students. The case not only recognises the legitimacy of the interest school students will take in these matters, but it accepts that even quite young students are able – or, at any rate, entitled – to make complex and important choices for themselves. The extent to which they are able to make these choices autonomously will depend, in part, on the information, advice and support that they receive.

The *Warnock Report*,[2] published in July 1984, focused a debate that had been proceeding in one form or another for at least a decade. On publication, the Government invited the nation as a whole to consider the findings and recommendations of the Report, so that appropriate legislation could be drafted on the basis of wider public debate. Among the issues Warnock considered were: artificial insemination and various techniques for the alleviation of infertility, including *in vitro* fertilisation, egg donation, embryo donation and the use of surrogate mothers. A major concern of the report was the legitimacy of research on human embryos. Many school students are voters, many others soon will be. Some may also be parents. School is an obvious and important source of the knowledge which will help to inform debate on these issues. It is also a forum in which discussion of the various questions involved may proceed in a structured and dispassionate manner, within a context in which back-up, in the form of further information and explanation, is readily available. If the Government seriously expected the debate it invited to take place, then discussion of these issues in school would have been essential.

I indicated at the outset that the facts of life are not what they were. One of the techniques that is responsible for this disturbing change is that of *in vitro* fertilisation. When this technique is used to fertilise the egg of one woman in the test tube and then transfer the resulting embryo to the uterus of a second woman so that she carries it to term and gives birth to the baby, then that baby has two perfectly reasonable candidates for the title 'mother'. One is the *genetic* mother, the woman whose genetic material has shared with that of the baby's father the responsibility for the genetic make-up of the resulting child. The other is the *surrogate* mother, the woman who has carried and nurtured the foetus and who has undergone the risks and pains of pregnancy and birth. This process has split our concept of motherhood in two. It makes no sense to argue as to which of the two women has the better claim to be called the mother of the resulting child. They are both in a sense its mother. But the question of which, if either, of the two might have the better claim to *custody* of the child is another matter entirely. If school students are to be able to understand and cope with the massive jolts that such developments give to very basic ideas and fundamental beliefs, they will need not only to be introduced to some of the basic science which lies behind these developments but also to acquire some familiarity with ways of thinking through the conceptual, social and moral consequences of these revolutionary techniques.

The 'biotechnological revolution' is not confined to human biology and to medical science. Many industrial processes in use in our society present social, as well as medical and moral problems. We must consider not only the *morality* of nuclear power, nuclear defence and the re-processing of nuclear waste, but also the medical and scientific implications. To participate in the debate, we need to be informed about the medical hazards that face those living near or working in nuclear installations, and also the possible dangers to society as a whole which derive from the presence of such installations within our borders or within those of our near neighbours. All responsible citizens need to assess these hazards and to weigh the advantages and disadvantages of running the risks of nuclear power. Again, schools are one of the few, if not the only, institutions to which many citizens will have access, which can hope to help with the clarification of the issues involved, and with providing at least *some* of the relevant scientific and medical information.

The so-called biotechnological revolution will continue to present us with complex dilemmas, the resolution of which will require specialised information. Should we welcome or fear the use of genetic engineering to modify plant and animal species? Is there an essential difference between attempts to remove dysfunction and attempts to enhance function in human beings? In other words, if we are in favour of helping to diminish various sorts of handicap, how can we be against attempting to make people stronger and longer-lived, more intelligent, or less susceptible to disease?

Medical and biotechnological issues have a proper and essential place on the school curriculum. More importantly schools have an indispensable role to play as educational resources for the community as a whole. This role can, in part, be discharged by helping school students to understand the issues that confront them as individuals and as citizens. The other part of this role – that schools operate as resource centres for the wider community – lies beyond the scope of this essay.

What follows is a case study of one particular medical issue. The discussion of this case will attempt to show that its inclusion in the school curriculum is essential, and I will say something about the issues with which a proper study of its complexities must be concerned.

II *A case study*

There can be few people in the United Kingdom who do not know the name of Mrs Victoria Gillick. The case with which her name is associated has been debated and gossiped about, and no one who reads a newspaper or watches television can fail to be acquainted, not only with the bare bones of the case, but also with at least some editorialising about the issues involved. And yet these issues have been at best only superficially examined even in the serious press. They raise problems of the most profound consequence for school students and present in sharp focus a range of the most controversial issues with which a school curriculum should concern itself. Let's look first at the facts of the case.

1 The facts

The case was originally brought by Mrs Gillick to obtain a judgement that it would be unlawful for any of her daughters (at the time she had ten children, five of them daughters under 16) to be given contraceptive advice or treatment without her express consent. She succeeded initially and in the Court of Appeal and for a while many thousands of young girls found that the contraceptive advice they had been receiving was no longer available. Eventually the House of Lords reversed earlier decisions. The Lords declared that girls under the age of 16 had the legal capacity to consent to medical treatment – including contraception – providing, as a matter of reasonable judgement in the circumstances, that the girl in question could give 'informed consent'. The term 'informed consent' is taken to mean that the girl can understand the nature of the decision she is making and has the sort of information on which a reasonable person could make a rational choice.

It is difficult to know just how many young women are affected by this House of Lords decision. In 1983 the number of live births recorded for women under 16 was 1249 and the number of abortions for women residents (the term 'residents' is used to distinguish these women from foreigners coming to the United Kingdom specifically to have abortions) was 4077. It is likely that many tens of thousands more young women are exposed to the risk of pregnancy.

It is clearly important that as many such girls as possible should fully understand the nature of the choice they may be making. It is, of course, equally important that a young man contemplating a sexual relationship understands the dimensions and responsibilities of his choice. It is to the complexities of the choices involved that we must now turn.

2 The choices

Although we will be talking about decisions and choices and the conditions under which they are made, these are, in a sense, ideal notions. The people involved clearly *do* make choices, but however rational, well-informed and mature they are, the processes by which they arrive at these choices will seldom take the form of reviewing alternatives and consciously weighing-up various considerations, or arriving at conclusions by anything analagous to formal argument.

When decisions are seen 'from the inside' they may appear to be spontaneous and unreflective, but this does not mean that they have not been informed and prepared for by much reflection and consideration of alternatives and consequences. Even after the event there may be wide scope for reviewing choices and assessing their ramifications. It is important to be clear about just what the choices involve, at whatever stage the information becomes relevant to, or usable by, particular agents. By looking at some of the ramifications of the kinds of decision we are talking about, we can see which of their dimensions might, or should, appear on the school curriculum. It may be helpful to deal with these decisions separately for boys and girls. Since the Gillick case concerned the choices facing girls, that is where we shall begin.

Women

It is unlikely that the decision to have sex for the first time is made in a cold-blooded or 'rational' manner. Nevertheless the decision has, in addition to its personal significance, moral, social, legal and even political dimensions that are worth spelling out.

If the girl making this choice is under 16 she cannot legally consent to sexual intercourse. The consequence of this is that when she does, *de facto*, consent, her partner will in the eyes of the law be tantamount to a rapist, because he will be having intercourse with a woman who is deemed to be incapable of giving the required consent. He will therefore (while not guilty of rape itself) be guilty of a criminal offence. Unless the man concerned is much older than the girl, he is unlikely to be prosecuted, but criminal he technically will be. Interestingly, the girl herself commits no offence, a fact which makes dubious the suggestion that – even before the House of Lords decision – a doctor who gave her contraceptive advice might be 'counselling or procuring' a criminal offence.

The decision in the Gillick case has revealed glaring anomalies in the law on consent to intercourse. For while a girl under 16 may under no circumstances be legally competent to consent to sexual intercourse, she can consent on her own account to medical treatment which may have much more far-reaching consequences for her. Indeed, she could presumably consent to being made pregnant by medical intervention by artificial insemination or *in vitro* fertilization, though not by the more normal non-medical method.

In deciding whether or not to seek medical advice on contraception, a young woman will have to decide whether or not to involve her parents or any other advisers. She will have to consider the risks (and maybe also the advantages) of sex itself – or at any rate of sex with the partner she has in mind – of various rival methods of contraception, of pregnancy and maybe of abortion or birth. Some of the costs and benefits of these decisions are also moral costs and benefits. Although these are unlikely to be foremost in her mind, the interests of a number of third parties, from her parents and friends to the child she may conceivably have, may also be worthy of some consideration.

All of this may seem obvious enough and so it may appear ponderous to give chapter and verse. However, some of these choices while apparently straightforward, (if difficult to resolve) are in effect exceptionally complex and deep. To show this and to make clear just where the school curriculum enters the debate I want to consider two opposed, if superficially crude, views of the rights and wrongs of choices like these.

A woman's right to choose

One very clear approach to the Gillick case and to the circumstances of those about whom Mrs Gillick and we are so concerned, is the view that women are entitled to self-determination in the fullest sense, and in particular, that they have a fundamental right to determine what happens in and to their own bodies, as far as this is technically possible. This approach is increasingly popular but it begs a number of important questions, upon which the tenability of the feminist position depends. Once these questions are raised, the role of education in providing information and a context for rational discussion of the issues upon which their resolution depends, becomes obvious.

Bluntly, a woman's right to choose may well depend upon whether or not what she wants to choose is right. If we take just one dimension of the decision of a woman to risk pregnancy we can see the point. The whole issue of the legitimacy of abortion turns not on the question of a woman's rights, important as these are, but on the moral status of the embryo or foetus. If there are good reasons to suppose that the life of the embryo is as morally important as that of any other member of the human species, then the legitimacy of abortion will depend upon finding convincing arguments for destroying the life of an individual member of the human species, an individual whose life is, *ex hypothesi*, of equal importance to any other – including of course the woman who wants an abortion. If, on the other hand, there are no good reasons, or inadequate reasons, for regarding the foetus as morally significant, or as possessing moral significance in any way approaching that of the mother, then the issue of the legitimacy of abortion is easier to resolve. In this case it is more probable that a woman might have the right to choose in the sense of determining what happens in and to her body, for there would be no conflict of interests or rights to resolve.

The issue of the moral significance of the foetus or embryo raises many questions. Some of these are factual, some theoretical, some conceptual and some moral. A person seriously attempting to understand the arguments for and against the legitimacy of abortion, will need to know what might be said in answer to a range of these questions. An obvious starting point would be the question 'when does life begin?' Clearly an answer to this question requires investigation on a number of fronts. Some basic biology and medical science would be required; an answer would have to deal with the development of the human egg and the life of the sperm before conception, to discuss what happens at conception, how the human egg cell divides, and how the emerging cell mass may become a single individual, twins or even a cancer (a hydatidiform mole) some time after conception. Even where the egg develops normally it cannot of course survive unless it implants, is suitably nurtured and so on. Once a reasonable grasp of the medical facts is obtained it becomes clear that these alone cannot solve the problem. The facts, such as they are, show that life cannot sensibly be said to begin at *any* particular point; the egg is, after all, alive before conception, as is the sperm. Nor does the human individual begin at conception, since at that point the cell may develop into more than one individual – or indeed into a mole.

Even when the egg has implanted and is apparently developing normally, we may ask what *sort* of life has been established, and what moral importance that sort of life has. The human embryo is to start with a very simple creature indeed, less complex than a tadpole. In virtue of what exactly might it be more morally important? If it is more important than a tadpole, is it of sufficient moral importance to be entitled to be valued equally with its mother, particularly when it can only emerge from the womb at some risk to the life of its mother?

Examining the nature and capacities of the foetus at various stages and comparing these with other creatures, will help to establish just what it is we are valuing when we value the foetus. It will also provide a framework for thinking about the value of other creatures with comparable capacities.

I make no attempt to answer these questions here. I wish simply to show that answers *are* required by anyone taking a view about the legitimacy of abortion and so, of necessity, by anyone taking a view about the propriety of risking pregnancy. More importantly for our present concerns, it is clear that much of the information required both for an answer and even to see that an answer of a particular kind is required, can be provided as part of the school curriculum.

Of course the problem is not circumvented by taking the view in advance that if pregnancy occurs abortion will be ruled out. It is still important for all concerned to know whether abortion should be ruled out on moral grounds, that is, whether the choice to have a child is a 'free' choice or one required by morality. If we now turn briefly to the other side of the Gillick case, the parental perspective, we can see that the same arguments apply.

A parent's right to choose?

Suppose our inclination is to think that Mrs Gillick is right and that ultimately it is up to parents to decide whether or not a girl under 16 should receive medical advice and treatment. Suppose we think that the parents are better placed to consider their daughter's best interests and to make mature judgements as to what those interests are. Or we might simply think that parents have the right to control the behaviour of their children under the age of 16, including their sexual behaviour. Well, suppose a particular young woman goes ahead regardless and becomes pregnant. She attends a good school and on the basis of information and opportunity for discussion of all the relevant issues, she has come to the conclusion that she would be justified in having an abortion and indeed wants one. To believe that her parents are entitled to have control of whether or not she obtains medical advice and treatment is to conclude that her parents are entitled to prevent her having the abortion she seeks and so insist that she has the child. Since pregnancy and giving birth are life threatening conditions (in the sense that the chances of mortality are greater than if she is either not pregnant or has an early abortion) this view involves the judgement that her parents are entitled to threaten her life or at least to prevent her removing that threat.

To come to a view about the legitimacy of a 'parents' rights' approach to these issues, one must also have in mind certain medical considerations, for instance, the dangers involved in various alternative procedures. Again, this is something that should certainly appear on the school curriculum, and I mean to include here both the medical considerations and their consequences for the moral and political views which bear upon them.

Men

To examine the consequences of the Gillick case from the male perspective is of course very different but no less educationally interesting or morally important. I will not attempt this in any detail, for in many ways the discussion parallels that above. To think through the implications of the 'women's rights' approach to the dilemmas of the Gillick case is to explore not only the male role in reproduction but also the nature of male assumptions about women. In reviewing the nature of the dilemmas faced by women it is impossible not to consider the extent to which men share responsibility for those dilemmas and also the limitations on their power or prerogative to influence the choice of those who are most closely concerned.

Conclusion

We have reviewed some of the major medical issues that have curriculum implications and examined one of these in detail to see just how its resolution can develop. We have seen how the ways in which it might develop are not only appropriately placed within the school curriculum, but also how the school is uniquely placed to help in the resolution. Schools have both a moral and a political responsibility to include discussion of issues of this sort and to provide, on the specialised curriculum, information relevant to their resolution.

The Gillick case illustrates the ways in which an issue which actually affects only a small proportion of the community may raise important questions of principle for the community as a whole. These are questions about which those who claim the right to speak or vote have a resonsibility to inform themselves, so that their voice will express a judgement rather than a prejudice. What better function can education perform than to help materially in this process?

Notes and references

1 Gillick v. West Norfolk and Wisbech Area Health Authority and the Department of Health and Social Security, 1985.
2 Report of the Committee of Inquiry into Human Fertilisation and Embryology, established in July 1982 to examine the social, ethical and legal implications of recent, and potential developments in the field of human assisted reproduction (HMSO, 1984).

Chapter 8

Religion and religious education

Enid B. Mellor

Religion, like Everest, is there – explicit in the beliefs and practices of its adherents; implicit in the questions, spoken and unspoken, which arise from a more than superficial consideration of almost any topic. Why am I here? Where did I come from? Where am I going? What happens when I die? Why should I be kind/truthful/reliable and all the other things that seem to be taken for granted? Is there such a thing as a just war? The ethical, social, philosophical and political issues raised in other parts of the curriculum come home to roost in Religious Education. Religion has things to say about them, although different religions do not always say the same thing. To the Religious Education specialist teacher the dictum of the Spens Report of 1938 that 'no boy or girl can be counted as properly educated unless he or she has been made aware of the fact of the existence of a religious interpretation of life'[1] is no more than a statement of the obvious.

Theoretical considerations

This said, the subject is controversial in almost all its aspects, presenting a problem from whatever angle we view it. Controversy resides even in its name. Do we teach Religion, Religious Studies, Religious Knowledge, or Religious Education? Or do we, as laid down by the 1944 Education Act[2] (and still appearing on the occasional school timetable or syllabus) provide Religious Instruction? No such hesitation surrounds other, long-accepted, disciplines; we teach History, Geography, Mathematics, Science, English and Foreign Languages with confidence. Ambiguity tends to appear, as the reader will no doubt already have noticed, when we approach the contentious areas of the curriculum.

Variety in nomenclature indicates a variety of views concerning what a subject is, and why it should be taught. 'Religion' might be defined in terms of, say, six major world faiths – Buddhism, Christianity, Hinduism, Islam, Judaism, Sikhism – accepted by tradition rather than by decree. Or it might extend to overtly secularist stances, (Humanism and Marxism are common examples) which present a coherent framework for living without reference to the supernatural.

This leaves us with the question of whether or not to include the new, and older, 'fringe' sects which attract adherents. Are they to be given a place in the curriculum, and if so, what are the criteria for choice? Do local adherence, representation within the school, or national statistics determine our decision? Do philosophical and theological definitions play a part? In the end, do we pay attention to our own teaching strengths and weaknesses? Is it proper to give value judgements, and if so, on what are these to be based?

Definition is thus bound up with intentionality. What we teach cannot be separated from our reasons for teaching it. Do we, as some religious communities wish, nurture a child in his or her own faith, and in so doing restrict and fragment the curriculum? Do we seek to present choices, and so come into conflict with the demand for nurture? Do we, if such a thing is possible, give objective information, and in our endeavours underplay or even ignore the passion and partiality of some religions? Do we try to encourage tolerance, understanding and empathy, and if so how do we deal with faiths which lay claim to the absolute truth and are not distinguished by an attitude of amiable acceptance of the beliefs of others?

In our endeavours we may be helped, or not (according to viewpoint), by the matter of legality. By law, Religious Instruction must be provided in schools. In county schools it must be taught in accordance with an Agreed Syllabus – agreed between representatives of the Authority, of teachers' associations, of the Church of England, and of 'such religious denominations as in the opinion of the Authority ought, having regard to the circumstances of the area, to be represented.'[3] Nowadays the last clause is usually interpreted as including representatives of a variety of faiths and life stances.[4] Yet compulsion is accompanied by freedom, for 'conscience clauses' give teachers the right to opt out of religious teaching and/or attendance at school worship, and parents the right to withdraw their children.[5] Denominational partiality is also guarded against by the 'Cowper Temple clause', enshrined in the Education Act of 1870, which required that 'no religious catechism or religious formulary which is distinctive of any particular denomination shall be taught.'[6] This was perpetuated in 1944 with the stipulation that worship in a county school

... shall not ... be distinctive of any particular religious denomination [and that the Religious Instruction] shall not include any catechism or formulary which is distinctive of any particular religious denomination.[7]

No other subject is at once so protected and so flexibly treated. The interpretation of the above clauses of the Act results in a variety of practice. For how much of a child's life is Religious Education compulsory? Does the requirement cease with the attainment of statutory school leaving age? What about the sixth form college? How much time in a week, a term, a year, should be set aside for the study of religion?

Can its existence be safeguarded during the integrated day of the primary school and in the integrated studies programme of the secondary school? Can the host of practical problems encountered in attempting to implement the conscience clauses be solved? Education and educationists speak with many voices in answer to these questions.

Intersecting, though not identical, with the Religious Education provisions of 1944 are those relating to voluntary aided and special agreement schools, where the 'providing body' is a religious institution. Here, denominational teaching can be given, and denominational control can be exercised over staff appointments and pupil admissions.[8] In these schools Religious Education is not subject to local authority control either by inspection or by syllabus requirements. How far, if at all, is the existence of such schools justified in the last quarter of the 20th century? If it is, ought it to be restricted to schools of the Judaeo-Christian tradition? Does the composition of our society now warrant the foundation and funding of, perhaps, Muslim and Sikh schools on similar lines?

The controversy surrounding these matters of nomenclature, definition, intentionality and legality, acute though it may be, is arguably less so than the uncertainty which surrounds the place in Religious Education of religious *experience*. Religion is more than a set of beliefs, of rules, of rituals; more than a body of literature or a social framework.[9] It reaches the core of the human spirit, its essence is inexpressible by many and expressed by very few. It is unprovable, immeasurable and yet totally real to those who know it. How can something of this be included in the curriculum? Is it even proper to think of doing so? Yet how can we omit it and claim to have engaged in Religious Education or indeed in education at all, since it

shall be the duty of the local education authority for every area, so far as their powers extend, to contribute towards the spiritual, moral, mental and physical development of the community by securing that efficient education . . . shall be available to meet the needs of the population of their area.[10]

The dilemma is especially felt in certain areas pertaining to the subject. Examinability is one such point of pressure: clearly we cannot and should not attempt to assess religious experience, and it may well be improper to try to measure sensitivity and receptivity to such experience. If so, is there any point in constructing a formal examination system around a subject which is essentially unexaminable? Commitment is another problem area. Many teachers are deeply religious, but how far should their commitment be admitted, shared, or even used as a resource? Others are uncommitted; can they teach with warmth as well as objectivity, with feeling as well as accuracy? The perennial question of fairness versus feeling remains unresolved.

Perhaps the most debatable and debated intersection between

Religious Education and religious experience is exemplified by the requirement of the 1944 Act, still in force, that 'the school day in every county school and in every voluntary school shall begin with collective worship on the part of all pupils in attendance'.[11] It is easy to condemn this provision out of hand, on principle; how can anyone be *told* to worship, especially in an assorted community where few if any shared values can be presupposed? It is still easier to complain about the non-eventful nature of the so-called 'Assembly', which may be a verbal noticeboard, a helping of moral uplift laced with reproof, or an attempt to encourage aesthetic and cultural appreciation using music, literature, movement or the visual arts as stimuli. It is more difficult to answer two questions basic to Religious Education. First, is there any 'mileage' in making an attempt to introduce children to religious experience and if so how do we go about it? Second, what *is* religious experience anyway? If religion is potentially present in all parts of life it is there in relationships; the school gathering with a common purpose, however prosaic, may be religious in the practical, if not the metaphysical, sense.

The teacher of Religious Education may feel, and often does, that the school assembly is not the context for introducing pupils to any sort of religious experience, however defined. Assembly is generally the province of the headteacher; it is honoured more in the breach than in the observance; if and when it does happen it is neither religious nor experiential. Many teachers (myself among them) would be glad to see the requirement for a compulsory act of worship excised from the Act, or at any rate re-sited so that it is not mixed up with the legislation concerning Religious Education in the classroom. Yet, surprisingly, these same specialist teachers will often accept some responsibility for Assembly – perhaps by direction from above, or perhaps through sheer exasperation at what is already happening. There is then a choice of strategies. In a denominational school one can hope for a nucleus of worshippers and an 'outer circle' of observers. In a multifaith school one can attempt some form of syncretism (usually a recipe for disaster), or ask representatives of the different faiths to be responsible in turn for worship in their own traditions, perhaps involving visiting speakers from the local communities. Or, as already mentioned, one can eschew explicit religion and concentrate on the ethical and the aesthetic. But almost invariably we must face the fact that school worship, once the seed-bed of children's religious experience, is so no longer. So we are left with the classroom; the problem has not disappeared, but has surfaced in a different setting and in one which may be even less congenial than the school hall.

With so many controversial questions attaching to a controversial subject we may feel that the only possible counsel is one of despair. In fact this should not be, nor is it, the case. Controversy is part of the stuff of religion; blandness would be so untypical as to be positively grotesque.

I find it hard to believe that any dedicated teacher of the subject would wish it otherwise, for where there is doubt, dissension, argument and experiment there is life. The subject is not dead.

Practical considerations

So to the practicalities. First, where in the school curriculum can this recalcitrant set of problems be accommodated? There is a case for answering 'everywhere', for few disciplines lack opportunity for philosophical, theological or ethical discussion, given the time and the will. This is particularly so in the field of multicultural education; it is difficult to overestimate the connection between religion and culture, yet all too easy to forget it. With a crowded syllabus and an unconfident teacher, time, or will, or sometimes both, can be lacking. So we need time set aside for dealing with religious topics both in connection with other subjects and in their own right.

Religious Education must be timetabled: timetabled adequately and timetabled by name. Where it is part of the integrated day or the integrated studies programme it must make its distinctive contribution. Examination provision apart, secondary school classes need at least the equivalent of two single periods a week for Religious Education. What other subject would be content with less? Neither breadth nor depth of teaching can be contemplated during 35 minutes (if one is lucky) in every seven days.

Second, who should be responsible for Religious Education? To write 'trained and qualified teachers' may read like a statement of the obvious. But far too often in the past, and in the recent past at that, piety and goodwill have been accepted as adequate substitutes for a degree in Religious Studies and a specialist professional training. The skills needed to study a sacred text, to approach a world faith or to consider a philosophical problem are not easily picked up as sidelines, though many teachers have done valiantly in equipping themselves at their own cost in time and money. Until there are enough specialists, in many schools the non-specialist must continue to struggle, with inevitable consequences for the academic achievements of the pupils and the academic status of the subject.

Third, what resources are available to help us? The local education authority inspector or adviser (provided there is one in the area) is invaluable: advising, encouraging, and (sometimes) warning; helping probationary teachers; organising conferences; encouraging applications for in-service training and higher degree courses. Often, too, the adviser is the driving force in setting up the conference which will eventually produce a new Agreed Syllabus,[11] as well as bearing much of the administrative and ideological burden inseparable from what may turn out to be years of patient negotiation. We need to appreciate the adviser's existence, make use of the adviser's services, and press relentlessly for an appointment where none already exists. Some expressions of support and appreciation from the teaching force might not come amiss from time to time!

Journals, resource centres (often with lending facilities), books for teachers and pupils (ranging from the stapled-together, produced-in-a-cellar type of leaflet to the lavishly-illustrated hardback), charts, videos, computer games and other offerings of modern technology are there for the taking – at a price. There, of course, is the rub. Religious Education teachers need to concentrate on deploying finances wisely and constructively. Many use their ingenuity to devise and produce their own materials, and increasingly this expertise is shared with colleagues in other schools.

Fourth, how do we cope when we actually face our classes? Here we have both a help and a constraint, additional to those imposed by external examinations. In the maintained sector, Religious Education must (unless good reason is shown for claiming otherwise) be taught in accordance with an Agreed Syllabus (see page 109). But the representatives of the denominations, faiths and life stances who are invited to help produce the syllabus may differ from area to area; as may the end-product of their deliberations.

Let us take two examples: Lincolnshire and the Inner London Education Authority.

Lincolnshire

Religious Education in Lincolnshire (1980) lists, on its standing conference, representatives of the Church of England, the Roman Catholic Church, and 'other denominations' (unspecified, but all with English-sounding names). The syllabus states

The content of religious education in Lincolnshire will be drawn largely from the study of Christianity in its many forms, this being the religious faith which has most influenced our culture. However, it is essential that children in today's world should also be given some understanding of other religious commitments and world views found in contemporary British society and in other parts of the world. (p 7)

There is little non-Christian content prescribed for the primary school in Lincolnshire. At secondary level it is suggested that Christianity and two other world religions should form the basis for the course, plus themes such as festivals, ceremonial and rites of passage, and sacred writings, giving examples from several religions. An educational reason – the danger of confusion – is given for this restriction, and the nettle of unfamiliarity in a largely monocultural area is firmly grasped.

The Lincolnshire child lives in Britain which is multicultural and multifaith, and we have a duty to educate him to understand the world in its wholeness and not just his own local environment. Problems of unfamiliarity can in any case be overcome by the judicious use of good textbooks, audio visual aids, and informed teaching. (p 16/17)

One gets the feeling that content in Lincolnshire may be manageable, but that the difficulty of 'bringing to life' a multicultural society should not be underrated. The 'good textbooks' and the rest will be needed – and more besides.

The Inner London Education Authority

The Inner London Education Authority's *Religious Education for our Children* (1984), on the other hand, had the benefit of the advice of Christian (including the Afro-Caribbean and Greek Orthodox Churches), Hindu, Jewish, Muslim, Sikh and Humanist representation. Behind its unwieldy aim:

> . . . to help young people to achieve a knowledge and understanding of religious insights, beliefs and practices, so that they are able to continue in, or come to, their own beliefs and respect the right of other people to hold beliefs different from their own

lies anxiety about nurture, and a realistic view of the conflicting truth-claims in religion. The syllabus prescribes that six world religions (Buddhism, Christianity, Hinduism, Islam, Judaism and Sikhism) shall be taught and (unlike Lincolnshire) also requires 'a non-ethical, non-theistic tradition such as Humanism' (p 16).

The actual teaching methods are much the same as in Lincolnshire – a mixture of the thematic and the systematic. Acknowledgement is made of our Christian sub-culture ('. . . . it is taken for granted that Christianity features clearly' p 7), though not as strongly as in the Lincolnshire syllabus. But the carrying out of these ideas must be at once easier and more difficult in the inner city. Easier, because of the multifaith environment with its places of worship, family customs, dress, and children who bring to the school a diversity of outlook; more difficult when (as in one girls' school of my acquaintance) 85% of the pupils are of Asian – often strongly Muslim – background, and yet Islam must be taught alongside five other faiths and Humanism. The solution in this school is to offer Islamic Studies in their own right, and to encourage parents to allow their children to learn of other faiths and cultures in the hope that 'knowledge and sympathetic understanding of these faiths and practices help children to learn to live together in harmony' (p 6).

In the end we return to the most important resource of all – the teacher. Here lies the real inspiration for the imaginative use of material (and often for the material itself); for the lively discussion sensitively handled; for the pupils' occasional surprised discovery that religion is fascinating and worth serious study at all levels. Here also lies the awareness which facilitates (for we can do no more) the rare moment of stillness when the group or an individual is touched by the mystery which is the heart of spirituality. Ultimately, in the quest for 'useful' subjects and vocationally-oriented schooling it is the committed and dedicated teacher of this contentious discipline who will commend it, with all its potentially life-changing consequences, to students, colleagues, governors, and to a needy and largely uncaring world.

Notes and references

1 The Spens Report on Secondary Education (1938) p 208.
2 The Education Act (1944) section 25.
3 *ibid* sections 25 and 27. See also the Fifth Schedule.
4 See, for example, *Religious Education for our Children*, the Agreed Syllabus of the Inner London Education Authority (1984).
5 The Education Act (1944) sections 30 and 25.
6 Elementary Education Act (1870) section 14(2).
7 The Education Act (1944) section 26.
8 *ibid* sections 25 and 26. See also the Third Schedule and *Faith, Culture and the Dual System* Bernadette O'Keeffe, (1986).
9 For a fuller discussion, see Schools Council Working Paper 36, *Religious Education in Secondary Schools* (London, 1971) pp 47 ff.
10 The Education Act (1944) section 7.
11 *ibid* section 25.

Some useful addresses

The Regional RE Centre,
West London Institute of Higher Education,
Lancaster House,
Borough Road, Isleworth,
Middx TW7 5DV   01-568-8741 Ext. 2656
Publishes *Media Review* three times a year, reviewing books, posters, videos, computer programs, multimedia packs.

The National Society's RE Development Centre,
23 Kensington Square,
London W8 5HN   01-937-4241

The Regional RE Centre,
Westhill College,
Selly Oak,
Birmingham B29 6LL   021-472-7275 Ext. 58

York RE Centre,
The College,

Lord Mayor's Walk,
York YO3 7EX 0904-56771

The Welsh National Centre for Religious Education,
School of Education,
UCNW,
St Mary's,
Bangor, Gwynedd LL57 1DZ 0248-51151 Ext. 6109

(All these arrange short courses for teachers and publish regular reviews
of materials)

Many Local Education Authorities also provide resource centres.
Periodicals are sometimes produced locally and distributed nationally,
for example, *RE News and Views* (termly from the Inner London
Education Authority), and *Resource* (termly from the Univeristy of
Warwick Institute of Education).

Organisations

General
The Association of Christian Teachers,
2 Romeland Hill,
St Albans,
Herts AL3 4ET 0727-40298
Publishes *Act Now* and *Spectrum* termly. Concerned with Christian
Education generally, and with Religious Education within that setting.

Christian Education Movement,
Lancaster House,
Borough Road,
Isleworth,
Middx TW7 5DV 01-568-8741 Ext. 2656
Publishes *British Journal of Religious Education* and *R.E. Today* termly.

Commission for Racial Equality,
Elliott House,
10/12 Allington Street,
London SW1E 5EH 01-828-7022

The Commonwealth Institute,
Kensington High Street,
London W8 6NQ 01-603-4535

Help is also often given by charities, by embassies, by museums, by travel
agents, and by local religious communities.

Buddhism
The Buddhist Society,
58 Eccleston Square,
London SW1V 1PH   01-834-5858

Christianity
The British Council of Churches,
2 Eaton Gate,
London SW1W 9BT   01-730-9611

St Paul Book Centre,
199 Kensington High Street,
London W8 6BA   01-937-9591

Hinduism
The Hindu Centre,
39 Grafton Terrace,
London NW5   01-485-8200

Islam
Islamic Cultural Centre and London Mosque,
146 Park Road,
London NW8 7RG   01-724-3363

Muslim Information Service,
233 Seven Sisters Road,
London N4 2DA   01-272-5170

Judaism
Central Jewish Lecture and Information Committee,
Woburn House,
Upper Woburn Place,
London WC1H 0EP   01-387-3952

Sikhism
Sikh Dharma Trust U.K.,
Guru Ram Das Ashram,
246 Belsize Road,
London NW6   01-328-4781

Suggested reading
Cole, W Owen: *Religion in the Multifaith School* (Hulton)
Cole, W Owen (ed): *World Religions: a Handbook for Teachers* (Commission for Racial Equality)
Copley, T E: *RE Being served?* (CIO Publishing)

Cox, E: *Problems and Possibilities for Religious Education* (Hodder)
Elias, J: *Psychology and Religious Education* (Florida: Kreiger)
Grimmit, M: *What can I do in RE?* (2nd ed) (Mayhew McCrimmon)
Harris, A: *Teaching Morality and Religion* (Allen and Unwin)
Hay, D: *Exploring Inner Space* (Pelican)
Hill, B V: *Faith at the Blackboard* (Paternoster Press)
Hinnells, J (ed): *The Penguin Dictionary of Religions* (Penguin)
Hull, J: *Studies in Religion and Education* (Falmer Press)
Hull, J: *New Directions in Religious Education* (Falmer Press)
Hulmes, E: *Commitment and Neutrality in Religious Education* (Chapman)
Jackson, R: *Approaching World Religions* (John Murray)
Lealman, B: *The Total Curriculum in Relation to RE* (CEM)
Lealman, B: *Implementing the Agreed Syllabus* (CEM)
Lealman, B: *Current Issues in Examinations* (CEM)
Mumford, C: *Young Children and Religion* (Arnold)
Nicholls, K (ed): *Voice of the Hidden Waterfall* (St Paul Publications)
O'Leary, D J and Sallnow, T: *Love and Meaning in Religious Education* (OUP)
Schools Council Working Paper 44: *Religious Education in Primary Schools* (Evans/Methuen)
Schools Council Working Paper 36: *Religious Education in Secondary Schools* (Evans/Methuen)
Sealey, J: *Religious Education: Philosophical Perspectives* (Allen and Unwin)
Smart, N: *Secondary Education and the Logic of Religion* (Faber and Faber)
Sutcliffe, J (ed): *A Dictionary of Religious Education* (SCM)
Want, D (ed): *Religious Education – and Microcomputers?* (MEP Centre, Chelmer Institute, Chelmsford)
Wright, D S: *The Psychology of Moral Behaviour* (Penguin)

Chapter 9

'Peace Studies' in the curriculum of educational institutions: an argument against indoctrination

D N Aspin

Introduction

In this chapter I am concerned to examine the *raisons d'être* behind the setting-up of schemes of 'Peace Studies' in the curricula of educational institutions. I aim to establish, so far as it may be possible to do so, whether any of the criticisms recently advanced by such writers as Cox and Scruton, and Marks, against the place of programmes in 'Peace Studies' in such institutions, have any legitimacy or force. Such an investigation is, it seems to me, especially important at a time when educational institutions in the UK are being forced to accommodate themselves to the demands for public accountability that come in the train of reduced public funds, falling numbers on school rolls, and the imperatives for curricula reflecting balance, breadth, relevance and differentiation that the policies of the government have imposed upon the education sector. If the charges of Cox and Scruton and Marks and the strictures of Sir Keith Joseph can be proved to be well-founded, then the possibility of funding, availability of teaching, and student interest continuing to be devoted to the area of 'Peace Studies' may well be seriously attenuated. This is quite apart from the scepticism that might be entertained by institutions generally about the implications of imputations of indoctrination arising out of such charges. It is with the querying and assessment of such charges that this chapter is largely concerned.

The characterisation of 'Peace Studies'

I take as conceded the case for the promotion of a set of *ends*, that we may characterise as coming under the broad heading of 'Peace Studies', 'Peace and Conflict Studies', 'Peace Education', 'Education for International Understanding', or whatever. Indeed the obligation on governments to give support to such educational undertakings follows from their agreement with prescriptions emanating from the United Nations

Organisation itself. In sessions in 1978 and 1982 the Reports produced as a result of special sessions devoted to the topic of disarmament contained such paragraphs as these:

Governments and non-govermental organisations are urged to take steps to develop programmes of education for disarmament and peace studies at all levels.

(Para 106)

In order that an international conscience may develop and that world opinion may exercise a positive influence, the United Nations should increase the dissemination of information on the armaments race and disarmament, with the full co-operation of Member States.

(Para 15)[1]

These recommendations accord well with the weight attached by the UNO to the principle of the *Universal Declaration of Human Rights*, in which the view is advanced that:

Education shall be directed to the full development of the human personality and to the strengthening of respect for human rights and fundamental freedoms . . . It shall promote understanding, tolerance and friendship among all nations, racial or religious groups and shall further the activities of the United Nations for the maintenance of peace.

All these undertakings may be presumed to be shared by signatory states, who are then to implement their recommendations in programmes of public policy. So much may be seen in the remarks of the Secretary of State for Education and Science, Sir Keith Joseph, in a speech made in March 1984.[2] He was, he said, supportive of the policies of the UK Government and stood 'ready to propagate and defend them in public on any political occasion.' He was in agreement that issues of peace and war should have a place in the classrooms of our educational institutions; he deplored attempts to trivialise the issue, cloud it with inappropriate appeals to emotion, and present it one-sidedly. He argued for a rational approach to the subject, urging that teachers' presentation of the issues should be balanced and objective, aimed at encouraging pupils to acquire competence in weighing arguments and evidence so as to enable them to arrive at rational judgements themselves. The only qualifications to these aims were found in Sir Keith's view that issues of war and peace would crop up naturally in the curriculum in such a way that no special provision needed to be made for a study labelled 'peace'; that the title of 'peace studies' ought really to be dropped because of its emotional overtones and superficiality; and that issues of the discussion of peace and war in the curriculum should be decided on 'educational' and not on 'political' grounds.

The 'Black Paper' view

There can be little doubt that Sir Keith's views are shared by many, both inside and outside the education service. Indeed Sir Keith's speech is only one manifestation of a point of view about the nature of educational institutions, curricula and programmes that has found expression from the time of 'Black Papers' and before. The reservations Sir Keith articulated concerning the status and purpose of 'Peace Studies' in some educational *milieux* were followed up and expanded in the criticisms advanced by Caroline Cox and Roger Scruton and by John Marks.

Marks' booklet *'Peace Studies' in our Schools: Propaganda for Defencelessness*[3] is in the same tradition of which Sir Keith's views are an expression. Deploring indoctrination and arguing for the need to have a range of information available, Marks gives a useful account of developments in Peace Education over recent years. He provides an outline of some of the courses available, and points to omissions in course content and bibliographies of material relating to the Soviet Union and the Warsaw Pact. He reminds us properly of the need for balance in peace studies courses, noting that, while references to conflict situations in Northern Ireland, El Salvador and South Africa are often to be found, there is no comparable list mentioning events in Afghanistan, Warsaw and Russia itself. In so far as this may be true of some courses, then Marks' criticisms of lack of balance are serious and to the point; in pointing this out, Marks does signal service to the cause of academic work in this area.

Where he is more contentious, however, is in his imputation of disingenuousness on the part of teachers responsible for such courses. For such people, he maintains, there is a clear political *agendum*, that some would see as part of the hidden curriculum of peace studies courses: the favourable representation of a view of the need for 'peace studies' that may be associated with the Marxist-Leninist political imperatives that underlie and govern 'Peace Studies' courses in state schools in countries under Soviet domination or control. Courses in peace studies in the UK, he claims, run a gamut from merely stressing the need for courtesy and good manners to outright political indoctrination. Marks maintains that 'politically contentious subjects should form no part of the curriculum for those below the age of 16'; he refers to those who 'would say that the teacher should at all times keep his political views to himself', and he echoes the view of Sir Keith Joseph that

We are surely right to expect our schools not to encourage pupils to take a view of notions which are wholly alien to our society – for example, that Government should be other than Parliamentary or that the rule of Law should be abrogated.

Such notions are, Marks maintains, often implicit in the views of some teachers of Peace Studies who cannot see the dangers of Communism and the reasons behind Russian initiatives for peace and peace education. To that extent, Marks holds, we are engaged in a battle, such that

f we fail to win the battle now being waged for the minds of the young, in a few years there may be no battle left to fight. As Plato wrote, more than 2000 years ago, of those who spoke incessantly of peace: '. . . on account of this fondness of theirs for peace, which is often out of season where their influence prevails, they become by degrees unwarlike, and bring up their young to be like themselves; they are at the mercy of their enemies; whence in a few years they and their children and the whole city often pass imperceptibly from the condition of free men to that of slaves'.

For Marks, therefore, 'peace studies' should be subordinated to the clear requirements of our own system of education, which has much more to do with teaching children the facts in an 'unbiased, objective way', that presents all sides to any question, keeps off politically-contentious ground and is only concerned with the 'inculcation of such moral precepts' as have 'always been an essential part of education'.

Peace studies as a discipline?

A similar point of view is to be found in the pamphlet by Professor Roger Scruton and Lady Caroline Cox, *Peace Studies: A Critical Survey*.[4] They operate with a similar notion of the 'true aims and content' that characterise 'essential educaton'. They contrast this with the indoctrination that they see present in many modern educational institutions, departments and courses in schools, colleges and universities in the United Kingdom – and nowhere more than in the School of Peace Studies at Bradford University, which is for them a test case. For, they argue,

If the Bradford School fails . . . to discharge the onus of justifying (Peace Studies), then we are entitled to assume . . . that it is not a genuine academic discipline.

The implication is clear: Peace Studies ought to be removed from the curriculum of any genuine educational institution concerned with the pursuit of truth and the promotion of academic ends. Such studies should receive no further research funds or public recognition and should be replaced by an education committed to 'the traditional concept of good manners . . . (that) has always been a part of education . . . ' – if the criticisms of the legitimacy of the claims of 'Peace Studies' to academic status advanced by Scruton and Cox can be substantiated.

What do those criticisms amount to? Scruton and Cox set them out in the introduction to their booklet:

Peace Studies is not a genuine educational discipline, and therefore cannot be taught as one.

The existing programmes proposed by major exponents of the subject clearly favour a conclusion which (they) believe to be mistaken.

The subject is taught in such a way as to discourage critical reflection, and encourage prejudice, about the matters of peace, war and disarmament . . .

The movement for Peace Studies in schools is part of a trend towards the politicisation of education, involving both the lowering of intellectual standards, and the assumption of foregone political conclusions. It is (their) belief that the foregone conclusions in question are immensely damaging to our national interests, and favourable to those of the Soviet Union.

The reality of Peace Studies ought not to be confused with its apparent, and innocuous, purpose – that of encouraging children to resolve their conflicts through tolerance and conciliation rather than by force, to understand each other's differences and to address one another always with the words and gestures of peaceful co-operation.

To sum up: 'Peace Studies' is not a genuine educational discipline; it is poorly taught; it represents a limited way of examining the current world situation and it is part of a trend towards politicising educational institutions and endeavours. Moreover, the intentions of its proponents and teachers are disingenuous, in so far as these are concerned, whether tacitly or overtly, to call our own national interests into question in favour of those of an alien political system and ideology. These charges, if true, are grave and it would be reasonable for any educationalist or academic to be sceptical about courses or their teachers susceptible to them. For they strike at the root of what such people regard as valid and supportable educational and academic enterprises, capable of the serious-minded and scholarly pursuit of the truth that is supposed to characterise the kinds of activity to which educational institutions are committed. The question must therefore be raised as to whether these criticisms are justified or not.

Criteria for an 'Educational Discipline'?

Scruton and Cox's view as to what will count as a criterion for 'educational' aims, methods and content, is set out thus:

The truly educational subject forces the pupil to understand something which has no immediate bearing on his experience. It teaches him intellectual discipline, by presenting him with problems too remote or too abstract to be comprehended within his own limited world. In other words, it asks him to stand back from his immediate concerns and make a considered judgement of matters which are interesting in themselves, whether or not he can see their relevance. This is part of what is contained in the idea of intellectual discipline, and one of the reasons for believing that education is at war with propaganda.

Whatever else education is about, therefore, it has nothing to do with the idea of 'relevance'; indeed 'genuine' intellectual disciplines are, for Scruton and Cox, 'respectable' *because of* their irrelevance to the lives of their students and all their main concerns. Their 'genuineness' evidently consists in their remoteness or abstractness; and their value is only assessed in so far as they are 'interesting in themselves'. On this basis, also, 'novelty' becomes suspect: any subject that is an addition to the *corpus* of existing educational subjects or disciplines has to justify its existence by the same criteria of admissibility against which initial claims for the inclusion of traditional intellectual disciplines were measured and which such disciplines themselves engendered and fostered. For these and similar reasons, therefore, 'Peace Studies' cannot be accorded intellectual respectability. It is on the basis of this epistemological criterion that Scruton and Cox's rejection of Peace Studies largely rests.

Let us get rid of their claim that 'Peace Studies' is taught 'in a biased and irresponsible way'. As a matter of contingent fact, this may well be true. That does not of itself, however, disqualify Peace Studies from serious claim to academic consideration. The same charge may equally apply to other subjects – from the teaching of English Literature by those committed to Leavisite principles or structuralist approaches, through the teaching of Philosophy by those who allow no place in their courses for phenomenological or hermeneutic perspectives, to the work of those teachers of the sciences whose schemes for school science rest upon and embody only inductivist or Kuhnian preconceptions. If Peace Studies is to be excluded on such grounds, so also must any subject that happens to be taught in that way.

The claim of Cox and Scruton is different, however: it is that Peace Studies is taught in a 'biased and irresponsible way' *and could be taught in no other way*. Their support for such a contention can only come from their own account of the nature of the subject itself. This, it has to be pointed out, they get not so much from any extended philosophical analysis of what the subject might be thought to consist in, what its cognitive content might be, the ends at which it might be aimed and so on, but rather from their examination of a very restricted number of courses, quotations and visits to schools. Such analysis as they offer or engage in is, at best, only partial; at worst, it is misconceived, because it appears to rest on assumptions about the proper content of 'academic' courses, the appropriate criteria for their evaluation and the desirable concerns of educational institutions that the authors themselves simply do not question or justify.

In this respect the views of Cox and Scruton do not differ in kind from those of Sir Keith Joseph when he required that teachers should uphold the view that government should be parliamentary and that the rule of law should not be abrogated. But it is far from proven that the only – or even the best – form of government should involve parliamentary institutions. Nor is it likely that there will never be occasions when some concerns might take precedence over the rule of law, particularly if the law is widely regarded as outmoded, deficient or discriminatory. It might be thought that even such an obvious 'political' aim as preparing future citizens for their lives in a participatory democracy must necessarily involve encouraging students to consider whether there might not sometimes be a case for seeking to introduce other forms of in-stitutionalising a society's political arrangements than those typically found in advanced Western societies; or for going against law, precedent and custom in pursuit of objectives that might reasonably be thought – and be widely agreed – to conduce to a wider public good.

As for Cox and Scruton's demand for irrelevance, remoteness and abstractness as the sole determinants of academic and educational respectability: their adducing of such criteria suggests covert prescription rather than any well-founded analysis of what 'true education' (whatever that might be) might look like. The demand of 'irrelevance' would seem immediately to rule out much of the staple of contemporary higher education, at any rate: medicine, law, engineering, economics, policy analysis . . . Such subjects can hardly be claimed to be unimportant or 'remote' from students' lives and a society's concerns, yet all these are lauded and laboured at throughout higher education. There might be some point in reminding Scruton and Cox that the original motivation for the establishment and growth of the institutions that were precursors of the modern university was primarily vocational in character. The change to a concern with the 'disinterested pursuit of truth for its own sake' only emerged as a post-Renaissance ideal. I conclude that the claims made for the academic respectability of a subject cannot be judged in terms of that subject's 'relevance', or lack of it; if that were to be so, many subjects and departments would have to disappear from the modern educational pantheon.

The criterion of 'remoteness' can, with parity of reasoning, hardly feature as a benchmark conferring warranted admissibility to academic status. The activity and achievements of some modern departments in institutions of higher education, such as Agriculture, Oceanography, or Business Studies, cannot be thought to be 'remote' from the concerns of their students and the interests of their countries or indeed people generally – yet all have won the highest intellectual credence and international reputation. So their academic respectability cannot consist in that. Perhaps Scruton and Cox mean something different by this notion, however, to the effect that a student can only acquire intellectual rigour by endeavouring to achieve understanding of subjects not yet connected with the cognitive apparatus she or he has – the whole range of ideas, concepts, categories that structure and define his or her consciousness. If that *is* what they contend, then it is difficult – if not impossible – to conceive how such understanding might ever be attained. Students seeking to acquire new ideas and master novel modes of thinking must necessarily approach them by means of conceptual frameworks and patterns of cognition of which they are already possessors. Seen in that sense, Scruton and Cox's reference to 'remoteness' is unintelligible. From this consideration one can only infer that what they are concerned with, in their demand for 'remoteness' as a feature of 'truly educated intellectual discipline' is the laying down of a prescription as to what 'truly' educational disciplines, *in their view*, ought to look like.

As the three examples cited above will show, work can be both far from remote and directly relevant – and yet at the same time intellectually demanding and academically rigorous. Nobel prizes will doubtless go to the discoverers of cures for cancer and AIDS and there would, one imagines, be few who would deny that the award of such distinctions is a mark of anything less than the highest intellectual respectability. Similar regard is connoted in the award of royal honours for the conception and articulation of a new mode of philosophical investigation.

It is doubtful, however, whether the development of any new mode of philosophical reasoning would meet Scruton and Cox's strictures against 'novelty' (one of the grounds on which they base their criticism of the work of the Bradford School of Peace Studies). Such arguments as theirs, one suspects, were used by the protagonists of the retention of such traditional kinds of knowledge as Rhetoric, Dialectics and Syntax – to say nothing of more up-to-date examples such as Euclidean Geometry or Newtonian Physics – in their attempts to hold off the encroachments of such new subjects as Geography, English Literature and the Social Sciences on the curriculum of their institutions. This antediluvianism has been exposed for the academic conservatism it is by the work of 'scientists' concerned with the development and growth of human knowledge since the time of Aristotle, and by the satires of such authors as Harold Benjamin, who describes the Cox–Scruton kind of view of educationally respectable knowledge as a plea to preserve the 'sabre-toothed curriculum' of earlier ages.[5] Given the recent emergence and crucial importance of such novel subjects as those of the bio-sciences or artificial intelligence, it cannot be maintained that the relative modernity of Peace Studies is a legitimate source of criticism.

Similarly, the strictures of Scruton and Cox against the inclusion of the word 'Studies' in the title of any subject or area aspiring to academic status cannot be taken seriously. The widespread regard for such schools or departments as Literary Studies, Modern European Studies, Business Studies or even a Research School of Pacific Studies (for example), rests upon an acceptance that the work done by such institutions involves standards quite as high and motives quite as disinterested as those that can be observed in operation in assessing the work of students and teachers in, say, Mathematics, Philosophy or Sociology. One could hardly contend that those working in the former fields are any less capable of critical appraisal, understanding, or the ability to 'assess or dispute a . . . proof' or what counts as one in the field in question, or to 'acquire any other intellectual accomplishment that would show itself in reasoned critical reflection, applicable beyond the range of examples which have nourished it', than the latter, at least in principle. There may always, of course, be individuals who become denizens of such schools in the hope of being recognised as academics – but that is equally true of inhabitants of some departments of philosophy or sociology. Equally, there may be some subjects that have taken the additional term 'Studies' with the intention of securing acceptability, validation, funding, CNAA recognition, and so on. But these are contingencies that do not vitiate the basic contention that work *can* be done in such places that has as much rigour and respectability as that in more traditional places where academic excellence is prized and criticial and creative thinking are seen to operate.

There seem to me to be no grounds *ex hypothesi* for excluding schools or departments of 'Peace Studies' or 'Peace and Conflict Studies', or courses of 'Peace Education' in schools and certainly not on grounds of their novelty or relatively recent provenance. For if there is any one criterion of academic institutions it is in their concern to promote innovation and development within existing subjects, in the areas between subjects and indeed of new subjects that have to be developed to deal with the continuing accretion of knowledge from the constantly expanding frontiers of the cognitive realm. Were this not so, we should never have had subjects so important, complex and demanding as cybernetics and bio-physics. New advances are always being made in the intellectual realm; every subject now accepted as 'traditional' was once thought 'new' and in this respect we do well to remind ourselves of Heraclitus' fragment 'No one can step twice into the same river, for fresh waters are always flowing down upon one'.[6] This is true whether we are talking about discoveries of the meaning of Linear B or the structure of the DNA molecule. We cannot rule out the possibility of our making discoveries, different in kind though equally important, in that new realm of human interest and enquiry we have happened to designate as 'Peace and Conflict Studies'.

The notion of 'Peace'

Scruton and Cox do not underestimate the importance of the issues of peace, war and disarmament. These, they say, are matters 'of the first importance for the future of this country and of mankind' and they themselves raise what they see as the questions that will arise in any investigation into the nature of peace and its preconditions.

With the first of these we are immediately into such a difficult and perplexing area that some have been led to question the existence of any subject including the word 'Peace' in its title, much less any claims it might have to intellectual respectability. If, as might be suggested, 'Peace' is a term empty of any explicit or positive content, being rather more of a slogan serving to rally those committed to a particular ideal or set of norms of a religious or political kind, then those concerned to study it from an academic standpoint would be committed to a search for a chimera and, at worst, liable to end up wasting their time or, at best, more likely to make progress on 'peace' issues *via* other avenues of intellectual enquiry.

Certainly problems of definition surround the concept 'Peace', as they do the other ends at which some courses of study in educational institutions aim, such as 'Health' or 'Freedom'. For some people the most that can be said about 'Peace' is that it is the absence of war; for others

it is a state in which countries live in peaceful coexistence with each other. For some, it is life free from fear. To others, it is a state of inner serenity . . . Peace is a very controversial word.

Harbottle[7] is right in that: dictionaries, etymologies and philosophical analyses offer different versions of the meaning of the term, among and between which there are some overlaps but many distinctions. In this respect, 'War' (and, for that reason, 'War Studies') is easier to grasp, for with that there are easily seen criteria that can generally be agreed to constitute the minimum conditions for intelligible application of that term to a particular phenomenon, though there might be differences of interpretation at the periphery (as in the case of the Falklands 'War', for example). We can readily see when a *de jure* or *de facto* 'state of War' might be said to be in existence between two sovereign states: it will involve, at least, the use of force to settle a dispute and bring about some desired end. Similarly, such terms as 'conflict' or 'dispute', applicable not only to the relations of sovereign states but also to individual people, can be characterised in terms of the different evaluations or judgements concerning some object, situation or course of action and the means by which two parties think it possible to secure the success of the opinion or judgement that they rate as more desirable or important.

When set against such relatively straightforward accounts, any attempt to elucidate 'Peace' by analogous criteria becomes problematic, for little except 'the absence of war' seems to be agreed. And that is unsatisfactory as a definition, for it is negative: 'p' as 'not-q' cannot be said to tell us anything about the nature of 'p' and the ways in which it can be identified. In this respect, similar dissatisfaction may be felt with the definition of 'Health' as 'the absence of illness' or 'Freedom' as 'the absence of constraint': all are, so to speak, arguments of a deficiency kind. If this is all we can come up with as an account of 'peace', then, it might be said, the reservations of Cox and Scruton are based upon a solid point: how can there be any sense in the notion of 'Peace Studies' when the principal object of such studies is no more than a negation? The SOED certainly suggests as much: 'freedom from . . .' and 'absence of . . .' such objectively identifiable things as 'war', 'strife', 'discord', 'fear' and 'conflict' make up almost all its characterisations of 'peace'.

Yet, just as there is a widespread feeling that 'health' amounts to more than the mere absence of disease, so there is considerable regard for the view that a state of 'not-war', 'not-conflict' or 'non-oppression' does not add up to the 'peace' that is represented widely as a desirable *terminus ad quem* for statesmanlike endeavour and practical politics. A recent report of a Peace Education Conference in New Zealand suggests a more positive account of 'peace':

it begins with the fostering of self-esteem or personal wellbeing in the individual, whether child or adult, and extends to
- respect for the rights of others
- mutual trust
- the pursuit of justice
- co-operative decision-making
- creative resolution of conflict within individuals, communities and the world.[8]

These kinds of aim seem to fit in well with one of the definitions of 'peace' suggested by the SOED – as whatever produces 'a state of calmness, tranquillity and repose', or what some people have called the notion of 'conviviality'. The aims also fit in well with a characterisation of the 'positive' side of Peace Studies by the Professor of Peace Studies at Bradford, James O'Connell.

The theme of peace . . . contains two basic elements, one positive and one negative: willing co-operation among persons for social and personal goals and the absence of violence (in the shape of direct physical, psychological or moral violence) . . . in the case of medicine, health provides a positive focus and disease a negative focus; and this double focus is analogous to the positive and negative foci that positive and negative peace provide to their subject.[9]

In other words, I suggest there is a possibility of characterising the notion of 'peace' in a way that goes beyond the privative aspect of the mere absence of conflict. This relates to the *desiderata* of a spirit of co-operation among individuals, communities and states, to enable them to bring off joint aims and projects that will conduce to the welfare of all, enhance and secure individual freedom and autonomy, and create and maintain an atmosphere of mutual toleration and regard. All these will make it possible for both individuals and states to work out patterns of preferred life-options for themselves, without any sense of threat or fear of constraint being felt. To this extent, and in this way, the aim of 'Peace Studies' is not all that different from the aim of some programmes of Health Education to promote the kind of 'health' described by the WHO as involving 'a positive state of physical and mental wellbeing'.

There is more to the positive aspect of 'peace' than that, however, and the reference to the ideal of an increase in personal autonomy that peace makes possible gives us a further clue. One version of the principle of 'freedom' is not to make it an *end* of ethical endeavour and social policy but a *beginning*, a presupposition of any kind of moral discourse. Thus, we can say, moral deliberation about right action starts from the premise that human beings are presumed to be free agents, until good reason can be given for laying constraints on them. Similarly, with the principle of justice and fairness contained in the idea of 'equality', we can say that human beings act upon the presumption of their equality until relevant and socially operative reasons can be given for making exceptions in their case and treating them differently – the onus of justification for doing so always resting upon those proposing to make the discrimination or impose the constraint.

It is just so with the concept of the prime principles of all moral discourse, that human beings will not have any purposes or projects of theirs disrupted by violence, aggression or conflict – with the correlative requirement that those who wish or propose to disrupt have the onus of accountability and the liability for the consequences. I can only see one difference here: there might, on occasion, be good reason – moral reason – for interfering with people's freedom or for treating them differently. But for me the analogy ends there. I can see no good reason why anyone should propose, as an act or policy capable of vindication, to impose aggression, violence or conflict on another human being. That view clearly arises from my own moral and metaphysical preconceptions – and no doubt proponents of the idea of a 'just' war would strongly disagree. Here is one possible area of further discussion and debate that could be quite as learned and academic as many of the controversies in departments of morals, theology or medicine, or topics on the programme of courses in 'Personal and Social Education'.

Clearly, parties to such a controversy would share much common ground and one of their shared premises might be a regard for some such positive conception of peace as has been adumbrated above. Why should this be, if the account of Scruton, Cox and others is correct? Perhaps the answer lies in the metatheoretical bases upon which Scruton and Cox's account of peace and Peace Studies rests. For we may object to their purported 'definition' of peace that they are working with a notion of definition that is itself at best contentious, at worst mistaken.

Wittgenstein can be of help to us here. He rightly warns anyone seeking to get clear about 'meaning' not to start off with preconceptions, but rather simply to 'look and see' how terms are actually used by participants in a particular universe of discourse: 'for a large class of cases, though not for all, the meaning of an expression is to be found in its use'.[10] The principle of 'Don't look for the meaning, look for the use', when applied to our investigation into the nature and point of Peace Studies will, I think, give us the criterion we need to render intelligible the aspirations and norms articulated by participants in communications about a universally-desired end of political and social life. Strangely, there seems to be no-one who does not share those aspirations. As Ted Wragg remarks.

I don't actually know anyone who is against peace. Try as I might to trawl through my memories of all the people I have ever known, I cannot for the life of me find one who is against the notion of living in peace.[11]

Why then the problem? A major difficulty is that not all people agree about the particular aims and projects that will conduce to the welfare of all, about what set of constraints they would be willing to accept consistent with developing their own preferred pattern of life options, or indeed about what individual or national freedom might consist of. What debates about peace often come down to is the articulation of notions of human being and human flourishing that are radically different. Thus discussions about the nature of peace often involve fundamental differences in our metaphysics of man and society – of what counts as human nature, human welfare, and an acceptable basis of social relations for its optimum realisation. This problem is exacerbated when the interlocutors in such a debate do not recognise even the most rudimentary ideas, concepts or categories required for other parties' ideological commitments and identities to be comprehended, much less evaluated or assessed for any potential worth they might have for protagonists in such a discussion.

A prime focus of research in Peace and Conflict Studies, therefore, might be the development of a language appropriate for the investigation and elucidation of such fundamental differences as outlined above. That may well involve us in an even deeper level of difficulty. If we are relativists, we will believe no such language could ever be developed. Or, we may hold that there are absolute and unvarying criteria of logic and rationality shared and exhibited by all human communication – so that it should be possible, in principle, to develop some sort of common logic for the elucidation and evaluation of even the most fundamental ideological differences as to what *counts* as human welfare and harm. The answer to this further question is far from clear; all we can be sure about is that those interested in and committed to the attempt to understand the nature of peace and conflict are not going to be short of work to do.

Peace Studies as a field of knowledge

Faced with the plethora of requirements – from logic, epistemology, ethics and metaphysics – and great amount of work to do, academics and teachers might be forgiven for throwing up their hands and passing on to problems they see as more immediate, such as maintaining their own institutions, preserving access to resources or funding, attracting student numbers, and so on. Two considerations might be advanced against such moves. First, I can think of no problem more demanding of solution that the question of how any form of peaceful life can be secured for all people, if the institutions about the continued existence of which academics are so concerned are to have any kind of future at all. Second, this problem is one that is not, in principle, beyond solution. We do not abandon the search for a cure for cancer or AIDS, for we believe that, given human ingenuity and resources, a cure can and will in time be found. We might argue, with parity of reasoning, that we need not abandon the search for concord and amity between individuals and societies, given that problems of conflict resolution and the inhibition and elimination of aggression are, in principle, capable of solution.

All that we need to abandon – though this is still a considerable matter requiring the most strenuous efforts of education and public support – is the myth that human beings are 'innately' violent and incapable of settling their differences by any other than aggressive means. It is not self-evidently true that human beings are 'by nature' or 'innately' disposed in this way or that towards our differences of view, at least not *a priori*; it may be an empirical 'fact' about present human forms of society and institutions that that is how we have *come* to resolve them. But that can be changed. What we need, in our attempts to secure such changes, is those qualities that are *propria* of our human being status – curiosity, a desire to explain and understand, and a creative imagination. Something that tends to bring all these into play is being presented with a problem.

It is one of these problems which Cox and Scruton delineate as the main focus of questions about peace – whether peace can be attained and, if so, how it can be maintained and secured. In this concern O'Connell sees an analogy between Peace Studies and what he calls 'area studies' such as Medicine and Human Geography:

In the case of human geography, economics and sociology are focussed by a concern for the uses of the earth; and in medicine a whole range of subjects from chemistry to psychology are joined by a concern to maintain and restore health.

On this basis Peace Studies is analogous to such 'area studies': it deals with a practical problem and draws upon the insights provided by a range of other forms of enquiry in the attempt to work out answers to the substantive issue which is its origin and prime focus.

At this point it might be interesting and helpful to take up a suggestion made by Anthony Weaver. In his postscript to a pamphlet of the Peace Education Project[12] he draws attention to the applicability of a particular curriculum theory to the educational potential of courses in Peace Studies. Referring to the trenchant rebuttals made by other contributors to the same pamphlet against the contention that 'peace studies are not a genuine discipline', he remarks that:

None of them . . . has explained with the clarity of Paul Hirst[13] that disciplines are primarily distinguished by their respective methods of enquiry, or to use his words 'criteria for truth' (eg experiments in science, logic in mathematics, examination of records and artefacts in history) whatever their content. And that subjects such as geography, engineering or education are best regarded as fields of knowledge to which the disciplines contribute . . .

For Hirst, disciplines such as philosophy, science and mathematics are discernible by their distinct concepts, networks of concepts, methods of enquiry and tests for truth. Writers such as Schwab[14] or Powell[15] have added other characteristic features, such as particular content, circumstances or outcomes aimed at by practitioners in the field – though their point is the same. We may think it reasonable to agree that Peace Studies, (when measured against such criteria) does not satisfy the requirements for 'disciplinary' status. What it *does* provide is a paradigm of what Hirst called a 'field of knowledge', in which subject practitioners draw upon contributions from the various disciplined modes of enquiry to help them formulate answers to the particular problems, practical or theoretical, upon which they are working. 'Theoretical' fields of knowledge, such as geography or the study of politics, are primarily concerned to provide explanations of phenomena and so to assist us in understanding what 'is'; 'practical' fields of knowledge, such as engineering, education or medicine, are centred upon the search for solutions to problem situations and thus aim to assist us in our deliberations concerning what 'ought to be'.

Here, I believe, we can see at least one account of the epistemological status of 'Peace and Conflict Studies' that may easily refute the objections advanced by Cox and Scruton and others: 'Peace Studies' may be defined as an 'area study' that is both theoretical and practical. 'Conflict Studies' helps us to understand and explain the causes and origins of human conflict, violence and aggression; 'Peace Studies' enables us to use that knowledge and understanding and, along with other considerations, to attempt to frame answers to the practical question 'What ought we to do in order to promote the absence of war, conflict and aggression and the attainment of amity, concord and mutual trust?' These two areas of reflection and deliberation provide us with the agenda and curriculum for any course of 'Peace and Conflict Studies' established in institutions devoted to the prosecution of similar questions relating to the promotion of human welfare and the diminution of harm.

The peace studies curriculum

'Health education' might offer a useful analogy. Here the imperatives are the inhibition and elimination of all those conditions, physical and mental, that militate against the individual's being able to perpetuate his/her existence to 'normal' term ('normal' is, of course, a term with highly evaluative overtones); and the promotion of the conditions and regimen of living that will enable the individual to rise above the level of mere existence and enjoy a life of some quality. The attempt to understand deleterious conditions and to conceive and elaborate policies and programmes of a positive or therapeutic kind will call on a range of disciplined forms of understanding and enquiry. These will include the natural and the social sciences; medicine, in many of its aspects – perhaps especially epidemiology and pathology; geography – demography and climatology; and perhaps above all, ethics. These are examples only, the list is not meant to be exhaustive. But it offers an illustration of the kinds and range of cognitive skills that might generate a curriculum for 'Peace Studies'. Given that 'Peace Studies' may be properly defined as an 'area study' or as a practical and theoretical 'field of knowledge', the only problem remaining for curriculum planners is to draw up a list of subjects that may be thought sufficient to constitute its staple.

I do not believe that any *definitive* or exhaustive list can be drawn up, however, for the reason that circumstances alter cases. The curriculum in one institution, where the concern is with global conflicts and the attempt to achieve peace, friendship and close co-operation in major projects between nations, would differ in many respects from that in another, in which the concern was much more devoted to local issues, such as strikes and/or community reconciliation, as for instance in Northern Ireland or South Yorkshire. But I do believe that some tentative guidelines may be laid down.

As a contribution to discussion, I should like to offer the following subjects as prime candidates for inclusion in a list of issues that, taken together, might make up a curriculum in Peace Studies. As with Health Education, I think that reference to moral considerations and principles would be paramount, at some stage and in some explicit form; clearly ethics will have to feature on such a curriculum. The human and social sciences, too, would give a great deal of indispensable information, as well as providing an appropriate set of disciplinary tools for the examination and understanding of the origins and causes of human conflict: history, anthropology, sociology, social psychology and psychology would seem particularly appropriate. Economics must also play a part as, one imagines, must human geography. Some understanding of religion would also seem to be required if, for example, we are to have any comprehension, from an informed point of view, of the conflicts currently bedevilling the Middle East. Critical and analytical skills, typical of philosophy, will also be needed if we are successfully to struggle with the basic questions of the nature of peace, the idea of a 'just' war and the status of the arguments advanced for policy proposals put forward in the attempt to promote and secure peace. Scientific understanding is going to be called on at many points throughout a programme of Peace and Conflict Studies as, for instance, when one is considering the likely consequences of the 'nuclear winter' that would follow the use of nuclear weapons; while the statistical procedures of mathematics would be needed for students to calculate probabilities and run thought experiments in this field. Medicine and the bio-sciences; cybernetics and systems theory; and policy studies – all would have contributions to make to this area of intellectual activity and educational interest. The range of subjects and disciplines that would be appropriate to advance understanding and assist deliberation in the field is as wide as the topics themselves. The ways and means of securing peace are various, depending on the level and complexity of the problems to which we may wish to address ourselves, as are the patterns of understanding required to analyse and elaborate what conditions promote the achievement of personal autonomy and what militate against it.

O'Connell has a slightly different list. For the Bradford School of Peace Studies, he identifies five 'areas of concentration' as critical to students' need to attain a structured understanding of the issues of peace:

Peace theory (the history and analysis of the concept and value of peace and related concepts and values: especially justice and freedom) . . . work is also done on non-violent methods of social change.

Nuclear and non-nuclear defence (. . . the School concentrates a great part of its work on the politics, technology, economics and ethics of the nuclear arms race as well as on the problems of proliferation).

Relations between economically developed and developing countries (Peace, justice and development form the strands of . . . research on relations between the world's regions) which include the use and allocation of energy resources, marketing of commodities, the export of technology and the sharing and education of skills.

Industrialised societies (three areas of choice: . . . [the problem of] race/ethnic relations in European countries; . . . the problem of industrial/social class divisions in Britain; the third area is the conversion of arms industries into industries for other purposes).

Regions in conflict (from among the many areas in which peace has broken down the School has chosen to specialise in Northern Ireland and the Middle East).

These are the areas of teaching and research for a particular department, with a particular background and interests. There, the problems, topics and issues are more specific and sharply focused, though they are nonetheless similar to the list suggested above in their range of reference and disciplinary perspectives.

Scruton and Cox have a slightly different list of contributory subjects and disciplines which, they aver, are necessary to a consideration of the questions raised in any attempt to understand the nature and the preconditions for peace. Their list is as follows:

Philosophy, and especially ethics, political philosophy and the theory of social choice;
Logic and mathematics, and especially probability theory, decision theory and the theory of games;
Military strategy;
History, especially the history of modern Europe and America, of the Second World War, and of the Soviet Union and its expansion;

Theology, and especially the theory of the just war, natural law and God's peace;
Economics, and especially the theory of the market and the comparison between
planned and free economies;
Sociology, and especially the theories of social conflict, of social cohesion and of
collective action;
Politics, and especially comparative systems theory, and the theories of
representative government, of mass movements and of totalitarianism.

Here there are different emphases to those of O'Connell and myself,
although there are some areas of overlap too. Here again, the curriculum
suggested is just as much a function of particular preconceptions as that
in the Bradford School of Peace Studies but this time from a different
point of view – that of the Institute for European Defence and Strategic
Studies.

The point is that all three suggested curricula are such as can be taught
in both schools and colleges and generate research at the highest level of
intellectual abstraction but at the most relevant points of social and
international applicability. Any of them would serve the purposes of
preserving and transmitting knowledge and at the same time critically
appraising and reinterpreting it where necessary. At the same time they
would help push back the frontiers of human ignorance in the attempt to
expand and ameliorate human understanding and our ability to predict,
plan for and control the future.

These are the purposes of any institution in the education service
seeking finance and support. The one difference between schools and
colleges and universities is that 'Peace and Conflict Studies' may be
appropriate as providing a forum for specific courses of teaching and
research in the latter, while in the former, the way in which such a subject
may best figure on the curriculum is a subject for further enquiry.

Some believe, for example, that a concern for peace ought to infuse all
a school's curriculum endeavours and indeed the whole institutional
ethos of a school, and that no specific timetable time needs to be
provided for it. Others consider that there ought to be specific courses in
International Understanding and Human Relationships and that a
specific section of those courses should be devoted to the topics of peace
and conflict. Yet others would wish to see a combination of the two;
others again would see all this coming under some other heading, of
which 'Personal and Social Education' and its like are the most widely
canvassed occasions for peace education in the UK. But such people
appear increasingly to assent to the proposition that courses of some such
kind, under such headings and for such purposes, should now feature on
the curriculum and in the programmes of educational institutions
generally.

It is also right to note, however, that many parents, politicians,
education authorities and academics have reservations about this. In
their eyes, such courses are part of a spectrum that extends from

recommendations about good manners to outright indoctrination, that often serves to promote outright political agenda.

The question of epistemological status

Few universities or schools, one imagines, would want to see themselves described as indoctrinatory. For, whatever the past history of the concept may have been, there is no doubt that these days the word 'indoctrination' carries the most injurious pejorative overtones. Any of the standard analyses of the term would show why this is so.[16] Few parents would be happy to see their sons or daughters exposed to teachers who intended to employ whatever means seemed most efficacious to bring about the uncritical acceptance, on the part of their charges, of highly contentious or even incorrigible theories and doctrines, in such a way as to become unshakeably committed to them as ideologies that then govern and shape their lives and which they are also concerned to propagate to others so as to secure similar commitment on their part. Parents would very soon make their objections known, as the affair of William Tyndale Primary School in London between 1975–6 illustrates.[17] For their part, universities would quickly be brought under the most critical scrutiny from external examiners and their funding bodies, possibly even to the extent of losing staff or recognition.

Schools and universities are not in the business of indoctrination when supported by subventions from the public exchequer; their overt purposes are those of education, which was once characterised by R S Peters as the initiation of the young into the various valued traditions of critico-creative thought, by means that require voluntariness and wittingness on their part and in such a way that their perspectives are transformed by the cognitive spill-over that their acquisition of the forms of public knowledge brings about in them.[18] It is in respect of such definitions of 'education' and 'indoctrination' that Cox and Scruton and Marks point the accusing finger at courses of 'Peace Studies', in whatever institution or form they are taught. Their contention is that the cognitive nature of Peace Studies is such that the subject is

not merely . . . often taught in a biased and irresponsible way, but that it could be taught in no other way.

This is to make a claim different in kind from the contention that the subject may, as a matter of empirical fact, often be taught in such a way; that could as well be true of subjects like History, Politics, Economics, Sociology and even English Literature. The claim amounts to a particular conceptualisation of the purported epistemological status of the subject matter of and methods appropriate to the teaching of Peace Studies. For Cox and Scruton there is too little of fact in it and too much of belief, opinion and even prejudice; too little of objective information and too much of material that, in the hands of some teachers having particular intentions regarding the aims of teaching such a subject, is potentially indoctrinatory.

To such a charge many of the foregoing considerations about the cognitive status of Peace and Conflict Studies may be thought to constitute adequate rebuttal. On some such basis we may, with diffidence, support the conclusions of Annabel Laity's critique of Scruton and Cox's document:

There is room for a genuine educational discipline in the field of human relations, rights and responsibilities, whether we call it peace studies or not.

It is possible to teach the above-mentioned disciplines without party political bias.

Given that political awareness is a most necessary equipment for those of us who live in a democracy we cannot dismiss the discussion of political issues from the school curriculum or university.[19]

This response is not based on contingencies about what might be the case in the teaching of Peace and Conflict Studies or in the development of curriculum schemes to facilitate it; it is a response that proffers an alternative articulation of the concept and epistemology of Peace and Conflict Studies, based upon the requirements that can be presupposed by the necessary commitment of the future citizen in a democracy to the idea and goals of 'education for democracy'. Such an aim requires just that open-mindedness and openness to counter-argument, refutation and falsification that is called for in the sort of society argued for by Karl Popper as the only one capable of functioning so as to secure maximum human happiness and to provide a bulwark against the exploitation, ignorance and servitude endemic in any totalitarian system.[20] In this respect, at least, Laity and her colleagues are surely on the same side as Cox and Scruton. The goals seem to be the same.

The problem is, however, that the epistemology seems to be the same. For the view of 'objectivity' evidently taken by both sides in this dispute is a function of foundationalist preconceptions about perception and knowledge, the foundation in question being a version of the empiricism that lies at the root of some recent attacks on the claims made for proper cognitive status to be accorded to moral discourse, aesthetics and religion. The principal tenets of this empiricism are similar to those held by positivists in the philosophy of science and verificationists in the philosophy of language: namely, that perception can be veridical, value- and theory-free, unmistaken and untainted by subjective prejudice; that there is a realm of 'facts' that can be logically distinguished from the realm of 'values'; that the collection of such facts is the function of the organs of perception; that 'truth' is only to be sought in the certainties of deductive reasoning such as mathematics and logic or in the highly probabilistic findings of the inductive methods of the natural sciences; and that human cognition can be reduced to some basic forms, whether these be the Humean distinction of two realms of proposition or the Hirstian categorisation of human understanding into seven basic 'modes of understanding', 'forms of knowledge', or whatever. On the ground of such epistemic preconceptions, both Cox and Scruton *and* Laity can argue for and against the possibility of coming to clear agreements as to the 'facts' that would be relevant to work in Peace Studies and of the separate exercise of making value judgements of and about them. Indeed there are some who might want to go further and claim that the possibility of 'education' is restricted to the realms of science and mathematics only; when one enters debatable fields such as the arts, literature, religion, sex and politics, one must take especial care, for all such subjects are potentially indoctrinatory.

It is surprising that such views continue to be held – and used as the basis for attacks upon such subjects as Peace Studies – when arguments in rebuttal of them have proved so fatally debilitating, for many years. As long ago as 1949 Popper[21] was pointing out that inductivist accounts of the 'true' nature of science rested upon a blatant *petitio principii*; as long ago as 1953 Wittgenstein's *Philosophical investigations* could be used to show that language has very many uses and forms of meaning, certainly many more than seven. Similar age can be claimed for arguments that persuasively call into question the validity of the alleged 'Fact-Value' distinction,[22] as also the idea of absolute objectivity and a theory-free account of 'truth'.[23] I do not believe I need multiply examples nor amplify the arguments that have been mounted by various critics against such views as those of Cox and Scruton and Marks, or versions of them, deployed against courses in Peace and Conflict Studies – views that rest upon such shaky epistemic foundations. For the interest of those who would wish to see those arguments rehearsed *in extenso*, tellingly developed and succinctly summarised, perhaps the most useful account for educational purposes might be something like that of Kevin Harris[24] – though he too has a case of his own to put forward. Like him and Chalmers[25] we may now draw on the work of Popper, Lakatos, Kuhn and Feyerabend to maintain, against the empiricist epistemology held by those who embrace postulates such as those implicit in the Cox and Scruton pamphlet, that observation is theory-dependent; that our selection of what is to count as a fact will itself be a function of our values and interest; that 'truth' has to be defined, if indeed it can be defined at all, as a criterion of what is interpersonally and conventionally agreed to be 'warrantably assertible' in any field of discourse; that human meanings are shifting, polymorphous and elusive; that the supposed distinguishability of 'fact' and 'value' may be nothing more than a positivist fiction; that human experience and understanding cannot be reduced to any basic building blocks upon which the whole of the structure of the human cognitive enterprise must necessarily be erected and that have to be 'presupposed' in all further attempts at sophistication within it. Armed with the counter-arguments that these tenets afford us, we may return to a critique of empiricist foundationalist epistemologies with greater power for their refutation. We may now rebut the contentions of such hostile critics as those cited, not merely by answering them in their own terms (as Laity and others do) but, more devastatingly, by showing that the basis of their criticism is itself, at best, highly contentious and, at worst, fatally flawed *ab initio*. This may even involve giving up the recourse one might want to have to the otherwise attractive curriculum defence offered by Hirst's theory; for, as a result of the *elenchus* of *its* foundationalism formulated by Walker and Evers,[26] it is doubtful whether we should be immune from criticism in seeking support for Peace Studies as a 'field of knowledge' from such a dubious source – for it too exhibits all the axioms and postulates to the falsification of which Australian critics of empiricist epistemology have devoted so much scholarly effort to such persuasive effect.

Epistemological support for peace studies

What then is left? Have we taken away the basis for a theoretically sound articulation of the epistemological status of Peace Studies, that will enable us to vindicate its appearance on the programmes of schools, colleges and universities? I do not think so, for from the above set of considerations we may derive other and better arguments in its support. Reference to the work of Popper, for instance, enables us to see Peace and Conflict Studies as a paradigm of science or of philosophy, as a species of critical problem-solving. Those active in teaching and research in this area are concerned with the attempt to find solutions to problems of a particularly pressing kind: what is peace, and how can it be secured? These problems seem to be capable, in principle at any rate, of solution, or of 'trial' or tentative solutions, to which all the critical apparatus of the falsification that is the mark of any 'open' academic community may then be brought to bear. On this basis it is then sufficient (for public utilities and education authorities) to agree that the need to find policies apt for the promotion of concord, amity and co-operation and the elimination of aggression and structural violence in the world we inhabit is now a matter of the most overriding importance if we are to survive at all and have teaching and research institutions to employ for the solution of other human problems. Having showed such agreement, they can then devote all their energies to its solution. Schools and courses of Peace and Conflict Studies would be seen as having priority in assignment of staff, provision of resources and research funding, and the involvement of all academics instead of, as is now sadly often the case, enjoying no more than the status and role of Cinderella – much less that of the Ugly Sisters, in which some modern critics of educational institutions cast them.

An alternative possibility would come from the arguments of Evers,[27] already referred to. His refutation of reductionist accounts of knowledge as partitioned into basic impermeable sets argues for an epistemic holism, in which the whole cognitive repertoire of any individual is related and, as it were, integrated into what Quine calls just one 'web of belief', giving that individual the theory that informs and predisposes all his/her attempts to understand reality and cope with its exigencies. On this account science and philosophy become, not so much exercises in problem-solving, but rather activities of critical reflection, criticism and correction of the theory of which one is a bearer – and of comparing that theory with others, to test its fecundity and explanatory power. Critical theory analysis and comparison in the realm of Peace Studies would then enable those engaged in it to re-examine the theories that structure and define their own approaches and thus to make whatever adjustments, criticisms or corrections seemed to be called for in their attempt to articulate and develop a whole network of theoretical understandings to be brought to bear on the problems with which they were required to deal. This last point is underlined by Walker:[28] he sees such problems as providing the stimulus and the occasion for our theories of the world to be brought into play, when questions of human interests and purposes arise. For him the pragmatic approach is always to be preferred and the test of whether a policy or programme works lies in its functional utility. His approach seems to point the way toward a revivification of Deweyan pragmatism; this would offer Peace Studies as a forum in which theory-building would have the formulation of policy as its primary focus, that would again require a range of cognitive skills and repertoire to operate upon its chief problematic.

Popperian evolutionary epistemology, Quinean holism, Deweyan pragmatism, all seem to provide the opportunity for the critical appraisal of problems, issues and theories with which the field of investigation under the rubric of Peace and Conflict Studies seems to be replete. All of them offer teachers and students a collection of material upon which they may choose to sharpen both their knowledge and their skills of conceptualisation and categorisation, and constitute what Latakos might have seen as a properly scholarly and progressive 'research pro- gramme'.[29]

Part of that programme may involve, at some stage, considering whether the title or nomenclature of the subject ought to be changed. Of course, as Laity intimates,[30] there seems to be no reason *a priori* why we should stick to one title rather than another. What is important is the kind of *problems* to be studied and the *policies* developed for their solution; it is this that will give such a subject what Powell insightfully calls its 'flavour'. For him what marks off one scholarly area of investigation from another is its content, the sources it is drawn from, the interests and background of those doing research on it, the considerations that make certain moves decisive in it, the context in which it takes place, the ends aimed at and the outcomes observed – all criteria the pragmatic quality of which both Walker and Schwab would, one feels, strongly approve. Under this rubric any convenient heading will do; whether we see teaching and research on these topics, problems and issues as coming under 'human relations, rights and responsibilities', 'personal and social development', 'the Humanities Curriculum', or 'Moral Education', what is important is that the study of those factors and conditions conducing to human welfare and minimising human harm is, at some stage and in some form or other, an element in the construction of such courses as a matter of necessity.

Education is, as Daveney convincingly argues,[31] in the last analysis a moral concept; it has to do with the ways in which we choose to institutionalise the child-rearing practices of our various communities with the overt intention of preparing them for a life in society that, we hope, will be better than our own. What we are after, as Mary Warnock tellingly noted,[32] is a society that, even if it is going to be at several removes from our own, will be one in which the knowledge we now hand on is enhanced and further developed so as to improve the lot of its denizens. Peace and Conflict Studies, however we name it and see it, is going to be an indispensable element in courses devoted to that end.

Assessment in peace and conflict studies

There is one final problem – last, but by no means least. It is that of assessment. Given that we can develop programmes, of the appropriate 'objectivity' and intellectual acceptability, and that we can provide material to buttress their claims to curriculum time, resource provision and training of the teaching staff required, we still have to elucidate the criteria of what might count as desirable outcomes and progress in them. In every course there has to be opportunity for us to evaluate the success of the course in achieving its objectives, so we may inject further material and prescribe further objectives to which its students may be helped to attain. What might such objectives and outcomes look like, if we are to justify the aims of a course in the analysis and understanding of peace and conflict as phenomena in human relations?

To this there can be no easy answer, and this is hardly the place to start upon an elaborate and complex enquiry. We may, of course, check a student's acquisition of factual information and ability to bring appropriate concepts, categories and skills to bear, with as much ease or difficulty in this subject as in any other. Students' understanding is perhaps more difficult to examine, though here too we may think that a few indicators, such as the ability to explain issues, to use relevant terminology with a degree of accuracy, to be able to give some account of the economy of the phenomena empathetically and to identify sympathetically with the experiences and feelings of others similarly exposed to them, would be all that one could reasonably require.

What might be looked for in any assessment of the success of students' progress in a course of Peace and Conflict education would probably be much harder to characterise, let alone specify and define. For here one might be seeking evidence of, not merely acquisition of information or skills – though they are important enough – but larger-scale and more general advances in attitude, values and beliefs, perhaps not without some change in the ones students already hold. The problem of attitude-change consists as much in endeavouring to bring it about as in the assessment of the extent to which attitudes may have changed as a result of exposure to educational experiences.

We may, perhaps, make some tentative suggestions. One way of our being able to establish whether peace education programmes had been successful might simply consist in our observing and enumerating the incidence of occasions of conflict or acts of violence in various sectors and at various levels of human society. These might range from a decrease in the number of fights in the school playground, through a decrease in the number of days lost due to withdrawal of labour, right through to a refusal at government level to settle differences over such issues as the sovereignty of the Falklands/Malvinas islands by recourse to physical means. On the positive side, we might look to the number and increased range and diversity of friendships struck or alliances formed, and their duration and fecundity in increasing the opportunities of both parties for further co-operation and mutual assistance. We might also seek for evidence of such increasing amity and mutual regard as we can see in the public behaviour of some individuals (whether children or international statesmen) and groups (whether sports teams or the nations themselves). Perhaps the most impressive criterion of achievement of that kind would be our awareness of the extent to which the concept of nationhood and of sovereignty might increasingly give way to acceptance of the need for us all to become sensitive and responsive to the imperatives of our global interdependence.

The concept of national sovereignty, we hear,

is outmoded. For the ecological warfare of the planet we need to become terrestrial people, to use Teilhard de Chardin's phrase, patriotic towards our geographical homelands and cultures, but emotionally and politically loyal to a world society.[33]

Evidence of that could be found in our commitment to the work of such bodies with global concern, as WHO, UNESCO and, of course, UNO itself. On such a criterion the absence by choice of some countries from the councils of these and similar bodies must be regarded as evidence of failure.

Such criteria may serve as minimal benchmarks against which work and progress in peace education courses might be assessed. But what of the more thorny questions of our being able to monitor and assess the advances and changes that those charged with the framing of such courses might aim to bring about in their students – changes in attitude, disposition and creative imagination, all aspects of what we might (*pace* Ryle[34]) call our students' 'inner forum'? Here we run into major problems: not merely those of being able to identify and characterise the disposition, emotions and powers upon which we wish our educational activities to be directed; but also the fundamental one of being able to know or understand other people's minds at all. Some have tried it: Wilson, with his delineation of the various components of moral understanding and action,[35] won a degree of interest and acceptance from many teachers and academics concerned with questions of what it might mean morally to educate our young and by what means we might attempt to do so most promisingly. But he himself always maintained that what was needed was a much more sophisticated understanding of the incredible complexity of moral thinking and conduct and this, for him, clearly pointed to the need for more research.

Concluding remarks

That is perhaps the point at which I should bring these tentative reflections to a close, even if only a temporary one. For enough has been said, I believe, to establish the idea that Peace and Conflict Studies have legitimate claim to the kind of epistemological status that can obtain for them a position on the curriculum in institutions devoted to education and to high standards of scholarly enquiry and achievement.

All that is needed now is for me to make some concluding remarks as to the implications of all this for the work of teachers in schools and of academics and research workers in universities and other institutions of higher education.

For teachers and those planning the curricula of schools and colleges I believe that the following requirements might result from an acceptance on their part of the case advanced above:

1   the insertion into the curriculum of some course, programme or element in which the problems, topics and issues of peace and conflict, their causes, understanding and management can be explicitly addressed and seriously studied. It makes no matter what such courses might be called: 'Human Relations', 'International Understanding', 'Education for personal, national and international security' have been variously suggested, and all have their proponents. Perhaps a beginning might be

made by addressing such topics in courses on 'Personal and Social Education' that are now widespread.

2   the choice of content and the range of matters to be tackled in such courses must be settled by teachers, in consultation with all the various interested parties – parents, LEA advisers and inspectors, other professionals in the education and social welfare services, and so on. Such discussions, if students are working at more senior levels in the schools, should not exclude the students themselves. Suggestions as to a range of suitable topics and issues may be seen in the specimen curricula set out on pp 133–36 above. It is in the nature of such courses that there will be constant dynamic change, as the examples of conflict and the various ways in which people, either individually or in groups, move towards its control and elimination, wherever and in whatever form it occurs, whether this be at the local or the international level, the individual or the global. A study of the problems tackled by the Marriage Guidance Counsellor could be quite as efficacious in giving students the kind of understanding that is sought in these studies, as would be one of the work of international relief and diplomatic arbitration and mediation agencies.

3   the teaching methods adopted will be, one imagines, much less likely to succeed if they are predicated upon the confrontational or the heavily authoritarian model still favoured by some teachers in this area. Much more likely to secure student progress will be those methods and approaches that are predicated upon negotiation, co-operation and mutual regard, that the work of some social psychologists suggests are most effective in preparing students for active commitment to, and participation in, the democratic form of social interaction and political arrangement. Clearly much thought will need to be given to working out and adopting an appropriate teaching style in this area of the curriculum.

4   the need to define the subjects elsewhere in the curriculum on which the teacher of Peace and Conflict Studies will want to draw. This will require the teacher not only to engage in some fundamental thinking as to the various kinds of contribution that the other subjects on the timetable can make to his/her own work, but also to negotiate with the teachers of those subjects ways in which he/she can work with them, draw upon their expertise and resources and perhaps even secure their agreement to working in what will be essentially a team endeavour – with all the professional problems and constraints that this will cause.

5   the speech of the Secretary of State, Sir Keith Joseph, at Sheffield in January 1984, and the imperatives of new methods and schemes of assessment and evaluation will require the teacher of Peace and Conflict Studies to work out, or begin to work out, ways in which the work and progress of students attending his/her courses in this area can be monitored and assessed. As a first necessity, the aims will need to be specified as clearly and precisely as possible, as well as the subordinate or

intermediary objectives, before the appropriate modes of evaluation can begin to be developed and deployed. It will require considerable effort on the part of the teacher to work out such schemes, that will probably draw heavily upon the work of the most up-to-date findings of research by those active in the academic fields of assessment and evaluation. It will also require patience, for it may well be that the outcomes aimed at will be such as will only emerge at a considerable remove from what is actually undertaken in the school and classroom.

These seem to me to be the minimum set of considerations to which those interested in and committed to teaching this subject in our schools will have to attend. There may well be others and discussion on this matter will perhaps start to be promoted in formal and informal groups, organised by LEAs and their Advisory services, public sector colleges or polytechnics, and university schools and departments of education, in single sessions, or on award- or non-award-bearing short or long courses devised for such ends.

This last will bear immediately obvious consequences for academics and researchers in the various kinds of institution referred to. Advisors and advisory teachers, lecturers and research workers may well think there to be a need and the possibility of a growing point for both teaching and research in the provision of courses and conferences in this important area of the developing curriculum. Not only will such colleagues need to devote time and energy to working out and putting on such courses and conferences; they will also have to undertake the expenditure of time, energy and resources on some of the difficult problems of theory and practice that the development and expansion of this area of curriculum advance portends – amongst them those problems in the philosophy of mind and in methodology of evaluation and assessment that I have briefly adumbrated above.

All this will, in its turn, require further support from local authorities, communities and government, not only in terms of the production of policies and the provision of resources, nor simply by means of a suitable level of funding for teaching and research (though that will be critically important to support these endeavours) but also in the patience, tolerance, understanding, interest, sympathy and willingness to be involved that the full range of activities in this area will draw upon and call forth from them. Few would surely disagree that there is no problem more urgent than that of the securing and maintenance of a just and lasting peace for the world and for all its peoples. It is appropriate that this problem should be brought to the forefront of our educational endeavours and research undertakings in this way and at this time, during the International Year of Peace.

Notes and references

1 *Final Document* of the First Special Session devoted to disarmament (quoted in Harbottle, qv) (UNO, 1978 and 1982).

2 Speech by the UK Secretary of State for Education and Science, Sir Keith Joseph, to the National Council of Women of Britain, London, 3 March 1984.

3 *'Peace Studies' in our schools: Propaganda for Defencelessness* John Marks. Women and Families for Defence, 1 Lincolns Inn Fields, London WC2, 1984.

4 *Peace Studies: A Critical Survey* Caroline Cox and Roger Scruton. Institute for European Defence and Strategic Studies, 13/14 Golden Square, London W1R 3AG, 1984.

5 'The Sabre-toothed Curriculum' Harold Benjamin, in *The Curriculum: Context, Design and Development* R Hooper (ed) (Edinburgh: Oliver and Boyd for the Open University, 1971).

6 Heraclitus Fragment B12 and B91. See *Heraclitus: the Cosmic Fragments* G S Kirk (Cambridge University Press, 1956).

7 'Is peace education what it should be?' Michael Harbottle, in *Educare* June–Sept 1985, Vol 2, No 2, p 7 ff.

8 *Report of the Peace Education Conference* Wellington, New Zealand, 26–8 Feb 1985. Department of Education, Government Building, Lambton Quay, Wellington, New Zealand 16.4.85.

9 'The School of Peace Studies, or: Can Peace Studies be Taught?' James O'Connell, unpublished paper. Available from the School of Peace Studies, University of Bradford, West Yorkshire BD7 1DP.

10 *Philosophical Investigations* L Wittgenstein (trans G E M Anscombe) (Basil Blackwell, 1953) Paras 19–23.

11 'Fighting the War for Peace' T Wragg in *Peace Education* J Thacker (ed), published as *Perspectives 2* by the School of Education, University of Exeter, St Luke's, Exeter EX1 2LU, 1983.

12 'Postscipt' A Weaver, in *Seeking Common Ground: PEP Talk* (Journal of the Peace Education Project) Summer 1985, Nos 5 and 6. Published by the Peace Education Project, 6 Endsleigh Street, London WC1.

13 'Liberal Education and the Nature of Knowledge' P H Hirst, in *Philosophical Analysis and Education* R D Archambault (ed) (Routledge and Kegan Paul, 1965).

14 'Problems, Topics and Issues' J J Schwab, in *Education and the Structure of Knowledge* S Elam (ed) (Chicago: Rand McNally for Phi Delta Kappa, 1964). See also his 'Structure of the Disciplines: Meanings and Significances' in *The Structure of Knowledge and the Curriculum* G W Ford and L Pugno (eds) (Chicago: Rand McNally, 1964).

15 'The Idea of a Liberal Education' J P Powell, in *The Australian University* 1965, Vol 3, No 11.

16 Most of the significant papers on this topic were published in *Concepts of Indoctrination* Ivan Snook (ed) (RKP, 1972).

17 Report of the Committee of Enquiry under the Chairmanship of Mr Robin Auld QC into recent events at the William Tyndale School, Islington (ILEA, 1976). Available from: Information Office of the GLC, County Hall, South Bank, London SE1.

18 'Education as Initiation' R S Peters, in R D Archambault *op cit*. See also his *Ethics and Education* (Allen and Unwin, 1966) Part 1, chs 1 and 2.
19 'The Peace Studies Debate' Annabel Laity, in *PEP Talk* Nos 5 and 6 (see note 12 above) pp 23 ff.
20 *The Open Society and its Enemies* K R Popper (RKP, 1943). In two volumes: Vol 1: Plato; Vol 2: Hegel and Marx. See also his *The Logic of Scientific Discovery* (Hutchinson, 1949).
21 'Instruction and Indoctrination' R F Atkinson, in R D Archambault *op cit*.
22 See *The Is/Ought Problem* W D Hudson (ed) (Macmillan, 1969).
23 See *The Theory of Knowledge* D W Hamlyn (Macmillan, 1970) pp 80 ff.
24 *Education and Knowledge* Kevin Harris (RKP, 1979).
25 *What is this Thing Called Science?* Alan F Chalmers, 2nd ed (Open University Press, 1982).
26 'Knowledge, Partitioned Sets and Extensionality' C W Evers and J C Walker, in *Journal of Philosophy of Education* July 1983, Vol 17, No 2, pp 155–70.
27 *Logical Structure and Justification in Educational Theory* C W Evers, PhD Thesis, University of Sydney 1983. See also his 'Epistemology and Justification: From Classical Foundationalism to Quinean Coherentism and Materialist Pragmatism' in *Epistemology, Semantics and Educational Theory* J C Walker and C W Evers (eds) Occasional Papers No 16 (Department of Education, University of Sydney, 1984) pp 1–29.
28 'Towards a Materialist Pragmatist Philosophy of Education' J C Walker and C W Evers, in *Education Research and Perspectives* 1984, Vol 2, No 1, pp 23–33.
29 'Falsification and the methodology of scientific research programmes' I Lakatos, in *Criticism and the Growth of Knowledge* I Lakatos and A E Musgrave (Cambridge University Press, 1970).
30 Annabel Laity, *op cit*.
31 'Education: a Moral Concept' T F Daveney, in *New Essays in the Philosophy of Education* Glenn Langford and D J O'Connor (eds) (RKP, 1973).
32 *Schools of Thought* Mary Warnock (Faber, 1978) Ch 1.
33 *PEP Talk* Nos 5 and 6, Introduction, p 3.
34 *The Concept of Mind* Gilbert Ryle (Hutchinson, 1949).
35 *The Assessment of Morality* John Wilson (NFER, 1973). See also his chapter 'Assessing the Morally Educated Person' in *Introduction to Moral Education* John Wilson, Norman Williams and Barry Sugraman (Penguin, 1967).

Further reading

Issues in Peace Education Colin Read (ed) 1984. Published for United World College of the Atlantic by D Browne Sons, Cowbridge, South Glamorgan.
Peace Education Perspectives 2. School of Education, Exeter University, 1983.
Peace Research in the 1980s Andrew Mack, 1985. Strategic and Defence Studies Centre, Research School of Pacific Studies, Australian National University, Canberra, Australia ACT 2601.

Chapter 10

The nuclear issue in the curriculum and the classroom

J J Wellington

The aim of this chapter is to consider how the issues and arguments surrounding both nuclear weapons and nuclear energy can best be included in the school curriculum and approached in the classroom. The controversial nature of the nuclear issue is examined, leading on to a consideration of the content and the approach which are best suited to an adequate and acceptable treatment of this complex area. Some fairly concrete and specific ideas on both classroom strategies and teaching resources are put forward. Finally, the idea that is perhaps central to this paper is discussed: that a full and balanced coverage of the nuclear issue, and indeed any controversial issue, can only be achieved by literally changing our view of the school curriculum. Philosophical discussion has been kept deliberately brief to allow more space and emphasis to the practical problems of including the nuclear issue in the curriculum and dealing with it adequately in the classroom.

Is the nuclear issue a controversial one?

As the introductory chapter to this book suggested, the problem of defining a controversial issue is itself a matter of controversy. The decision to label the nuclear issue a 'controversial' one may be seen as highly problematic or indeed blatantly politically biased. For some, the very act of writing about or discussing the nuclear issue, or worse still including it in the school curriculum, is seen as a clear indication of a partisan stance.

My twin aim in this section, therefore, is to suggest why the nuclear issue is indeed a controversial one, and furthermore to justify its inclusion in the school curriculum.

A working definition was suggested earlier in the book. A *controversial* issue must:

- involve value judgements so that the issue cannot be settled by facts, evidence or experiment alone;

• be considered important by an appreciable number of people. The nuclear question, including both nuclear weapons and nuclear energy, surely qualifies on both counts. Many of the issues involved are considered to be of the utmost importance by a variety of people: politicians, industrialists, citizens of all kinds, parents and pupils. That can hardly be denied. Although opinions necessarily vary, such issues as the transport and storage of nuclear waste, the siting of *Cruise* missiles, the discharge of radioactive material, the purchase of *Trident* and the future of the nuclear industry are seen as vital by people with a range of political persuasions and scientific backgrounds. Moreover, these issues cannot be settled by *factual* or *scientific* means alone. There is no correlation between level of science education and viewpoint on the nuclear issue. Distinguished professors of physics, from Edward Teller to Martin Ryle, have differed in their stance on the nuclear issue throughout its 40-year history, and they will continue to do so. None of the contentious questions involved in the nuclear issue will ever be settled by scientific experiment alone.

Thus the debate on the future of nuclear energy and weapons must be a controversial issue according to the two criteria suggested above. There remains the problem of justifying its inclusion in the school curriculum. I suggest that this can be done on two grounds, both of which will be elaborated upon throughout the article. The first is based on the *content* involved, the second on *process*. Let us take content first. Despite the fact that the nuclear issue is a major concern for many children and adults (a point discussed later), our education system does not, and has not, prepared people to make informed and rational judgements in this complex field. Ignorance abounds. The Bishop of Salisbury has suggested, in a valuable discussion on 'education for nuclear matters', that science education has been particularly at fault:

Experience of the public debate on nuclear weapons . . . has convinced me of the need for a massive and urgent campaign of public education in this complex field. Let us begin at the beginning. Take the most basic difficulty of all, that most people in this country . . . have had little or no proper grounding in science. And what scientific education they have had often has not equipped them to understand terms like 'radiation' or 'radio-activity'.[1]

One of my aims in this paper is to outline how a suitably-balanced treatment of the nuclear issue can both inform people of the facts *and* enable them to make considered and rational judgements. The latter can be achieved by virtue of the *processes* and skills which can be developed in considering the nuclear issue (skills which may well transfer across to the handling of other controversial issues). That alone is sufficient justification for including a topic as complex as the nuclear issue in the school curriculum. The abilities to distinguish truth from propaganda, to weigh up evidence, to detect bias, to examine the origins of written material, and most of all to explore the sources of people's own information and views can all be enhanced by tackling the nuclear issue. The development of those abilities will, however, depend on the approach or pedagogy of the teacher.

Dealing with the nuclear issue: a balanced approach

The skills of listening, communication, examining evidence and working in groups can all be developed in dealing with the nuclear issue. Whether or not these skills are developed depends totally on the style and approach of the teacher. The Humanities Curriculum Project (HCP) gives firm and useful guidelines on pedagogy for the nuclear issue.

1   Teachers should not use their authority as teachers as a platform for promoting their own views.

2   The mode of enquiry in controversial areas should have discussion rather than instruction as its core.

3   Discussion should protect divergence of view among participants.

4   The teacher as chairperson of a discussion should have responsibility for quality and standards in learning.[2]

These suggestions, or rather premises, are embodied in the notion of procedural neutrality central to the HCP, ie that the teacher should act as an impartial chairperson in any controversial discussion by treating all opinions equally and consistently, and not expressing his or her own viewpoint.

The other strand to neutrality (expressed in point 2 above) is also found in Stenhouse.

The basic classroom pattern should be one of discussion. Instruction inevitably implies that the teacher cannot maintain a neutral position.[3]

In my view, however, this principle cannot fully be maintained when dealing with the nuclear issue. In many cases the provision of information, and even direct instruction, is central to an adequate treatment of the nuclear debate. I do not pretend that information and instruction are always value free, since so many 'facts' come from either one 'side' or the other, but an informed value judgement is surely a more worthwhile educational aim than is a value judgement, gut feeling or intuition. The aim of nuclear education is to equip pupils to make such informed evaluations.[4] Ignorance may be bliss but it is anathema in education.

Other objections to 'neutrality' as a teaching principle have been raised. First, one small but potentially confusing point in the classroom is the ambiguity of the word 'neutral'. In the nuclear issue, to take up a position of neutrality is itself a positive decision, based on a certain viewpoint. Indeed the concept of 'neutrality for Britain' in relation to nuclear weapons is usually associated with so-called left-wing tendencies. Hence the danger of a 'neutral' label attached to the classroom teacher when dealing with the nuclear issue.

Second, in actual classroom discussion, teachers frequently encounter two problems:

1   There is often not a 'divergence of view among participants', or at least an equally-distributed divergence.

2   Several viewpoints, some of them extremely important, are never expressed at all, eg the idea of minimum deterrence.

Is the teacher then under an obligation to present these viewpoints (in the second case) or perhaps to support the minority viewpoint more strongly than others? Such an attempt by the teacher, to play devil's advocate, may be necessary in maintaining balance in a discussion. Does this run contrary to the principle of neutrality? Which is of overriding importance: balance or neutrality?

On a practical level, teachers have complained that it is impossible to maintain neutrality and impartiality. This may appear to be the fault of the teachers themselves. Perhaps more fundamentally, some teachers have felt guilty of moral dishonesty in adopting neutral, impartial viewpoints on issues which they see as fundamental to the world's future.

The above objections of moral dishonesty, practical difficulty and the need for factual information make the concept of 'procedural neutrality' hard to realise in nuclear education. Perhaps a more attainable goal in the teaching approach is the idea of balance. This can be expressed as follows:

1   All viewpoints should be expressed in the discussion (even if they are not held by all participants) with equal force and fairness, and should be given equal time and space.

2   The necessary scientific principles (but not highly technical details) for understanding the nuclear issues should be explained and presented in a form which all can understand.

3   Arguments, information and opinion from all sides should be presented as 'evidence' in the discussion.

This may be as hard to aspire to as the principle of neutrality, but at least the notion of balance provides a measurable aim in considering content in nuclear education. Practical considerations of how this notion of balance can become reality form the theme of the next sections which consider *content, classroom ideas* and *teaching resources*.

The question of content, level and age range

Content and ignorance

It may be argued that the choice of content in the nuclear issue is far less important than process, ie the development of skills and approaches which can be used in examining any controversial issue. But there cannot be process without content, and vice versa. To parody a well-known passage from the German philosopher Kant:

'Process without content is blind'
'Content without process is empty'.[5]

An additional, and more practical reason for including an appreciable amount of content in nuclear education is the level of ignorance among pupils and adults as revealed by various studies. Barbara Tizard[6] reports some of these studies (at home and abroad) which show how ill-informed people are. For example, in one British study, only 58% of 15–18-year-olds questioned knew that nuclear weapons were used in World War II. Only half the sample knew that *Polaris* was a weapon system of some kind. My own discussions and experience with both pupils and adults in the last ten years point to even greater ignorance and misunderstanding of scientific principles. I do not suggest that every citizen needs to know the internal structural details of the nucleus in order to make an informed judgement on the nuclear issue, but many adults and school pupils believe (falsely) that a nuclear reactor could explode like an atomic bomb if an accident occurred. Others believe that so-called 'alternative' sources of energy could be simply substituted for fossil fuel and nuclear electricity generation if only the political will was there. From the other angle, an informed analysis, using scientific principles, of America's so-called 'Star Wars' programme or Strategic Defence Initiative would show that its probability of providing foolproof defence and making nuclear missiles obsolete must be close to zero.

For these reasons I believe that the history and facts, including a few basic scientific principles, should be covered in a balanced nuclear education.[7] The arguments used and presented in newspapers, magazines and on television should also form part of the content of nuclear education. The various viewpoints between the two extremes of deterrence and unilateral disarmament can be presented as evidence for discussion.

In my view, then, the relevant history, facts and arguments could form the content of nuclear education as a vehicle for developing worthwhile skills. The questions of to whom this content should be presented, and at what age and level, are perhaps more difficult to answer.

Level and age range

An oft-quoted statement of Jerome Bruner is commonly used to support the belief that many complex ideas can be introduced to younger children

. . any subject can be taught effectively in some intellectually honest form at any stage of development.[8]

This may be true of subjects with cognitive content only, but does it apply to controversial issues, which often involve a complex web of intellect, emotions and attitudes? Would it be appropriate, for example, to introduce ten-year-olds to the horrific effects of a nuclear explosion? They may be capable of grasping certain relevant intellectual ideas, including in my view the principle of nuclear fission, but should they be exposed to the feelings of horror, anxiety, helplessness and awe which nuclear education might generate?

These worries are lucidly discussed by Tizard.[9] She suggests that 10–12-year-olds are often more anxious about nuclear war than are adolescents, yet they are less well informed and hardly aware of the complex political issues involved. The question of suitable level and age range in nuclear education needs far more study and research by practising classroom teachers.[10] At what age are children capable of handling and discussing controversial issues in a constructive and beneficial way?

The question of appropriate age range for considering the nuclear issue is unanswered, and needs delicate and tactful investigation. Tizard sums up this problem by saying

Anecdotal information suggests that very young children may have bizarre and confused conceptions about nuclear war. The question of what kind of nuclear education is possible for young children, which will both protect them from experiencing too much fear, and yet take account of their interests and anxieties, requires further discussion.[11]

Attitudes and emotions

The problem and place of attitudes and emotions in the nuclear issue is of central concern in discussing classroom approaches. No solutions are offered here, but I would like to make three points which are relevant to teaching and learning:

- the use of concern and emotion as a justification, or source of motivation, for dealing with the nuclear issue;
- the idea of 'useful' and 'useless' or 'constructive' and 'negative' emotions;
- the mysterious relationship between knowledge and attitudes.

First, the fact that children are concerned and anxious about the threat of nuclear war is often used as a justification for the inclusion of nuclear education in the school curriculum. This is probably acceptable as one strand of justification (together with the others discussed above) but should not be overestimated. Many children are either unconcerned about the nuclear issue or, perhaps more accurately, prefer not to think, read or talk about it. This may be considered an ostrich-like approach but in fairness to such children it is probably closer to being a safety or defence mechanism. The complexity of this attitude, as it were shutting-off emotion, is a major factor in considering one's teaching approach to the nuclear issue.

It may be the case that the arousal of emotion, for example, by using horrific visual aids or video material, is counter-productive. Stradling discusses the advantages of a low-key approach by quoting from a fourth-year pupil after a session by some peace activists at the pupil's school:

They are very brave to do what they did. They believe in it but I think that might put people off. It's like assembly where you don't listen just because you know the people believe in it strongly.[12]

The dangers of 'overkill' in nuclear education may therefore be as great as those of an inadequate, a superficial, or a low-key factual approach.

There is also the danger that nuclear education may arouse numbing or 'negative' emotions in school pupils or adults. Feelings of anxiety, apathy, helplessness or hopelessness may all result from the wrong approach. Tizard discusses this danger and the emotional defence mechanisms which people employ in relation to the nuclear issue

It is not at all clear that increasing their anxiety will stimulate thought, or change their attitudes, although this may occur in some cases. Beyond a certain level, anxiety overwhelms the capacity to think. But people's anxiety rarely remains at this level, if only because it is a very unpleasant emotion.[13]

The third complex relationship which must be a major factor in dealing with any controversial issue is the unknown connection between knowledge and attitude. Does the provision of information affect people's attitude to an issue? It has been suggested, for example, that giving facts and information about nuclear weapons merely reinforces an existing view and, worse still, creates greater polarisation within a group. This contention needs further classroom, teacher-based research. Health education about the effects of smoking, as Tizard points out, often consists of providing information and arousing anxiety. Has 'smoking education' affected adolescents' attitudes on this issue? Cynics may argue that even including it in the school curriculum is likely to have negative results.

The intricate and unexplored relationship between knowledge, attitudes and emotions is a key factor in nuclear education, particularly in determining teaching approach. There are so many other, more potent, influences on pupils and adults which affect their attitudes to the nuclear issue that the part of nuclear education should not be overestimated. Perhaps the best that can be hoped for is that pupils make informed value judgements based on a balanced presentation of the history, facts and arguments, as opposed to biased assertions based on ignorance, prejudice or catchy slogans.

Ideas for the classroom

Up to this point, the problems of approaching the nuclear issue in the classroom have been considered at a fairly general level, by considering the questions of process, content and the prior attitudes and emotions of pupils. This section and the one which follows suggest specific classroom approaches, first by considering a range of classroom ideas, and then by discussing the use and evaluation of the teaching resources available to schools. All the ideas discussed are intended to incorporate the threefold notion of 'balance' suggested above.

Simply asking (or expecting) pupils to read material on the nuclear issue, and then perhaps to discuss it, may not be appropriate for many classes in comprehensive schools. More active learning and involvement is often needed. The following classroom activities can be used as alternatives to 'read and discuss':

- brainstorming
- examining photographic and other illustrative material
- role play and simulation
- pupils interviewing each other
- questionnaires, eg on knowledge or attitudes
- full debate with speakers and chairperson
- active reading for learning
- learning through writing

These possibilities are discussed briefly below.

Brainstorming

A useful idea, valuable in setting off open thinking on a new topic, is the activity of brainstorming. This is likely to work best with a small group. It is an effective and often enjoyable way of gathering people's ideas, associations and impressions about almost any topic. For a teacher it is probably most effective and illuminating before any discussion or instruction has occurred. A topic or idea is chosen, for example the atom; deterrents; the Soviet Union; Cruise missiles; nuclear weapons; disarmament; the USA; the hydrogen bomb or any other subject chosen by the group or the teacher. Members of the group are then asked to say aloud the ideas, images, associations or feelings which come into their heads in connection with the topic. A group member or the teacher writes them down without judging or evaluating them in any way. All responses, however funny or tangential, are written down. In the classroom, a blackboard, large chart or overhead projector transparency can be used. Responses start slowly and the ice may be hard to break, but gradually the process gathers speed. The central topic can be written in the centre of the board or chart, and ideas gradually written down and perhaps linked to form a sort of web. After the brainstorming session the web or chart can be studied and discussed. Which ideas come up most often? Which feelings are most obvious?

An open, non-evaluative session of this kind can form an excellent starting point

- interest and awareness are aroused;
- the teacher is provided with useful information on the views and prior knowledge of the pupils;
- people learn the attitudes and impressions of others in an enjoyable and non-argumentative way.

With a larger or less manageable group, pen and paper can be given to individuals. Each person is asked to write down the first three words or ideas that come into his or her mind in response to a given word. This can be done individually or in small groups. The responses can then be collected and made into a large chart for display.

Brainstorming is not a new idea. It may not work well for every teacher with all classes but it can be a good way of making an unbiased, open-minded start to a topic, or to the nuclear issue generally.

Interviews and questionnaires

Another way of arousing interest is to ask members of a group to interview each other, either in small groups or in pairs. The interview could be about each others' views, opinions and attitudes, about their anxieties or worries, or even about their existing knowledge on different subjects. Results should remain anonymous, and they may prove as interesting to the teacher as to the group members themselves. These results could also be collected and displayed. Teachers may wish to devise their own interviews to suit particular classes, or better still, ask the pupils to make up their own interviews to try out on the others.

A similar way of 'raising consciousness' is to use a questionnaire. Again, this could explore

- attitudes and opinions;
- worries and anxieties;
- existing knowledge.

The questionnaire could be given to each individual in the class, and the results then be collated to form a sort of class profile, perhaps using a bar-chart (histogram) or a pie-chart to show people's opinions and attitudes visually (a simple computer database is ideal for collating and displaying results).

Examining and using pictorial material

Photographs, clear illustrations, projected slides or overhead projector transparencies can all be used as alternatives to written material for generating discussion and presenting evidence. Old photographs, newspaper cartoons or modern pictures can be very useful stimulus material.

To start a discussion a teacher could:
* invite general comments from anyone in the group;
* focus on particular aspects of the picture, eg the people and their expressions, the likely time when (say) a photograph was taken, sizes and scale etc;
* ask for impressions and associations which the picture conjures up (rather like brainstorming);
* invite speculation on why the picture was taken, what point it is trying to make, why a cartoon was drawn etc;
* if people are shown, discuss what individuals might be saying or thinking.

Similar ploys can be used to start off written work. Pupils might be asked to write down three words or ideas which the picture brings to mind. Or they could write down what the characters in a picture might be saying, perhaps in a comic-strip type of balloon. Their suggested speeches could be compared and talked about.

These and other ploys can all be valuable starting points in using pictorial material. Figure 1 shows a summary of these ideas, taken from *Learning to Teach Through Discussion*.[14] This booklet contains a wealth of valuable ideas for teachers on handling small-group discussions, examining evidence and dealing with controversial issues.

Role play and simulation

A great deal of excellent work has been published on the use of games, role-plays and simulations in teaching which cannot be summarised here.[15] The nuclear issue is ideally suited to the use of role play and simulation – actual classroom practice will depend on the style, inventiveness and imagination of the teacher. Two suggestions are given below:

1   *Multilateral disarmament negotiations*, eg the Geneva Talks. Pupils are asked to 'take sides' in the talks. After studying the facts on the missiles and weapons which each side possesses, they simulate negotiations, for example, over reducing the number of land-based missiles on each side. Each side discusses this in groups before making an 'offer' to the other side. Bargaining chips could be used and presented in the negotiations. Different parts of the nuclear arsenals (eg land and sea-based weapons or strategic, theatre and tactical weapons) could be compared and used in bargaining.

A simulation of this kind could be a whole-class activity or, better still, conducted in small groups (of, say, eight people). The different groups could compare progress at the end of the session. Details and organisation would obviously depend on the class teacher and the nature of the group. However, a simulation of this general nature could highlight two important areas:

Figure 1 Using pictorial material as a stimulus

Some ideas to try out:

1 *In discussion*

a Ask for general comments
b Focus upon a particular aspect – actions, facial expressions, position of objects or people
c Pupils may imagine what individuals are saying or thinking
d If this picture were the first in a series of two or three, what would be in the next pictures?
e Two (or an appropriate number of pupils) may pretent to be a person in the picture and carry on a conversation
f Pupils may be asked to use one word to put across what 'feeling' the picture tries to transmit
g Pupils may speculate on the photographer's intentions or motives

2 *Written work*

a Before discussion pupils may write words, randomly, which the picture brings to mind.
b Choose one character, or let pupils choose, and ask for comments about their thoughts.
c Ask pupils to imagine a comic-strip balloon from the mouth(s) of one or more characters and write in it what they are saying.
d Ask pupils to decide which person in the picture they would like to be and to say why.

- the wide range of weaponry (size, position and strategy) possessed
- as a result of this, the tremendous difficulties faced by talks of this kind, and therefore multilateral disarmament in general, eg problems of comparison, verification and mistrust.

2 *The decision to drop the Hiroshima bomb.* A similar group discussion, with different sides representing different viewpoints, could be based on the 1945 decision to use the Hiroshima bomb. How should it have been used – as a demonstration on a remote Pacific island, or by dropping it on a city without warning? What dilemmas did the decision-makers face? Would the bomb have been used if Japan had had its own atomic weapon? The following groups could be represented:

- the politicians, eg President Truman;
- the military men, eg General Groves;
- the atomic scientists, eg Robert Oppenheimer, Leo Szilard.

Outcomes which different groups could argue for – and against – are as follows:

- a bomb dropped on a city without warning

- a bomb dropped on a city after a warning
- a warning demonstration of the bomb, arranged in a remote area
- simply telling the enemy of its existence.

Such a simulation would highlight the complexity of the decision by encouraging group members to study the important factors, for example, the previous heavy American losses; the huge investment in making the first bomb; the supposed fanaticism of the Japanese generals; the consciences and guilt feelings of certain scientists; the sheer momentum of the Manhattan Project and so on.

Other ideas for the classroom

Three further activities based on the nuclear issue are described below:

1 *Looking at language*

A specific activity, which may well stimulate wider reading is to look at the *language* used in discussing the nuclear issue. Particular words can be studied. For example, it is thought-provoking to list the names given to nuclear missiles: Cruise, Trident, Titan, Lance and Minuteman. How do these compare with less attractive labels such as SS-4, SS-5 or SS-20? Is there any purpose behind such carefully-chosen names? How do these names compare with those used by the car industry: Cavalier, Sierra, Jaguar, Fiesta, Panda? What images do different naming words conjure up? The car industry uses names to suggest comfort, masculinity, speed, or relaxation. How important are names and their images in the nuclear issue?

The words used by different sides to describe their opponents in the nuclear debate are also worth studying. The language used in the nuclear debate is interesting both for its emotive content and for the images and connotations it carries.

2 *The statements game*

One way of getting pupils to write and then discuss is to ask them to make short written statements on a small card. Initially, these could be statements on any aspect of the nuclear issue, such as

- 'I wish nuclear weapons had never been invented.'
- 'Britain should get rid of its nuclear weapons.'
- 'Without our own nuclear weapons Russia would invade this country.'

and so on. After the statements have been written on separate cards, various activities could follow with the class:

1 The statements could be either passed around or exhibited for the others to read.

2 Each statement could be numbered and individuals asked to write down whether they *agree, are not sure* or *disagree* with that statement.

The views and opinions of the class would then be open to everybody, yet would remain anonymous.

3   Another ploy would be to arrange the class statements in a long line. They could then be sorted out into groups representing (it is hoped) different shades of opinion. This sort of 'secret ballot' approach could be used with statements on specific issues, eg the idea of multilateral disarmament, the notion of a total arms freeze, ways of stopping nuclear proliferation, and so on.

An alternative to starting from pupils' statements, which may be very restrictive, would be for the teacher to write statements about an issue, on separate cards. These could be taken from different leaflets and publications on the nuclear issue and quoted verbatim. Similar activities to those above could then follow, ie writing *agree*, *not sure* or *disagree* for each one, arranging and classifying the statements (which are statements of fact, which of opinion, where might these statements have come from?) and so on.

3 *Newspaper studies*

Another activity to encourage reading and writing would be to examine media coverage of the nuclear issue from different sources. For example, an editorial in the *Sun*, letters to *The Times*, features in the *Guardian*, *Daily Mirror* reports and editorials, or cartoons from different sources. Wall displays and collages could be made showing the quantity and quality of newspaper coverage, and in some cases magazine articles. Different newspapers could be compared. If possible, old newspapers or copies of parts of them could be used to show coverage of present and past incidents, eg newspaper reports of the Hiroshima bomb.

All the language activities described here – looking at words and phrases, the statements game and newspaper studies – are fairly simple and can be easily adopted and adapted by class teachers for their own use.

The ideas presented in this section are offered as alternatives to a straightforward 'read and discuss' approach. This approach has its place, but pupils may soon tire of it. The value in many of the activities suggested is that the existing knowledge and prior attitudes of the group can be revealed, sometimes anonymously. This feedback is as essential to a teacher dealing with a contentious issue as it is in teaching other aspects of the curriculum, eg scientific concepts. In short, the teacher can start from where pupils are, in both their previous information and existing attitudes. In addition, the activities allow the general principle of balance to be monitored and preserved throughout.

Specific examples of several of the classroom ideas described above are contained in a form which teachers can photocopy for their own use in *The Nuclear Issue.*[16]

Points which arise in classroom discussion

In carrying out many of the classroom ideas suggested above several conceptual confusions are likely (from my own experience) to arise which need to be clarified. The onus of clarification will inevitably fall upon the teacher, who may be called upon to make distinctions between some of the conceptually confusing notions involved, such as disarmament, deterrence, pacifism and so on. This short section highlights just three of the important distinctions which need to be made, and which (again in my experience) are often confused in discussions of the nuclear issue at *all levels*.

Deterrence and self-defence

One of the confusions which often arises in discussion is that the idea of deterrence is equated with the idea of self-defence. People suggest, for example, that unless we have deterrence we do not have self-defence. This is a conceptual mistake which needs to be clarified. In fact, deterrence is one form of self-defence and (in the opinion of many people) an effective one. But it is not the only form of defence. In philosophical terms, deterrence is a sufficient but not a necessary condition of self-defence. The point can perhaps be made by describing the defence systems of certain other countries, eg Sweden, which has a strong and expensive policy of non-nuclear defence.

Deterrence and non-nuclear deterrence

This is similar to the distinction made above. A country may have a policy of deterrence yet not possess nuclear weapons. This was presumably the position of many countries before the advent of nuclear weapons. It might be argued that in the nuclear age a policy of non-nuclear deterrence is ineffective, obsolete and naive. However, the logical extreme of this argument is that every country should have its own nuclear deterrent, 'If it's essential for one it's essential for all.'

Pacifism and nuclear pacifism

Is it possible to be a 'nuclear pacifist' without being a pacifist in the broader sense? This is a key question in any group discussion and it underpins the other distinctions made above. A person can argue that it makes sense to have a strong and modern defence system yet not possess nuclear weapons. In other words, a person could advocate nuclear pacifism, that is, deny the wisdom of using nuclear weapons as a threat, without believing in pacifism as a general principle. An equally important point follows from this. A person may advocate nuclear disarmament without advocating disarmament in its full sense. This is a simple point, yet it is often ignored or forgotten.

The above are all conceptual points which will often help to inform and clarify a discussion on the nuclear issue with either children or adults. They are of more than academic interest – to pursue them fully could result in radical differences in viewpoint and policy. Further discussion of some of the complex issues involved in the nuclear debate can be found in:

British Nuclear Weapons: For and Against by J. McMahan (Junction Books, 1981);

Defence and Energy Issues, Science in Society, Book P (Heinemann/ ASE 1983).

Both books are well worth reading for teachers about to tackle the nuclear debate in the classroom, but they are probably unsuitable for direct classroom use.

Teaching resources for the nuclear issue

Resources and sources

Many of the resources available on the nuclear issue are said to come from one 'side' or the other. It would seem that most resources originate from the anti-nuclear or 'peace' groups. Contributors on the pro-deterrence side are often larger, government-related organisations such as the Foreign and Commonwealth Office, the Ministry of Defence, or the British Atlantic Committee. Between the two extremes there have been movements such as 'Tories against Cruise and Trident' (TACT). But, to my knowledge, there are no apparent teaching resources from groups arguing a line between the two 'poles' of unilateral nuclear disarmament and nuclear deterrence. A selective list of teaching resources is given at the end of this chapter. The list is necessarily highly selective – a comprehensive guide to teaching resources is contained in *Nuclear Issues in Education: a teaching guide.*[17]

Balance

A teacher is faced directly with the question of balance in choosing and using resources in a classroom. There are three questions to be faced in considering balance in this context:

1 *Quality*: should the quality of resources from different sides be considered in balancing the equation? Resources from one source may be dull, boring and unimaginative; they may be printed on poor-quality paper, with little visual impact; they may be cheaply produced and presented. Should they be balanced against glossy, well-produced materials presenting the opposite viewpoint? How far should quality be considered in determining balance?

2 *Quantity*: 'never mind the quality, feel the width'. How literally should a balance of quantity be taken? Should a 20-minute talk by a speaker from (say) the Ministry of Defence be balanced by a talk of equal duration from a CND speaker? Similar problems occur in balancing videos, films, leaflets and booklets on the criteria of quantity and quality.

3 *The sphere of balance*: how wide should the circle be drawn in considering whether or not school pupils receive a balanced presentation of the nuclear issue? Should the 'sphere of balance' include the home (eg parents' views), newspaper reports (eg editorials in the popular press) and television programmes, all three of which are likely to be more influential than school curricula? Some teachers argue that pupils do not receive a balanced presentation outside school, therefore their own job is to redress that balance within the school. There are two problems with attempts to widen the sphere of balance. First, how is a teacher to judge or even to collect information on the 'facts' and views fed to pupils outside school? This is an impossible task. In addition, the information and attitudes pupils encounter outside school will vary enormously from one to the other. To redress the balance for all would require a separate curriculum for each pupil. Second, it would be politically unacceptable for teachers to present an unbalanced treatment of the nuclear issue within schooling even if they argued that their aim was to compensate for indoctrination from outside. Balance will be measured within the school domain by parents, politicians, governors, education authorities and the media, whether teachers like it or not.

Evaluating material on the nuclear issue

One of the key problems for a teacher in approaching the nuclear issue is that of evaluating the resources available. Many of the resources on offer, and indeed often freely sent to teachers, suffer from a major problem. They are frequently unreadable. Many leaflets and pamphlets from both poles would score as badly on the FOG readability index as a legal document. In addition, much of the jargon or terminology of the nuclear issue is totally new and may be off-putting to pupils with its talk of pre-emptive strikes, strategic and tactical weapons, civil defence plans, and so on. Add to this the over-complicated scientific explanations often included and you have a recipe for classroom confusion.

Three other points need to be borne in mind by a teacher evaluating material on the nuclear issue: bias, accuracy, and datedness.

The development of an ability to detect bias is perhaps one of the main aims of or justifications for dealing with any controversial issue. Most people would agree that pupils should be educated to detect bias in a leaflet, book or television programme on any contentious topic. But this is not an easy aim to achieve. The notion of 'bias' is a difficult one. From which standpoint should bias be judged? Is there some acceptable 'centre of gravity' from which views or resources from either side can be evaluated? In short, does bias lie in the eye of the beholder, or can it be judged objectively? The problem of bias will face teachers both in discussions and in evaluating teaching resources.

An equally difficult quality to achieve in a teaching resource – and also to judge – is that of *accuracy*. In presenting scientific principles, strict accuracy sometimes has to be sacrificed for the sake of simplicity and readability. A fully accurate and technical account of, say, a nuclear explosion would neither be accessible nor relevant to debate on the nuclear issue. Another problem in the nuclear debate is that many 'facts' are in conflict. Exactly how many missiles the USSR possesses, and of what strength, is usually treated as a matter of opinion rather than a matter of fact. Similarly, there are conflicting data on other nuclear arsenals, on the countries capable of making nuclear weapons, on the effects of nuclear explosions and on the hazards of radiation. The boundary between fact and opinion is never sharp.

The third criterion in evaluating teaching resources on the nuclear debate is that of datedness. New situations, developments in the arms

Figure 2 Evaluating classroom materials: some points to consider

---

Use and organisation
How did you use the material in your classroom? (Whole-class discussion, or small-group use, work in pairs . . . ?)

Pupils' reactions
How did pupils react to it? (Were they stimulated by it? Were they kept active?)

Activities
What activities were pupils involved in? (Individual written work, writing in pairs, talk and discussion, role play . . . ?)

Level
Was the level of the material suitable for the pupils involved? Were the reading level and the conceptual level suitable? If not, for whom would the level be more appropriate?

Bias
From what source did the materials come? Are they very obviously biased, or more subtly biased? Would it be acceptable to use them with school pupils?

Accuracy
Are the materials accurate? When were they published? What original sources, if any, are referred to?

---

race, changes in the nuclear industry and even novel scientific ideas regularly arise which render previous knowledge and strategic thinking obsolete. Two major examples are the proposed Strategic Defence Initiative (or 'Star Wars' programme) in the USA, and the theory that a nuclear winter would result from a number of nuclear explosions. Both appeared in the media somewhat suddenly in 1984, and both have affected people's thinking about the duration of the concept of deterrence in a fundamental way.

I will not dwell further on the problem of finding and evaluating suitable resources on the nuclear issue (Figure 2 sums up some of the main points on evaluation). My main aim in this section, as in the bulk of the chapter, is to illustrate the complexity of the task of handling the nuclear issue in the classroom and including it in the school curriculum. The place of the nuclear issue in the curriculum is the final point I wish to consider – it is perhaps the most complex problem of all.

Including the nuclear issue in the school curriculum

The place of nuclear education in the curriculum is a matter of some debate which again cannot be explored fully here.[18] I am firmly of the opinion that a 'piecemeal' approach should be adopted to the nuclear issue, ie that the issue should be covered adequately and fairly across the curriculum rather than within its own timetable slot. This can be called the 'horizontal' as opposed to the 'vertical' approach. This approach, if coordinated properly and supported by readily usable teaching materials, can produce a far broader and more balanced treatment than a vertical approach. It has been suggested that nuclear education should be subsumed under a curriculum label of 'Peace Studies' or 'Peace Education' and this is sometimes the case. I believe that this approach is undesirable if the procedural principle of balance is to be explicitly applied to the inclusion of the nuclear issue in the school curriculum. A cross-curricular approach involving a range of teachers from different backgrounds and disciplines is likely to result in a more balanced, broad and pluralistic approach. I have argued these points more fully elsewhere.[19].

It has also been suggested that the nuclear issue should be dealt with mainly within science education, since the invention of nuclear weapons was largely a product of the sweat and genius of scientists. Although science teachers do have a vital role to play in nuclear education, it surely cannot be treated as their responsibility alone. It cannot be desirable, educationally, that the facts and arguments concerning nuclear energy and nuclear weapons should be seen as the sole province of the science staff, who often have little experience in, or enthusiasm for, dealing with controversial issues.

The main danger in a horizontal approach is that a lack of planning and coordination could result in one of two things. At one extreme the key issues (*if* they could be agreed upon) might be covered by so many teachers in so many subjects that 'overkill' would result. Pupils might be heard to remark: 'Not nuclear weapons again'. At the other, poor planning and careless coordination could result in a failure to cover all the issues equally well, or – worse still – in the involvement of only a few staff from a narrow range of subjects, eg the humanities.

These problems can be overcome in three ways: by liaison between the staff involved; by possession of a suitable bank of resources which teachers can draw upon; and by the choice of a senior member of staff to coordinate the varied approaches and establish an overview of the nuclear issue in the curriculum. The suggestions are fine in principle. However, the difficulties of managing and organising the three strategies in a school environment are extremely difficult, if not insurmountable. Such difficulties will occur when any issue or 'skill' is introduced to a school curriculum in a *horizontal* fashion rather than having a timetabled slot. This is true of language development, computer-assisted learning, multicultural education, the issue of gender, peace study, problem-solving, study skill or computer awareness. Few schools have succeeded in enabling those skills or issues to permeate their activity in a crosscurricular or horizontal way.

As long as school organisation is dominated by a vertical, 'timetabled-slot' approach to curriculum planning, a coordinated, horizontal treatment of the nuclear issue is likely to be a rarity. My own view, which I have argued for elsewhere,[20] is that new developments in education and society will bring about a more 'two-dimensional approach' to curriculum thinking, involving a horizontal treatment of key issues and skills across the curriculum in addition to the traditional vertical view based on 'forms of knowledge' translated into subject specialisms. In short, a gestalt switch is needed in curriculum philosophy.[21]

When such a switch comes about, then many of the controversial issues discussed in this book may receive the balanced, broad and pluralistic approach which they deserve.

Notes and references

1 From 'The Future and the Bomb' in *Lessons Before Midnight: Educating for Reason in Nuclear Matters* Bedford Way Papers, No 19 (Heinemann, 1984).

2 These guidelines are put forward and discussed in *The Humanities Curriculum Project: an Introduction* J Rudduck (Schools Council Publications, 1983).

3 First put forward in *The Humanities Curriculum Project: an Introduction* L Stenhouse (Heinemann, 1970).

4 The term 'nuclear education' is used here largely for convenience, and is not intended to denote any grandiose plan, curriculum or subversive activity. The

term will be used to signify; 'education, as opposed to indoctrination, in the history, facts and arguments surrounding nuclear weapons and nuclear energy'.

5 This is a distortion of one of Kant's major themes in *A Critique of Pure Reason* (Macmillan, 1968).

6 'Problematic aspects of nuclear education' B Tizard, in *Lessons Before Midnight* Bedford Way Papers, No 19 (Heinemann, 1984).

7 A full discussion of the unique role which science education can play is given in 'Nuclear weapons and science education' J J Wellington, in *School Science Review* March 1984, pp 440–7.

8 *The Process of Education* J Bruner (Harvard University Press, 1960) p 33.

9 Tizard, *op cit*.

10 This is surely a situation requiring the kind of 'action research' advocated by Donald Schon in *The Reflective Practitioner* (Temple Smith, 1983).

11 Tizard, *op cit*.

12 R Stradling provides valuable accounts of approaches to contentious issues in an excellent compilation entitled: *Teaching Controversial Issues* (Edward Arnold, 1984).

13 Tizard *op cit*.

14 *Learning to Teach Through Discussion* J Rudduck (ed) Centre for Applied Research in Education, University of East Anglia, Occasional Publications No 8, 1979.

15 Full discussion of games and simulations can be found in: *Learning and the Simulation Game* John Taylor and Rex Walford (Open University Press, 1978); *Simulations: A Handbook for Teachers* Ken Jones (Kogan Page, 1980); *Games and Simulations in the Classroom* (Schools Council, 1975); *Designing your own Simulations* Ken Jones (Methuen, 1985).

16 *The Nuclear Issue* J J Wellington (Basil Blackwell, 1986).

17 *Nuclear Issues in Education: a teaching guide* is obtainable from Newcastle-upon-Tyne Education Committee, Pendower Hall Teachers' Centre, West Road, Newcastle NE15 6PP.

18 Some of the problems were introduced in 'Teaching the unteachable' J J Wellington, in *Physics Education* 1982, Vol 17. This article led to further debate.

19 'Including the nuclear issue in the school curriculum: a balanced approach' J J Wellington, in *Cambridge Journal of Education* 1985, Vol 15, No 3.

20 A two-dimensional view of curriculum is discussed in *Children, Computers and the Curriculum* J J Wellington (Harper and Row, 1985) pp 245–250.

21 Philosophical arguments for a change in our view of the curriculum have been put forward in 'Determining a core curriculum: the limitations of transcendental deductions' J J Wellington, in *Recent Developments in Curriculum Studies* P H Taylor (NFER/Nelson, 1986).

An extensive, annotated list of teaching resources and sources related to the nuclear issue can be found in: *The Nuclear Issue* J J Wellington (Basil Blackwell, 1986) pp 17–21.

Additional bibliography

The articles and books listed below are all recently published discussions of controversial issues in the curriculum which have not been considered elsewhere in the text. They are provided here, as an additional bibliography, under the following headings:

1 General discussions of controversy and indoctrination in the curriculum
2 Political education
3 Religious education
4 Personal, social and moral education
5 Multicultural education
6 Peace education
7 Women's studies
8 World studies and global education
9 Science education

1 General discussions of controversy and indoctrination in the curriculum

Dearden, R F *Theory and Practice in Education* (London: Routledge and Kegan Paul).

Dobson, A P 'Towards an understanding of indoctrination' in *Teaching Politics*, Vol 9(3), Sept 1980; pp 216–27.

Durham, M 'Left-wing indoctrination widespread in schools' in *Times Educational Supplement*, 22/2/85; p 7.

Elliott, R K 'Objectivity and education', in *Journal of Philosophy of Education*, Vol 16(1), 1982; pp 49–62.

Gardner, P 'Another look at controversial issues and the curriculum' in *Journal of Curriculum Studies*, Vol 16(4) Oct/Dec 1984; pp 379–85.

Garner, R 'HMI discounts danger of indoctrination' in *Times Educational Supplement*, 26/10/84; p 8.

Hare, W *Controversies in Teaching* (Brighton: Wheatsheaf, 1985).

Hudson, W D 'Educating, socializing and indoctrinating: a reply to Tasos Kazepides' in *Journal of Philosophy of Education*, Vol 16(2) 1982; pp 167–172.

Hull, J 'Controversy, social education and the "core"', in *Forum*, Vol 26(1) Autumn 1983.

Kazepides, T 'Educating, socializing and indoctrinating' in *Journal of Philosophy of Education*, Vol 16(2), 1982; pp 155–165.

Newfield, J W and McElyea, V B 'Affective outcomes, indoctrination and the use of case rhetoric in curriculum guides', in *Journal of Curriculum Studies*, Vol 16(1), Jan/March 1984; pp 100–102.

Newfield, J W and McElyea, V B 'Affective outcomes, indoctrination and the use of structural/procedural objectives in curriculum guides', in

Journal of Curriculum Studies, Vol 16(2), April/June 1984; pp 195–197.
Palmer, F 'Dr. Scruton and co.', in *Times Educational Supplement*, 28/6/85; p 16.
Rudduck, J and Plaskow, M 'Bring back the neutral chairman', in *Times Educational Supplement*, 21/6/85; p 4.
Stenhouse, L and Verma, G K 'Educational procedures and attitudinal objectives: a paradox', in *Journal of Curriculum Studies*, Vol 13(4), Oct/Dec 1981; pp 329–337.
Stradling, R 'The teaching of controversial issues: an evaluation', In *Educational Review*, Vol 36(2), 1984; pp 121–129.
Thiessen, E J 'Indoctrination and Doctrines', in *Journal of Philosophy of Education*, Vol 16(1), 1982; p 3–7.
'New Law no answer', Editorial comment in *Times Educational Supplement*, 7/6/85; p 2.
Tyack, D B and James, T 'Moral majorities and the school curriculum: historical perspectives on the legalization of virtue', in *Teachers College Record*, Vol 86, Summer 1985; p 513–537.
Ward, L O *The ethical dimension of the school curriculum (Conference Papers)* edited by Lionel O Ward. (Swansea: Pineridge Press, 1982).
Wilson, J 'Example or timetable? a note on the Warnock fallacy', in *Journal of Moral Education*, Vol 14, Oct 1985; pp 173–176.
Wood, N 'How to handle controversial subjects in class', in *Times Educational Supplement*, 21/1/84; p 10.
Young, R E 'Teaching equals indoctrination: the dominant epistemic practices of our schools', in *British Journal of Educational Studies*, Vol 32, Oct 1984; pp 220–238.

2 Political Education

Davies, L 'Political Education, gender and the art of the possible', in *Educational Review*, Vol 32(2), June 1984; pp 197–195.
Gregory, I 'Political education: what warrant in democratic theory?', in *Westminster Studies in Education*, Vol 6, 1983; pp 3–12.
Harber, C 'Politics and political education in 1984' in *Educational Review*, Vol 32(2), June 1984; pp 113–119.
Jones, B 'Who cares about political education', in *General Education* No 36, Autumn 1982; pp 3–5.
Passmore, B 'Call to outlaw preaching of politics in schools', in *Times Educational Supplement* 31/5/85; p 6.
Phillips, G 'Taking political autonomy seriously; a reply to Gregory', in *Westminster Studies in Education*, Vol 6, 1983; pp 13–20.
Porter, A 'Much ado about nothing?: a critical consideration of the problem of bias and indoctrination in political education', in *Teaching Politics*, Vol 9(3), Sept 1982; pp 203–208.
Reid, A and Whittingham, B 'The Constitutional Classroom: a political

education for democracy', in *Teaching Politics*, Vol 13(3), Sept 1984; pp 307–330.

Warnock, M 'Teachers, politics and morals', in *Times Educational Supplement*, 7/6/85; p 4.

Wringe, C *Democracy, schooling and political education* (London: Allen and Unwin, 1984).

3 Religious Education

Aspin, D N 'Church schools, religious education and the multi-ethnic community', in *Journal of Philosophy of Education*, Vol 17(2), Dec 1983; pp 229–240.

Blake, N 'Church schools, religious education and the multi-ethnic community: a reply to David Aspin', in *Journal of Philosophy of Education*, Vol 17(2), pp 241–250.

Cowell, B 'The role of Christians in religious and moral education', in *Journal of Moral Education*, Vol 12(3), Oct 1983; pp 161–165.

Day, D 'Religious education 40 years on: a permanent identity crisis?', in *British Journal of Religious Education*, Vol 7(2), Spring 1985; pp 55–63.

Day, D 'Christianity in our multi-faith community', in *Spectrum*, Vol 15(2), Spring 1983; pp 20–24.

Greer, J E 'Religious education and moral education: an exploration of some relevant issues', in *Journal of Moral Education*, Vol 12(2), May 1983; pp 92–98.

Hammond, J 'The political implications of teaching the Bible', in *British Journal of Religious Education*, Vol 5(3), pp 151–155.

Hayward, M *et al* 'Religious Education', in *Times Educational Supplement*, No 3572, 14/12/84; pp 33–38.

Jackson, R 'Hinduism in Britain: religious nurture and religious education' in *British Journal of Religious Education*, Vol 7(2), Spring 1985; pp 69–75.

Kazepides, T 'Is religious education possible?: a rejoinder to W H Hudson', in *Journal of Philosophy of Education*, Vol 17(2), Dec 1983; pp 259–265.

Key, W K and Francis, L J 'The Seamless Robe: interdisciplinary enquiry in religious education', in *British Journal of Religious Education*, Vol 7(2), Spring 1985; pp 64–67.

Lodge, B 'Dunn wants assemblies in RE to retain Christian bias', in *Times Educational Supplement*, 3/5/85; p 12.

Lodge, B 'RE status and substance criticized' in *Times Educational Supplement*, 10/5/85; p 3.

Ouellet, F 'Religious education and the challenge of inter-cultural communication', in *British Journal of Religious Education*, Vol 7(2), Spring 1985; pp 81–86.

Sealey, J A 'Religious education: a component of moral education?', in *Journal of Philosophy of Education*, Vol 17(2), Dec 1983; pp 251–254.

Thomson, B 'Syllabus making in a multi-faith society', in *CEM Magazine*, Autumn 1983; pp 10–11.

Wilson, J 'A reply to John Sealey', in *Journal of Philosophy of Education*, Vol 17(2) Dec 1983; pp 255–258.

Wright, D 'Religious education from the perspective of moral education', in *Journal of Moral Education*, Vol 12(2) May 1983; pp 111–115.

4 Personal, social and moral education

Anderson, J 'The Lifeskills teaching programmes', in *Journal of the Institute of Health Education*, Vol. 22(1), 1984; pp 12–17.

Bates, I *Schooling for the dole? the new vocationalism* (Basingstoke: Macmillan).

Blackham, H J 'Moral education and its near relatives' in *Journal of Moral Education*, Vol 12(2), May 1983; pp 116–124.

Cohen, B 'Ethical Objectivity and moral education' in *Journal of Moral Education*, Vol 12(2), May 1983; pp 131–136.

David, K *Personal and social education in secondary schools* (York: Longman for the Schools Council, 1983).

Fleming, D and Lavercombe, S 'Talking about unemployment with school leavers', in *British Journal of Guidance and Counselling*, Vol 10(1), 1982; pp 22–23.

Gardner, P 'Defending moral education', in *Journal of Moral Education*, Vol 13, May 1984; pp 75–82.

Pring, R *et al* 'Life Skills', in *Times Educational Supplement*, No 3598, 14/6/85, pp 35–39.

Pring, R *et al* 'Personal, social and moral education' in *Educational Analysis*, Vol 5(1), 1983; pp 1–114, (whole issue).

5 Multicultural education

Education for a multi-cultural society/evidence to the Swann Committee . . . (London: N U T, 1982)

Conference: 'Education in a multi-cultural society', University of London, Goldsmiths College, March 1980.

Holmes, B 'Diversity and unity in education' (Conference proceedings) edited by Brian Holmes (London: Allen and Unwin, 1980).

Jeffcoate, R 'Evaluating the multi-cultural curriculum: students' perspectives' in *Journal of Curriculum Studies*, Vol 13(1), Jan/March 1981; pp 1–15.

Lashley, H 'Education, institutional racism and black youth' *Head Teachers' Review*, Winter 1983; pp 19–21.

Little, A and Willey, R (Project on) *Studies in the multi-ethnic curriculum* (full report) (London: Schools Council, 1983).

Lynch, J 'Human rights, racism and the multi-cultural curriculum' in *Educational Review*, Vol 37(2), June 1985; pp 141–152.

Partington, G 'Multiculturalism and the common curriculum debate', in *British Journal of Educational Studies*; Vol 33(1), 1985; pp 35–36.

Ruddell, D 'Colonial curriculum and mutlicultural curriculum: two British responses to black pupils' in *Curriculum*, Vol 5(1), Spring 1984 pp 18–23.

Ruddell, D 'Racism awareness: an approach for schools' in *Remedial Education*, Vol. 18(3), 1983; pp 125–1129.

Smith, C 'Teaching issues of race in secondary schools' in *Cambridge Journal of Education*, Vol 12(2), pp 115–121.

Smolicz, J 'Multiculturalism and an overarching framework of values: some educational responses for ethnically plural societies', in *European Journal of Education*, Vol 19(1), March 1984; pp 11–23.

Troyna, B and Ball, W 'Styles of LEA policy intervention in multicultural/ antiracist education' in *Educational Review*, Vol 37(2), 1985; pp 165–173.

Wright, D R 'What do pupils learn about race?' in *Education Journal*, Vol 6(1), April 1984 pp 1–5.

6 Peace education

Blake, N 'Peace Education and National Security', in *Journal of Philosophy of Education*, Vol 19, No 1, 1985.

Burns, R and Aspeslagh, R 'Concepts of peace education: a view of Western experience' in *International Review of Education*, Vol 29(3), 1983; pp 311–330.

Connell, W F 'Curriculum for peace education', in *New Era*, Vol 64(1), 1983; pp 11–19.

Garden, T 'Peace and war studies: is the chalk mightier than the sword?' in *Conference*, Vol 20(3), Autumn 1983; pp 9–11.

Haavelsrud, M and Galtung, J 'An introduction to the debate on peace education', in *International Review of Education*, Vol 29(3), 1983; pp 275–280.

Heater, D 'Peace: what is relevant?' in *Times Educational Supplement*, 8/6/84; p 2.

Marks, S 'Peace, development, disarmament and human rights education: the dilemma between status quo and curriculum overload', in *International Review of Education*, Vol 29(3), 1983; pp 289–310.

'Peace Education bibliography' in *Education Libraries Bulletin*, Vol 27(1) Spring 1984; pp 44–48.

Natase, A 'The culture of peace and peace education' in *International Review of Education*, Vol 29(3), 1983; pp 391–401.

7 Women's studies

France, M 'Why women's studies?', in *Women's Studies International Forum*, Vol 6(3), 1983; pp 305–308.

Gardiner, J 'What is women's history?' in *Times Educational Supplement*, No 3590, 19/4/85; p 22.

Spender, D *et al* 'Women's Studies' in *Times Educational Supplement*, No 639, 1/2/85; pp 25–29.

Yates, L 'Is women's studies a legitimate school subject?' in *Journal of Curriculum Studies*, Vol 18(1), Jan/Mar 1986; p 17.

8 World studies and global education

Brown, C 'National identity and world studies' in *Educational Review*, Vol 36(2), June 1984; pp 149–156.

Hicks, D and Fisher, S 'World studies: a global perspective in the curriculum' in *Curriculum*, Vol 3(2), Autumn 1982; pp 6–12.

McConnell, J 'Religious education and world studies' in *New Era*, Vol 63(2), April/June 1982; pp 47–50.

Schools in a world of change: NCTCL 9th annual course, conference. (Maidenhead: NCTCL, 1979).

Selby, D 'World studies: towards a global perspective in the school curriculum' in *Social Science Teacher*, Vol 13(2), Spring 1984, pp i–viii.

Webb, D and Cogan, J 'A global approach to the school curriculum' in *Curriculum*, Vol 3(2), Autumn 1982; pp 13–17.

9 Science education

Eijkelhof, H, Kortlund, K and Van der Loo, F 'Nuclear weapons – a suitable topic for the classroom' in *Physics Education*, Vol 19(1), Jan 1984; pp 11–14.

King, W K 'Social and Cultural Responsibilities of Science in the School Curriculum: objectives and teaching methods' in *CASME Journal*, Vol 5(2), 1985; pp 29–43.

McLelland, G 'The limits to a physics teacher's social responsibility', in *Physics Education*, Vol 18(3), May 1983; pp 114–116.

Turney, J 'A crop of controversies' in *Times Educational Supplement*, 14/6/85; p 13.

Zeidler, D L 'Moral issues and social policy in science education: closing the literacy gap' in *Science Education*, Vol 68, July 1984; pp 411–419.

Notes on the contributors

Jerry Wellington taught in Tower Hamlets, East London, before joining the University of Sheffield as a lecturer in Education. His most recent publications are *Children, Computers and the Curriculum* (Harper and Row 1985) and *The Nuclear Issue* (Basil Blackwell 1986)

Jean Rudduck is Professor of Education at the University of Sheffield. Her main publications include *Learning Through Small Group Discussion* (1978), *Making the Most of the Short In-Service Course* (1981) and *The Sixth Form and Libraries: Problems of Access to Knowledge* (1984), co-authored with David Hopkins.

David Bridges is Deputy Principal of Homerton College, Cambridge. A former history teacher, turned philosopher of education, he has recently been extensively involved in classroom and institutional action research and has a particular interest in discussion. Publications include *Education Democracy and Discussion*.

Graham Pike is Research Fellow and David Selby is Director at the Centre for Global Education, York University. Information on the Centre and a publications catalogue are available from: The Secretary, CGE, University of York, York YO1 5DD (Tel 0904 413267).

Judith Byrne Whyte is Senior Lecturer in Education at Manchester Polytechnic. She is the author of *Beyond the Wendy House* (Schools Council/Longman 1983) and *Girls Into Science and Technology* (Routledge and Kegan Paul 1986) and editor of *Girl Friendly Schooling* (Methuen 1985).

Alma Craft is a Principal Professional Officer at the School Curriculum Development Committee. Her paper draws on the fuller discussion presented in *Agenda for Multicultural Teaching* (Longman 1986), co-authored with G Klein.

Rob Fiddy is Senior Research Associate at the Centre for Applied Research in Education (CARE) at the University of East Anglia. Currently undertaking the local evaluation of TVEI in Norfolk, Suffolk and Essex, his research interests include pre- and post-vocational education with particular reference to youth unemployment. He has recently edited *In Place of Work: Policy and Provision for the Young Unemployed* (1983) and *Youth, Training and Unemployment: A Collection of National Perspectives* (1985) both published by The Falmer Press.

John Harris is Senior Lecturer in Philosophy in the Department of Education, University of Manchester. He has written many articles on philosophical subjects, and is the author of *Violence and Responsibility* (1980) and *The Value of Life: an Introduction to Medical Ethics* (1985) both published by Routledge and Kegan Paul.

Enid Mellor is Lecturer in Religious Education at King's College, London and has taught Religious Education in schools, colleges of education and university departments of education. She is author of *The Making of the Old Testament* (1972).

David Aspin is Vice-Dean of the Faculty of Education, King's College, University of London and Professor of Education (Philosophy) in the University of London. Recent publications include 'Friedrich Froebel: Visionary, Prophet and Healer' (1983), 'Church Schools, Religious Education and the Multi-ethnic Community (1983) and 'Metaphor and Meaning in Educational Discourse' (1984). Professor Aspin is a member of the Religious Society of Friends and a member of QSRE (the Quaker Board for Social Responsibility and Education).

Index